THE STATE AND ECONOMIC LIFE
EDITORS: Mel Watkins, University of Toronto; Leo Panitch, York
Univeristy

5 RICHARD M. BIRD AND SUSAN HORTON
Government Policy and the Poor in Developing Countries

The past decade has seen the governments of developing nations undertake a series of policies aimed specifically at alleviating the poverty of
their nations. Today those governments are forced to re-evaluate such
policies in the face of a negative international economy.

In 1985 a group of economists, political scientists, anthropologists, and
others attended a conference at the University of Toronto on poverty-
related policy in developing countries. The six papers in this volume were
originally presented at this conference; they explore a range of policies
which affect the poor. An introductory paper provides an overview.

Two papers discuss broad issues, agricultural policy and stabilization
policies. The other four deal with how government fiscal policy affects
the poor, both through taxation and through key areas of government
expenditure. Each of these papers uses household data to show that
ostensibly equity-oriented government policies are often far from that in
practice.

The exhaustive state-of-the-art literature surveys combined with case
studies will be illuminating for those studying development policy as well
as for practitioners.

RICHARD M. BIRD is Professor of Economics, University of Toronto.

SUSAN HORTON is Assistant Professor of Economics, University of
Toronto.

THE POLITICAL ECONOMY OF WORLD POVERTY

a series edited by Albert Berry, Cranford Pratt, and Richard Sandbrook
at the University of Toronto

The books in this series aim at increasing our understanding of the economic,
political, social, and cultural processes and institutions that promote or impede
the development of the Third World and the amelioration of its poverty.

GOVERNMENT POLICY AND THE POOR IN DEVELOPING COUNTRIES

edited by
Richard M. Bird and Susan Horton

UNIVERSITY OF TORONTO PRESS

Toronto Buffalo London

© University of Toronto Press 1989
Toronto Buffalo London
Printed in Canada

ISBN 0-8020-2672-9 (cloth)
ISBN 0-8020-6710-7 (paper)

Canadian Cataloguing in Publication Data

Main entry under title:
Government policy and the poor in developing countries

(The Political economy of world poverty; 5)
Rev. papers presented at a conference held at the
University of Toronto, Apr. 25–26, 1985, sponsored
by the Development Studies Programme and the
Institute for Policy Analysis of the University.
Includes index.

ISBN 0-8020-2672-9 (bound). – ISBN 0-8020-6710-7 (pbk.)

1. Poor – Government policy – Developing countries –
Congresses.   2. Economic assistance – Developing
countries – Congresses.   3. Developing countries –
Economic policy – Congresses.   I. Bird, Richard M.,
1938–   . II. Horton, Susan.   III. Series.

HC59.72.P6G67 1989   338.91 '09172 '4   C88-094889-2

Contents

Acknowledgments

The original versions of the papers included in this book were presented at a conference held at the University of Toronto, 25–26 April 1985, and sponsored by the Development Studies Programme and the Institute for Policy Analysis of the University of Toronto, with assistance from the Social Sciences and Humanities Research Council of Canada. The authors would like to thank the conference participants and particularly the designated discussants for helpful comments, which have improved the papers. In addition, the editors are grateful to Mohammed Halfani, Rohinton Medhora, Margaret Sanderson, and Rodney Schmidt for research assistance and to Jessie Leger, Lorelle Triolo, and Rita Mollica for assistance in organizing the conference and in preparing the final manuscript.

This book has been published with the help of a grant from the Social Science Federation of Canada, using funds provided by the Social Sciences and Humanities Research Council of Canada.

Conference Participants

(with affiliation at time of conference)

Roy W. Bahl *Director, Metropolitan Studies Program, the Maxwell School, Syracuse University*

Jonathan Barker *Department of Political Science, University of Toronto*

R. Albert Berry *Department of Economics, University of Toronto*

Richard M. Bird *Director, Institute for Policy Analysis, University of Toronto*

John Buttrick *Department of Economics, York University*

Malcolm Gillis *Institute of Policy Sciences and Public Affairs, and Department of Economics, Duke University*

Gerald K. Helleiner *Department of Economics, University of Toronto*

Susan Horton *Department of Economics, University of Toronto*

Yukon Huang *Chief, Bank Assistance Policy Division, Country Policy Department, the World Bank*

Emmanuel Jimenez *Education Department, the World Bank, and Department of Economics, University of Western Ontario*

Stephen R. Lewis, Jr *Botswana Project and Department of Economics, Williams College*

Stephen Mayo *Water Supply and Urban Development Department, the World Bank*

Barbara D. Miller *Senior Research Associate, the Maxwell School, Syracuse University*

Winnie Mitullah *Institute for Environmental Studies, University of Toronto*

Joan Nelson *Overseas Development Council*

Richard W. Osborn *Department of Preventive Medicine and Biostatistics, University of Toronto*

Barry Pinsky *Research Associate, Centre for Urban and Community Studies, University of Toronto*

Richard Sandbrook *Director, Development Studies Programme, University of Toronto*

W. Paul Strassmann *Department of Economics, Michigan State University*

Richard Stren *Department of Political Science, University of Toronto*

Vito Tanzi *Director, Fiscal Affairs Department, International Monetary Fund*

Lance Taylor *International Nutrition Program and Department of Economics, Massachussets Institute of Technology*

Stephen G. Triantis *Department of Economics, University of Toronto*

John Whalley *Centre for the Study of International Economic Relations and Department of Economics, University of Western Ontario*

GOVERNMENT POLICY AND THE POOR IN
DEVELOPING COUNTRIES

1
Introduction

R.M. BIRD AND S. HORTON

The study of economic development is, by definition, concerned with the poor, understood broadly as those who inhabit poor countries. In recent decades, however, this concern has become more sharply focused on the effects of growth, change, and government policy on the poorest people in the developing countries – often defined as the lower 40 per cent of the income distribution. The earlier, sanguine view that the benefits of generalized economic growth would inevitably 'trickle down' to the lower strata of society faded during the 1960s in the face of the increasing evidence of persistently large income disparities in many developing countries, even fast-growing ones, and the realization that the poor may not gain much from development immediately, even in absolute terms.

A new view, therefore, became dominant in the late 1960s and early 1970s. Those concerned with the well-being of the poor in developing countries were henceforth both to pay special attention to the effects of development policies on the poor and also to introduce policy measures specifically designed to help them directly. The resulting change in policy emphasis was perhaps most marked in the adoption, at least in part, of the 'basic-needs' approach to development (which focused on the provision of basic services such as food, water, shelter, and health care to the poor) by such agencies as the World Bank. An increasing number of researchers, both within and outside the agencies, also began to attempt to analyse and quantify the effects of government policies on the poor – both policies intended specifically to assist the poor, and other, more general policies, such as monetary and trade policy.

Over the last decade, a substantial body of research on the effects of different policies, both foreign and domestic, on the poor has thus accumulated. At the same time, however, two new factors have led to yet another change in emphasis both in the policies of the major international lending agencies and in the orientation of many researchers concerned with developing countries. One important factor has been the marked slowdown in world growth since the first OPEC crisis of 1973–4. The ensuing difficulties facing many developing countries, often exacerbated by the unkindness of nature and the unfortunate effects of ill-judged government policies, have to some extent inevitably turned attention back to the 'basic need' of these countries for economic growth – and away from the basic needs of the poorest members of society. At the same time, and for much the same reasons, a second factor is that many observers have become increasingly convinced that, at least to some extent, governments in both the developed and developing worlds have brought these problems upon themselves. Just as Keynesian 'fine-tuning' of the economy is out of fashion in most Western countries, so many Western observers of development have perceptibly shifted away from the view implicit in much of the earlier development literature that, once a problem was defined, the solution necessarily lay in the implementation of an appropriate government policy. The latest 'new view' on development, although not always clearly articulated, appears to be that government intervention, particularly when information is poor, is as likely to hurt as to help the growth prospects of developing countries – and, by implication, the chances for the poor in those countries to attain a better life.

From one perspective, this latest development may appear to bring us back full circle to the trickle-down theory mentioned earlier. In reality, the demonstrated fallibility of governments does not, of course, mean that the distributive results of the unfettered market are any more acceptable now, either in principle or in practice, than they were twenty years ago. It does suggest, however, that a closer look at the effects of government policy on the poor is necessary. If governments are to do less – or, at least, to do different things – in the name of increasing growth than before, then those concerned with the well-being of the poorest members of society must inevitably scrutinize what they do more closely and carefully than before. It is no longer enough, if it ever was, to look at official rhetoric or even at budgetary allocations by expenditure function and draw conclusions about the distributive effects of government policies.

This conclusion is reinforced by the fact that the evidence appears to support the common perception that even those policies specifically intended to aid the poor have not been very successful – and, indeed, have sometimes had quite perverse results. Expenditure policies, intended to make housing, health, education, and so on more accessible to the poor, for example, seem seldom to have reached their supposed target groups, and have often ended up subsidizing more favoured segments of society. Partly for this reason, there has been increased emphasis recently by the World Bank and others on ways of charging users and hence recovering costs in some of these expenditure areas – although one might think that such plans may run into the same obstacles that have generally made attempts to make tax systems more progressive in developing countries both difficult to carry through and disappointing in their results.

The new emphasis in development policy on 'getting the prices right,' like the marked stress on cutting down the scale and scope of government activities, also makes the question of the compatibility of these policies with improving the well-being of the poor in those countries especially important. Like the concern with the efficacy of specifically 'pro-poor' policies mentioned above, this question underlines the importance both of understanding the effects of what has been done in the past and of trying to think through as best we can the lessons suggested for the future by this experience.

One important aim of the conference at which the papers in this book were first presented was thus to survey the extensive research that has been done in recent years on government policy and the poor in developing countries. The unanticipated difficulties encountered in implementing policies aimed at the poor and the current constraints on such policies make it especially important at the present time to learn as much as possible from previous experience.

In addition to depicting the 'state of the art' with respect to research and knowledge in their respective areas, the authors of the papers were also asked to reflect on the implications of their discussion for future research in the field. Partly to make the discussions more concrete and partly to illustrate the variability of the development experience – and the consequent fragility of generalizations – authors were also asked, if possible, to incorporate one or more case studies into their papers. In the customary fashion of academics, each author of course interpreted these instructions in his or her own way, the result being a medley of variants more or less within these terms of reference. Finally, although all but one of the authors are economists, the obvious need to complement the economic approach by other perspectives was recognized by assigning discussants and inviting participants from such disciplines as political science, sociology, anthropology, and public health.

Although the resulting papers by no means constitute an exhaustive review of government policy and the poor in developing countries, they do encompass a wide range of experience and research in a variety of relevant senses. The topics covered included short-run stabilization and adjustment programs, long-run sectoral development policies in the agricultural sector, budgetary policies (both taxes and expenditures), and specific programs intended to aid the poor (such as food subsidies and sites-and-services programs). The specific cases referred to in different papers range from 'successes' in Asia (agricultural development in Taiwan) through more mixed experiences in India, Brazil, and Jamaica, to apparent 'failures' in sub-Saharan Africa (the food-subsidy program in Tanzania). The experience of the authors and conference participants similarly ranges from active officials of international lending agencies, to long-time academic observers of the development process in one or another part of the world, to actual participants in that process, as well as across the spectrum of disciplines noted earlier.

The papers presented here in most cases incorporate revisions made as a result of the conference discussion. Nevertheless, they by no means encompass the full scope of the broader issues that were raised about economic and non-economic dimensions of the impact of government policies on the poor in developing countries. The remainder of this introductory chapter, therefore, attempts to fill in some of this missing context, first by summarizing briefly the main issues raised in each of the papers nad the subsequent discussion and then by identifying several recurring themes that seem central both to our present perception of the effects of government policy on the poor in developing countries and, perhaps more important, to the further research that is obviously needed on this subject in the future.

1 Stabilization and the Poor

Perhaps the major stimulus for this volume lay in our perception that governments throughout the developing world were cutting back on poverty-oriented programs as part of their adjustment to their present difficult economic circumstances. It is appropriate, therefore, that the first paper, by Gerald Helleiner, focuses specially on this issue and that this paper gave rise to some of the liveliest discussion at the conference.

Helleiner's focus is one the immediate, short-run effects of International Monetary Fund – 'IMF-type' – adjustment programs on the poor, with special emphasis on conditions in sub-Saharan Africa. He divides such programs into three distinct components: restructuring, restraint, and policy change. While he recognizes that the three are often closely related, in his view the debates over development policy that have taken place between the international lending agencies and the governments in a number of countries are usually not directly related to the resolution of the immediate crisis at which stabilization programs are supposedly aimed. They rather illustrate the tendency to use the occasion of a crisis to press ideological or other points. Consequently, his discussion concentrates on the more relevant short-term policies that are customarily implemented in the course of such programs.

Helleiner repeatedly emphasizes the danger of applying what he sees as the generalized 'cookbook' recipes of the typical stabilization program to the wide variety of circumstances found in developing countries. Identical policies will have very different effects depending on the particular conditions prevailing in a country at the time they are applied. He is especially concerned that inadequate attention has been paid to the effects of adjustment programs on the poor – a concern strengthened by his perception that government expenditures are, as a rule, more equitably distributed than are private expenditures, so that cutting back public expenditures is likely to hit the poor especially hard. Finally, while he notes that this proposition has not been tested, he also mentions the common belief that such cut-backs often affect social programs most – and hence, again, the poor.

These general concerns about the 'anti-poor' nature of most stabilization programs are illustrated in the particular case of Tanzania. Helleiner argues, for example, that while problems such as the inefficiency of public-sector operations may well be central to Tanzania's future economic performance, they are not particularly relevant to its short-run stabilization problems and should not, therefore, be seen as central in discussion on an appropriate adjustment program. He also objects strongly to the failure to consider explicitly the distributional impact of such programs, noting that in principle a given restraint target can be reached in many ways, each with different distributional implications. He is particularly concerned about the need for much more attention to this problem in the very low-income countries of sub-Saharan Africa, where, he argues, there is often an especially strong case for financing a more gradual adjustment program, with more attention being paid to its impact on the very poorest.

The two formal discussants of the Helleiner paper took very different approaches. To oversimplify, one focused on the relationship between the international financing agencies and the developing countries in the formulation of stabilization programs and the other focused on the political dimensions of such programs within developing countries. The argument of the first discussant was essentially that adjustment was necessary with or without international financial assistance, that when adjustment packages were negotiated the results reflected not any kind of 'cookbook' approach but rather the outcome of prolonged consideration of all feasible alternatives by both sides, and that to the extent the required policy measures affected the poor adversely it was hard for the international agency to do anything about it.

More specifically, this discussant noted that it was often difficult to provide for more gradual adjustment programs because the resources available were limited and because the governments in power in many developing countries were often too politically volatile to make commitments for more than a few months in advance. With regard to the impact of stabilization programs on the poor, three points were made. First, the absence of adjustment would also, in most cases, be detrimental to the poor. Second, in practice it is difficult to protect the poor both because few feasible selective policy instruments exist and because the urgency of the situation usually forces recourse to blunt instruments that may not rate very high on the equity scale. Few countries can effectively implement, on short notice, targeted policies to help the poor; most can increase import duties and excise taxes overnight, once they choose to act. Third, government policies inevitably reflect the existing political structure, and that structure seldom gives the poor much weight.

The second discussant essentially elaborated this last point, stressing in particular the need to take into account not only the reality of policy actions but also the perceptions by different groups of the costs and benefits of such actions. For example, the economic crisis preceding a stabilization program has usually caused political unrest. Whether the program adds to, or alleviates, that unrest depends on a variety of factors, not least of which is whether groups think they bear the burden of adjustment and the ability of such groups to make their protests felt politically. The perceived equity of an adjustment program may indeed be an important factor in this calculus – but it is perhaps unlikely that in most countries the politically significant upper and middle classes are especially concerned with the treatment of the poor. Even in those countries with more economic room to manoeuvre than exists in the poorest countries of sub-Saharan Africa, this discussant argued, the result was more likely to be pressure to spare the middle classes and organized labour than to protect the poor. For these and other reasons, the political issues with respect to stabilization were often quite different from the equity issues.

The ensuing discussion touched on a number of additional points of interest, ranging from the appropriateness of conventional macro-economic policy prescriptions in developing countries to the role of the construction sector in adjustment. In traditional macro-economics, for example, stabilization policy refers to the appropriate mix of monetary-fiscal policy; in some developing countries it appears that the problem is sometimes the absence of any such coherent policies and also that such conventional remedies as tight money may easily make things worse rather than better, particularly in less-diversified countries suffering powerful external shocks.

As one participant noted, in a sense the acid test of the new classical macro-economics, with its emphasis on the expectations of agents and adjustment paths, lies precisely in the developing countries.

While there was by no means complete agreement with Helleiner's view on the relative equity of public expenditure, there was also substantial discussion of the sectoral impact of adjustment programs, particularly in terms of the composition of public expenditures. One participant argued that the major impact of cut-backs was on construction. Other participants suggested that investment in machinery and equipment, particularly imported equipment, was more often affected severely. While others noted that there was little evidence that social programs were especially adversely affected, it is hard to say what this means in terms of effects on the poor. Education expenditures, for example, may be maintained to protect the jobs of middle-class teachers rather than for any higher purpose: schools may be built and teachers paid even in the face of crisis – but there may be no funds for books, chalk, or pencils and paper. What much of this discussion perhaps revealed as much as anything else was the extent to which everyone tends to generalize from his or her particular experience, as well as the lack of any systematic and detailed study of the expenditure impacts of adjustment programs.

2 Taxation and the Poor

With the second paper on taxation, the conference moved from the high-profile area of stabilization policy to the less dramatic, but in the long run perhaps no less important, area of the impact of budgetary policy on the poor in developing countries. The paper by Richard Bird and Barbara Miller reviews an extensive array of studies on the incidence of taxes and user charges and reaches a number of clear conclusions. First, the tax systems in most developing countries are not, contrary to popular belief, particularly regressive. Second, taxes nevertheless still account for a significant fraction of the income of the poor, particularly the urban poor, so that the design of tax systems and their impact on the poor remain important policy issues. Finally, it is particularly important in considering this area to carry out detailed analysis, preferably on micro-data sets, because of the great heterogeneity of those classified as 'poor' in most developing countries and the consequently widely varying effects of different tax regimes within the group of the poor.

Bird and Miller consider in some detail two particular aspects of revenue systems: urban finance and indirect taxes. The financing of urban services through property taxes and user charges is shown to have widely different effects depending upon the precise structure of the policy instruments, how they are administered, and the economic and political environment within which they are applied. Similarly, in the case of indirect taxes – by far the most important taxes affecting the poor – they again stress the heterogeneity of results and the need for detailed quantitative studies, illustrating the point with a case study from the authors' ongoing work on Jamaica. In particular, they make a strong case for the need for some exemptions from general sales taxes on equity grounds.

Although both formal discussants of this paper seconded its conclusions on the hazards of generalizing about taxes and the need for more attention to equity within, as well as between, groups, they also raised some questions on the approach taken in the paper and introduced a number of additional considerations. One discussant, while supporting the use of micro-data, emphasized in particular the need to use more explicit models of fiscal incidence than those employed in the studies reviewed in the paper. Allowing for saving and the openness of the economy, for instance, might affect the results considerably. As another example, if taxes affect the real value of urban wages, then the decision to migrate from rural to urban areas might be affected, with implications that can only be traced out – albeit imperfectly – in a more explicit general equilibrium framework.

The second discussant argued that administrative considerations cast serious doubt on the argument by Bird and Miller for sales-tax exemptions and, more important, that it did not make much sense in the context of many developing countries to discuss the effects of taxes on the poor without simultaneously discussing the effects of inflation both on taxes and on the poor. Indeed, the two discussants in different ways raised a question that received substantial attention in the ensuing general discussion also: Are the effects of taxes really very important in the face of such pervasive phenomena as inflation, exchange-rate overvaluation, price controls, and other economic forces affecting the well-being of the poor on both the sources (income) and uses (expenditure) sides? The answer given by Bird and Miller is essentially twofold. First, as noted above, taxes on the poor are important, even in light of all these other factors. Second, in any case, governments and others constantly act as though equity in taxation does matter – even though it may well be true, as suggested in the discussion of the Helleiner paper, that they are not primarily concerned with the plight of the poor, let alone that of different subgroups within this broad category.

Another point raised in the general discussion that recurred at various times throughout the conference concerned the treatment of the parallel (or underground) economy. While the discussion of this issue was quite inconclusive, it was apparent that there was a strong divergence – perhaps based in part on experiences in different countries – between those who felt that, on the whole, the parallel economy was a natural and perhaps even healthy reaction to fumbling government intervention, and those who argued strongly that the development of a parallel economy usually brought with it all kinds of undesirable economic and political problems. It was also apparent that the amount of actual knowledge on the precise level, nature, and implications of the parallel economy was not large.

3 Education, Health, and the Poor

While the Bird and Miller paper argued that taxes do have important effects on the poor in developing countries, it did not take issue with the conventional view that the most important budgetary impacts on the poor are through expenditure policies, particularly 'social' programs. The next three papers discuss, in turn, four of the most important areas of social expenditure: education, health, housing, and food subsidies. Their general conclusion is that most of these programs do not, in fact, seem to have done much for the poor.

In his paper on health and education expenditure, for example, Emmanuel Jimenez first demonstrates that the public sector plays a dominant role in the provision of these services in most developing countries and that expenditures on health and education constitute a significant proportion of total public expenditures. He then evaluates these expenditures in a number of countries in terms of their efficiency and equity aspects, and finds them to be severely deficient on both counts.

In terms of equity, Jimenez argues that education in particular is provided in such a way in most countries as to give more benefits to the rich than the poor for a whole series of reasons, ranging from the relative degree of subsidization of particular services to the nature of the rationing systems applied (as illustrated in particular for Colombia). Similarly, in terms of efficiency also, he concludes that too many resources go to higher education rather than primary education. The situation in health, while perhaps not so dramatic, is similar. His recommended solution is on the one hand to lower the subsidies on those services used primarily by the rich through imposing user charges and to use the funds thus obtained to expand the services benefiting the poor, and on the other hand to relax the prohibitions on private provision of health and education services that exist in most countries.

Although the two formal discussants of this paper took quite different tacks, one concentrating on health and one on education, in fact the general tenor of their comments was similar. Both raised questions about the sense of orienting the paper around the concepts of equity and efficiency in the abstract without recognizing explicitly the political reality that in many countries expenditure patterns serving the needs of the elite were precisely what was wanted and not an unintended result to be 'cured' by the application of a quick policy fix. The very different characteristics of health and education were also stressed, as was what was considered to be the evidence that the general underfunding of these fields was at least as important as the misallocation of that funding stressed by Jimenez. Doubt was also cast on both aspects of his proposed solution. If private expenditures or user charges are increased, for example, does it make sense to assume that the level and composition of public expenditures will change as assumed in the paper, given the underlying political structure? And is private-service provision likely to be any better on equity grounds?

The subsequent general discussion again raised, even more strongly than in the case of the tax paper, substantial questions about the underlying model of incidence in this paper. It is far from clear, for instance, that allocating the budgetary costs of particular programs to income groups is a particularly meaningful exercise in either political or economic terms. Politically, grouping people by area, occupation, or ethnic category may be more relevant; economically, the 'benefit incidence' may be much more obscure than these calculations assume and the 'expenditure incidence' (that is, who actually receives the funds – doctors, teachers) more important.

4 Housing and the Poor

The second paper on expenditure programs, by Stephen Mayo and David Gross, takes a narrower focus. Rather than giving a broad survey of housing in developing countries, Mayo and Gross concentrate on a particular type of housing program launched some years ago in an attempt to overcome some of the problems of public housing in reaching the poor in such countries: the site-and-service approach. Their discussion of the extensive experience with sites-and-services programs in a variety of countries, like that in most of the other papers, stresses strongly the importance of the details, in this case of both housing demand and the design of housing policies, in determining the impact of these programs on the poor. In particular, they argue that most programs have consistently overestimated the willingness and ability of the poor to pay for housing and have consequently either not reached the intended target group or have done so only as a result of heavy and unsustainable subsidization. Their suggested solution to this problem is to lower housing standards even further and also to design the subsidy element more explicitly to assist the poor.

While neither formal discussant of this paper raised any objections to its characterization of sites-and-services programs as basically ineffective in reaching the poor, both noted that the housing problem in developing countries really had to be considered in a broader context. One discussant stressed that it was not possible to assess the effects of sites-and-services programs on the micro basis used in the paper; what was needed, for example, was a clearer understanding of the historical situation at the time the program was introduced. The other discussant emphasized the quantitative unimportance of sites-and-services programs, which had housed perhaps only 3 million of the 270 million people who moved to urban areas in developing countries in the 1972–84 period. As well, the discussant questioned the extent to which such projects were little more than political showcases for governments. This discussant's preferred approach would be to have less government intervention directly in housing and more concentration on providing infrastructure to create income-generating opportunities for the poor.

In the ensuing discussion, it became apparent that the sites-and-services approach had its detractors and defenders among the conference participants. Some argued that these projects, usually sponsored by the international agencies, undermined the capacity of local governments to provide housing. Others picked up some of the points raised in earlier discussions, noting the extreme difficulty, even in theory, of analysing the incidence of such programs and their political implications. The principal arguments in support of the sites-and-services approach appeared to be twofold. First, it was better than the only viable alternatives, that is, either doing nothing or else building so-called public housing, which really went almost entirely to the middle class, especially to government employees. Second, the indirect effects of sites-and-services projects in training officials and others in the realities of housing, finance, and other aspects of urban planning had generally been beneficial. Whether 'doing good by stealth' in this way was an efficient use of scarce resources is a question that remained unanswered.

5 Food Subsidies and the Poor

Unlike the developed countries, the developing countries do not have a large and varied spectrum of income-transfer programs that can be deliberately manipulated to achieve any desired distributive outcome. In a number of developing countries, however, in recent years an explicit attempt has been made along these lines in a limited way in the form of food-subsidy programs. Susan Horton's paper first reviews the extent and importance of such programs and then examines in detail the case of one particular food-subsidy program in Tanzania. As she notes, food-subsidy programs can be implemented either implicitly (through producer taxes or quotas, for example) or explicitly, through budgetary outlays. Such programs may also to some extent have specific nutritional goals as a target in addition to a distributional intent. In practice, however, food-subsidy programs often have a strong urban bias, not least for political reasons. Horton's examination of the Tanzanian case generally conforms with her general discussion. She finds, for example, that instead of the subsidy alleviating inequality, its removal would do so because the benefits went not only to urban areas but often to the better-off inhabitants of those areas. The Tanzania example is a particularly negative one: programs in other countries have been more progressive. There are also ways to restructure existing programs so as to benefit the poor more directly; however, the paper concludes that food subsidies are probably not a good policy instrument in African countries.

The first discussant again sounded a familiar note, raising a number of questions about the nature of the incidence analysis and noting the need to consider how subsidy programs are financed and the desirability of probing into the 'black box' of the family in order to understand the effects of subsidies on nutrition and productivity. In some countries, for example, the diets of men, women, and children may differ significantly, so that the choice of the food to be subsidized might be strongly targeted in unforeseen ways.

The second discussant of the Horton paper reverted to another theme that had come up several times in earlier discussion: the need to consider such policies in an appropriate macro-economic context. Food-subsidy programs may, for example, sometimes be a way to maintain aggregate demand. More important, their effects on agricultural prices and hence agricultural development need to be taken into account explicitly in any analysis of their impact. Finally, the dearth of knowledge about the comparative administrative costs of different delivery programs, in this or in other fields, was also stressed.

This last point was picked up in the subsequent discussion from a political perspective, when one participant noted that the question from the governments' point of view was partly whether such subsidy programs were the most cost-effective way of keeping their clientele happy. Other commentators noted that in some countries (e.g., Bangladesh) food subsidies had proved almost the only way to get anything to the rural poor, even if not very efficiently. Still others, while agreeing that food-subsidy programs were inevitably blunt instruments, noted that this was true of almost all policies in developing countries. Finally, various questions were raised about Horton's analysis of the Tanzanian case. In particular, it was noted that the effectiveness with which the program was policed was an important determinant of the size of black markets and hence of the leakage away from the poor – and this characteristic of the program was said to have deteriorated over time.

6 Agriculture and the Poor

A common theme running through all the papers dealing with public expenditures and revenues is that the major impact of such policies is almost invariably on the urban poor (or rich). Most poor people in poor countries, however, live in rural areas. It is, therefore, particularly appropriate that the last paper in this volume, by Albert Berry, deals with the effects of agricultural and rural policies on the poor. Berry essentially sets out a 'professional's model' of agricultural policy, based largely on Taiwan, and then examines why this model seems so seldom to be followed elsewhere, illustrating his analysis by case studies of India and Brazil.

In the course of his discussion, Berry makes a number of general points that are of interest. Noting, like every other author, the very considerable differences between countries, he argues that in the absence of any convincing general development model, history is our best and almost only guide to what works. One important lesson he derives from his own analysis of historical experience in a number of countries, for instance, is that the precise manner in which a policy is implemented is often more important than the details of the policy itself. In an expression that should be familiar to all students of public policy in any country, policy without implementation is nothing, policy plus implementation is policy – and implementation without policy is also policy. That is, what matters is not what people say they are doing or want to do but what they actually do.

More specifically, Berry considers that there are three ingredients of a successful agricultural-development policy: increased output, widespread distribution of the benefits, and some control on population increase. The principal policies he identifies as key to achieving these results include agricultural research and technical improvements, population policy, land reform in at least some instances, and the implementation of adequate health, education, and food policies in rural areas.

The first discussant supported the emphasis on research and population policy but argued that the set of policies influencing pricing and financial conditions – monetary, fiscal, and exchange-rate policy, for example – was considerably more important than Berry indicates. If these policies were off base, both agricultural and general development would be very adversely affected. In Kenya, for example, inappropriate policies had exacerbated the external crisis of recent years, while in Botswana generally sound policies had greatly moderated its effects.

Picking up two themes that had surfaced at several earlier points, the second discussant noted first that it was essential to relate policies to politically relevant groups and not just to such statistical abstracts as deciles. Second, this discussant again stressed that politicians were endogenous to the system and simply could not be treated as something to be tacked onto the end of the economic analysis. For example, could one learn anything useful from the Taiwan experience without knowing that the government was authoritarian in character?

A related important point made in the subsequent discussion was that the Berry paper – indeed, all the papers in this book – follows the conventional rather than the radical or Marxist approach to the problems with which it is concerned. That is, it ignores what some consider to be the basic issue of conflict between classes and the role of government in this conflict as an instrument of the dominant class. A recent survey suggests that the implications of this radical perspective have not really been thought through in detail or empirically tested, but that there is much more scope for careful, scientific work along these lines (Griffin and Gurley, 1985).

It was also argued that the fashionable plea for adopting the 'right prices' was not well founded if it was assumed, as often seemed to be done, that development would follow automatically without a good deal of government intervention. Countries such as Taiwan, Korea, and Brazil are by no means models of liberalism in trade policy, for example. In reply, other participants noted the obvious and avoidable damage done by mistaken trade and interest policies in various countries. Perhaps the best conclusion on this issue as it affects agricultural development came from one participant who noted that to say a country must get prices 'right' means nothing in the absence of a great deal of information about specific circumstances. Mexican wheat is not Thai rice, and generalized advice to raise agricultural prices, for example, is probably just as wrong now as was the generalized advice to squeeze prices in agriculture that was current twenty years ago.

7 Policy Conclusions and Future Research Directions

While many different points are raised in the papers included in this volume – or were touched on in the conference discussion summarized in part above – four themes recurred again and again: the need to identify precisely the poor with whom we are concerned; the heterogeneity of the developing countries and the consequent difficulty of establishing the valid generalizations; the relative desirability of government intervention; and the divergence between the conventional economic approach to these problems and broader 'political-economy' approaches. In addition to illustrating the diversity of the experience and the prior beliefs of conference participants, as well as the relative newness of research on these subjects, each of these themes also suggests potentially fruitful areas for further research, which are developed briefly in this section.

It is not a trivial matter to define who 'the poor' are. Clearly, the absolute level of poverty is important: if those who are already poor become absolutely poorer in the course of economic development, there are obviously grounds for concern. Even if such an increase in absolute poverty were thought to be only transitory, or perhaps even an almost inevitable part of the structural changes accompanying development, such an outcome would obviously be most undesirable, given the low initial level of well-being of the poorest people in developing countries. In a sense, therefore, perhaps the most fundamental concept of poverty is in terms of absolute income standards. As the debate on 'poverty lines' in this country has shown, however, it is not that easy to define precisely who is to be considered poor in absolute terms. Because even the lowest poverty line that might be reasonably drawn in Canada would probably include 99 per cent of the population in many developing countries, it is clear that the application of 'absolute' poverty standards has a strong relative component.

It is also clear that most of us are not concerned with absolute poverty alone. Relative position enters into people's perception of their well-being, so that if the poorest fall behind only in relative and not in absolute terms, there is still reason for concern. As a rule, therefore, income or expenditure deciles (or some similar percentile measures) tend to be used to identify the poor within any particular country. The 'bottom 40 per cent,' for example, is perhaps the most common definition of the poor in the literature. This approach, too, has its problems. Should per capita or per household measures be used? Income, expenditure, or consumption (that is, including services from durable goods such as housing)? Weekly, monthly, annual income, or income over some longer period? Apart from such definitional questions, there is also the problem that undue focus on relative measures may lead us to miss the more important changes in absolute levels of well-being. If the level of living of the poor is doubling every ten years – as has probably happened in Japan, for example – are they likely to be too upset by the fact that their relative share of the rapidly growing national pie is simultaneously shrinking? Should anyone be concerned? Why?

One reason for raising this essentially philosophical question is that abstract measures such as income deciles are not likely to have any very direct relation to policy matters in any case. Whether one is a Marxist, a neo-classical economist, or a pragmatic policy-maker, what matters is not a decile grouping but a class (the urban labour force), a factor of production (labour), or such politically relevant groups as the urban employed or landless rural labourers. However one looks at them, the fact is that the poor is most countries come from very heterogeneous groups. About all they have in common is their lack of productive assets such as physical capital, human capital, access to infrastructure, and access to political power. This commonality is obviously important, although not a very useful basis for policy interventions. What is even more important in the present context are the considerable differences that exist among different groups of the poor in different countries. In some countries, for example, urban labourers may be the poorest of the poor; in others, they may be thought of as well up the social and economic ladder. In all countries, different policies are needed to help different poor groups – and the same policy may have very different effects on different groups. Poor urban labourers with jobs, for instance, are clearly helped by effective labour legislation such as minimum wages; those who do not get jobs as a result of the higher costs of employing labour are just as clearly hurt.

Even within any well-defined group of the poor, there are still substantial problems in discovering and appraising the effects of any particular public policy. There may well be serious problems of horizontal equity. Two poor households equal in all respects except that in one someone smokes and in the other no one does, for example, will be treated very differently by a tax system relying heavily on tobacco taxes. Does this difference matter? There is no simple answer to this question. This same example can be used to bring out another problem in analysing the impact of public policy on the poor, namely, the tendency to treat the household as a 'black box.' Does it make any difference if only men smoke? Or if men and women pool their earnings? Or if only the income of women goes to feed children? There is almost an infinite variety of such questions that might be asked about relationships within the variety of basic social groupings that constitute the essence of social reality in different developing countries. Again, it is hardly surprising that there are unlikely to be any simple answers.

What seems needed to improve knowledge – and ultimately policy – with respect to these problems is, first, a much clearer definition of the precise nature of the object of inquiry (the poor) than is found in much of the literature. Second, it would also be helpful if we were told more precisely why this particular definition was chosen and what the implications of choosing it are. Third, more effort needs to be made to distinguish among different groups of poor people in terms of their relevance to policy, whether as politically salient groups or as possible target groups for particular policy measures. Fourth, in an increasing number of developing countries, more use can be made of micro-data sets to explore these matters. And, finally, a good deal more thought needs to be devoted to the precise meaning and interpretation of the very differentiated results of particular policies that tend to be revealed when one does look closely at their micro effects.

Just as the heterogeneity of the poor in any one country makes it both difficult and perhaps dangerous to generalize too quickly about the effects of particular policies on them, so the heterogeneity of developing countries makes generalizations equally difficult. Very different effects may result from implementing the same policy in different economic and institutional circumstances. The person who initially receives a subsidy or pays a tax, for example, is not necessarily the one who ultimately receives the benefit or bears the tax burden. The ultimate effect of taxes and subsidies upon income distribution depends on the elasticity of supply of factors, the elasticity of demand for products, factor mobility, the degree of openness of the economy, and the degree of monopoly power prevailing in the markets in question, among other things. All these factors obviously vary greatly from country to country.

Similarly, the effects of macro-economic policies and structural-development policies depend very much on the precise circumstances of the country in question, on the precise design of the policies, and – by no means least – on precisely how they are implemented. As in the case of fiscal policies, the indirect or secondary effects of such policies may turn out to be as important as their direct effects if not more important. All in all, despite the very considerable amount of research surveyed in this volume, the inevitable conclusion is that we do not as yet know nearly as much as we should before making pronouncements about the effects of this or that policy on the poor in developing countries.

Two types of research that may help alleviate this situation are comparative studies and detailed historical case studies. Although both of these approaches are decidedly out of fashion in economics today, work along these lines, especially quantitative work at both micro and macro levels, seems more likely to add to knowledge in these important areas than do either abstract theorizing or simplistic empirical studies based on published aggregate data. Several examples of such research are offered in the papers in this volume. Many other useful studies obviously remain to be done on such questions as the composition of expenditure cuts in countries undergoing adjustment programs and the administrative costs of different ways of delivering relief to the poor.

To do such studies correctly requires not only intimate institutional knowledge of the countries in question but also considerable analytical and technical skills in order to be able to piece out a coherent and accurate story from the usually fragmentary and contradictory data and information that can be unearthed. As Bent Hansen (1985) recently noted, 'protection of the poor is ... a serious matter and a difficult one to solve in a satisfactory way, at least in LDCs.' Only a very close examination of the successes and failures of actual policies in a variety of developing countries, and an attempt to disentangle the universal from the particular features of these cases, seem likely, over time, to provide enough of the kind of information needed to enable us to get a firm grasp on this serious and difficult problem.

In the absence of an adequate accumulation of careful case studies and comparisons, what most commentators on policy and the poor tend almost inevitably to do is to draw on their own limited experience and perspectives as the basis for often sweeping generalizations. In no respect is this more likely to be done than with regard to the desirability of government intervention. Given that there appears to be virtually general consensus in the literature that the effects of government policy on the poor in most cases has in practice been less beneficial than hoped, what is to be done?

One extreme view is that not only is there nothing that the governments in most developing countries should do – or at least nothing that they can do, given their limited (and often shrinking) administrative capacity – but that they should cease doing much of what they are now doing, precisely because it is inappropriate and fumbling government intervention that lies at the roots of much of the observed failure. At the opposite extreme, there are still those who hold the faith with respect to the ability of governments to resolve most of the ills of mankind, once freed from the toils of the international capitalist system and the evils of political systems controlled by the economically powerful.

Although most researchers who have studied this subject would not adhere to either extreme view, many clearly lean in one direction or another. Some, for example, would like to see less government and more private activity in such fields as housing, food marketing, and even health and education. Others, noting the prevalence of market imperfections and externalities in some of these areas, doubt the benevolence of the workings of the unfettered market with respect to the poor and assert the continued need for government intervention in these and other areas. Even the latter group, however, nowadays appears often to agree that governments in most developing countries would be well advised to confine their activities to those important areas in which they must and can do something – and should collect better information about the effects of what they are doing.

The papers in this volume, for example, contain many suggestions about ways in which government policies might be reoriented and improved in implementation in order to improve their effects on the poor. More emphasis on primary education and preventive health care, particularly in rural areas, some downgrading of housing standards and increased affordability, increased targeting of food subsidies, and more explicit attention to the distributional aspects of stabilization programs are instances of the sorts of recommendations that are made. In almost all cases, however, it is also noted that a good deal more work is needed in order to do such things right, such as research on the parallel economy and particularly on the administrative aspects of public policy.

Finally, apart from ideological or other reasons for favouring government over private action or vice versa – or for attributing the present ills of the poor in developing countries primarily to external or internal forces – another clear dividing line in the literature surveyed here is between those who take a conventional economic approach to this problem and those who insist that only a broader, interdisciplinary, 'political-economy' approach can get us very far with respect to these issues. Like most of the authors in this book, the editors are economists and are therefore inclined by training and preference to analyse problems as economists customarily do. Moreover, we are firmly of the opinion that such analyses, as exemplified by several of the papers included here, make an invaluable contribution to the study of poverty in developing countries. More and better studies along these lines are therefore essential in the future if we are ever to get a handle on this serious and important problem. The marginal social utility of such contributions, it seems to us, will as a rule surely be much greater than that of yet another twist on some well-honed theoretical model or another econometric run at some set of published numbers.

Nevertheless, it is also clear from the papers in this book that economics is not enough. What determines the success of particular policies? Why are some policies implemented in some countries and not in others? What are the relationships between economic position and political power, and how do these relationships affect what is done – or what can be done? Are policy changes that will help the poor easier or harder to bring about when times are difficult? Under what conditions is it possible to 'do good by stealth,' that is, to introduce policies that aid the poor in addition to achieving some other, more obvious, purpose? What are the most policy-relevant characteristics of the poor, and how do these characteristics relate to the policy instruments available? Is it possible for the design and implementation of policy to be, so to speak, insulated from the pressing realities of daily life (as seems often to be assumed implicitly in economic analyses), and, if so, under what conditions? There is an almost infinite variety of such questions that are highly relevant to the problem of protecting and improving the lot of poor people in developing countries – and the answer to none of them lies in economic analysis alone.

Interdisciplinary work in the social sciences is in some disrepute today, in part for good reasons. Nevertheless, it is our firm conviction that further progress in understanding the interaction between poverty and policy lies not only in the further refinement and development of the tools of each discipline – as urged above for economics – but also in the greater openness and willingness of each to learn from the others. Economists, for instance, must learn to pay much closer attention to the institutional details that are usually – for good and understandable reasons – neglected in their standard disciplinary tool-kit, but which are so often critical in determining the outcome of their recommendations in the real world. At the same time, political scientists, sociologists, anthropologists, and others would do well to pay more attention to the important lessons economics has to offer with respect to the workings of markets and the effects of different incentive structures on human behaviour. And both groups would do well to spend much more time first learning from those engaged in actually doing things – educators, physicians, builders, tax collectors – exactly what they are doing and why. Social scientists can then try to fit these realities into their disciplinary paradigms to the extent possible, rather than assuming they have the answers before they understand the questions.

References

Griffin, K., and J. Gurley. 1985. 'Radical Analyses of Imperialism, the Third World, and the Transition to Socialism: A Survey Article.' *Journal of Economic Literature* 22: 1089–1143
Hansen B. 1985. Book review in *Journal of Economic Literature* 22: 1206–7

2

Stabilization, Adjustment, and the Poor

GERALD K. HELLEINER

The impact of stabilization and adjustment programs upon income distribution and the poor is a matter over which argument rages. 'Usually,' Lance Taylor has said, 'income [re]distribution against labour and the poor is implicit in stabilization attempts' (Taylor, 1983, p. 200). Particularly controversial in this context is the appropriate role of the international financial institutions, particularly the International Monetary Fund (IMF), in the construction and support of such programs. On the one hand, the managing director of the IMF declares (de Larosiere, 1984):

It is often said that Fund programs attack the most disadvantaged segments of the population, but people forget that how the required effort is distributed among the various social groups and among the various public expenditure categories (arms spending or social outlays, productive investment or current operations, direct or indirect taxes) is a question decided by the governments ... A question that may be raised in this connection is whether the Fund should exert pressure in the determination of government priorities and even make the granting of its assistance contingent on measures that would better protect the most disadvantaged population groups. An international institution such as the Fund cannot take upon itself the role of dictating social and political objectives to sovereign governments.

On the other hand, 'by remaining aloof from such questions [of income distribution] the Fund tacitly accepts the distributional policies of the government in power, whether it likes them or not. This, more often than

Permission to reprint an edited version of this paper, which first appeared in *World Development* 15, no. 12 (Dec. 1987), has been granted by the publisher (published by Pergamon Journals, Ltd., Oxford, United Kingdom).

not, implies a *de facto* alignment with forces opposed to reduced inequalities ... the politics are inescapable' (Killick et al., 1984, p. 198).

No less important are the instances in which Fund programs seem to be resisted by equity-oriented governments on the ground that they do not take sufficient account of their likely effects upon poverty and income distribution. There are many sovereign governments, like that of Tanzania, that profess a particular interest in such objectives as 'avoiding measures which would place the burdens of short-term adjustment on the most vulnerable groups' (United Republic of Tanzania, 1982, p. 5). An International Labour Organization (ILO) mission report on Tanzania, addressing 'the problem of how to protect, strengthen and expand past achievements on basic needs against the threats that stem from the deterioration of the external environment and from some failures of domestic policy' (1982, p. 2), notes that these threats 'could be aggravated by orthodox remedies for balance of payments adjustments, such as cuts in recurrent Government expenditure on the social services and a drastic switch from food production for domestic consumption to export crops ... [Their] concern is to propose adjustment policies that would not hit the satisfaction of basic needs of the poor' (p. 3).

UNICEF (1984, p. 169) has also offered a view quite different from that of the IMF: 'The tendency for governments faced with recession to cut back on child-focused social expenditures (and measures which support poorer families) arises from many sources, domestic as well as international. But international influence is often critical, especially when linked to the negotiation of an IMF agreement or an international loan ... as a clear condition of an agreement, as the technical advice of international experts or as the orthodox wisdom promoted in courses or less formal contacts.'

There must always be a wide range of possible policy packages from which a borrower can and should choose in order to achieve precisely the same impact upon external balance, and therefore the capacity to repay international loans. Insistence upon any *one* policy package is analytically indefensible. (Realistically, the likelihood that any externally recommended policy package will 'stick' clearly increases with the degree of local [borrower] input into its construction [see Stewart, 1984, pp. 203–4] – and that is true whether the borrowing government is interested in equity or not.) There can therefore be no *analytical* escape from consideration of the questions of income distribution in assessments of global or national economic experience and policy alternatives.

Not least among the reasons why professional attention must be directed at the effects of macro-economic experiences and policies upon distribution and/or poverty is the fact that these are now widely regarded as important components of overall macro-economic performance. They also have obvious political implications, although there is no easy link between poverty and political instability (Nelson, 1984). Whether they are consciously intended (or professionally analysed) or not, all policy packages imply certain distributional effects. One does not have to raise the fear (or hope?) that international lenders may 'override a sovereign government on distributional questions' in order to make the case that 'distributional issues are a legitimate object of Fund concern' (Williamson, 1982, p. 34). Evidently, the effects of recent macro-economic experiences and policies upon poverty are already matters of grave concern to UNICEF and the ILO, among others (Cornia et al., 1987; ILO, 1986). They deserve more professional attention and analysis than they have so far received. In an admirable summary of the issues Killick et al. reaches a similar conclusion (1984, pp. 242-6, 285; see also Addison and Demery, 1985; Loxley, 1986).

In this paper an attempt is made to survey the recent literature on the impact of stabilization and adjustment programs on the poor and to consider some of the key issues in the context of a particular equity-oriented low-income country. Section 1 considers some of the approaches and issues in earlier analyses. In section 2 the analysis of stabilization and adjustment is segmented into consideration of the effects of restructuring policies, macro-economic restraint, and strategic policy change. Section 3 reviews available evidence on the recent experience of Tanzania with external shock, efforts at stabilization, and relations with the IMF. A brief conclusion may be found in section 4.

1 Previous Analyses and Approaches

Most theorizing about income distributional effects of macro-economic change has addressed only the question of functional distribution and has done so in terms of comparative statics rather than via analyses of adjustment paths (Knight, 1976; Bruno, 1979; Ahluwalia and Lysy, 1981). The usual existence of a large informal sector and the frequent importance of a smallholder farm sector, within both of which incomes are an amalgam of returns to labour, capital, and land, greatly complicate theoretical analyses of the distributional impact of policy changes that depend upon expected changes in factor earnings. Functional distribution of income, while theoretically tractable, therefore usually proves hopelessly unusable for the kind of distributional policy discussion at issue here.

Until recently, the only publicly available analysis of distributional considerations in stabilization emanating from IMF sources was a theoretical paper (Johnson and Salop, 1980) that provided a promising beginning but did not carry us too far. Its starting-point was the presumption that external imbalance is the product of over-expansion of demand, rather than exogenous shock, and that what is at issue is 'reversal of the increased expenditure ... [and] ... unwinding structural changes' (p. 8). Its main focus was upon functional, regional, sectoral, and public-private distribution rather than directly upon size distribution (by household or individual) or distribution by socio-economic group, in which real-world analysts are generally more interested. Recent empirical study within the IMF of some of the distributional aspects of IMF-supported programs has been broader in its sweep but quite inconclusive in its results (Sisson, 1986). World Bank analysis of the distributional implications of structural adjustment programs has also been perfunctory or inconclusive (Yagci et al., 1985, pp. 129–32).

What changes in size distribution of income ought one to expect during periods of macro-economic difficulty? Whatever the debates about its empirical verification (Anand and Kanbur, 1986), if the Kuznetsian U-curve were to be taken seriously, one might argue that at low levels of income, periods of unusual adversity might be accompanied by reduced concentration in the overall distribution of income (although presumably not by any alleviation of poverty). In parts of sub-Saharan Africa, where non-market activities are still significant or constitute a realistic alternative for the energies of participants in a deteriorating market economy, recent experience seems consistent with such expectations. Anecdotes abound, for example, of relatively buoyant (low-level) non-market and rural economies in the face of significant recent overall economic decline. At higher levels of per capita income, in contrast, on the right-hand side of the Kuznetsian U, deterioration of income might typically be accompanied by greater distributional concentration. To the extent that some developing countries had been able to 'advance' the Kuznetsian shift to increasing equity through policies of 'redistribution with growth,' they, too, could expect macro-economic set-backs to reduce the equity of overall distribution. But the original Kuznetsian hypotheses, and most other analyses of interrelationships between growth and income distribution, relate to long-run change rather than to short- or medium-term fluctuations. More to the point in current debates over stabilization and adjustment are the questions relating to changes in the distribution of income over relatively short periods and, particularly, to the welfare of the bottom end of the distribution.

Analysis of the distributional incidence of short-term cut-backs in consumption of goods and services or sectoral restructuring requires knowledge of the context within which they are made. What may seem to be a 'neutral' recommendation of proportional cut-backs for all (e.g., Feinberg, 1982) will, in fact, generate greatly differing distributions of interpersonal or intergroup sacrifice depending on the initial distribution of income. What is regarded as 'fair' or politically feasible can vary with the original distributional context. That context may be the product of political circumstances as well as Kuznetsian ones. Suppose there has relatively recently been improvement in the level of living of bottom-end income recipients or reduction in their numbers or both – with or without overall income growth. (In some circumstances such improvements can contribute to external imbalance.) Can one expect these bottom-end gains to be protected during a subsequent macro-economic adjustment program, particularly one that requires overall retrenchment at least for a time? *Should* this be a domestic or international objective? Cross-national absolute standards have always proved exceedingly difficult to develop, and even more difficult to protect.

Further complexities arise from the fact that immediate (short-run) distributional or poverty effects of macro-economic imbalances or stabilization and adjustment programs may be quite different from longer-run effects. Short-run cut-backs in the consumption levels of the poor may be outweighed by future gains for them that current austerity helps to make possible; then again, future social benefits may not accrue to them at all. Where, in addition to the usual distributional issues, there are also intertemporal reallocations of consumption, the appropriate methodology for assessing distributional effects is presumably the calculation of changes in the present value of future income streams, consequent upon the introduction of alternative stabilization programs. Apart from the inherent difficulty of undertaking plausible calculations of this type with respect to an uncertain future, there is the usual analytical imbroglio over the choice of an appropriate discount rate. Wishful thinking on the part of policy-makers is likely to generate considerably smaller calculated effects upon the 'permanent income' of the poor than upon their immediate income levels. Moreover, the poorest can be assumed to employ a significantly higher rate for the discounting of the future than others do. And the question as to whether there may have been other ways in which to assign the burden of short-run cutbacks always remains. For these reasons, while longer-run effects upon poverty and income distribution should also where possible be addressed, the *prime* issue should normally be the degree to which the *immediate* burden of adjustment falls upon the poor.

Analytical problems and statistical deficiencies have long blocked satisfactory analysis – either at the level of specific countries or more generally – of the question of exactly 'who are the poor?' There are even more ambiguities and unresolved issues relating to the question of the adequacy of the provision of basic needs (Streeten, 1984). The most convenient procedure has typically involved the identification of certain socio-economic categories as 'target groups,' e.g., small farmers, landless workers, unskilled labourers, informal-sector workers, members of particular ethnic groups or castes, women, children. As far as global poverty issues are concerned, it should be self-evident that the lowest-income countries, where the largest numbers and proportions of 'the poor' are concentrated, are those in which macro-economic difficulties are most likely to generate increased absolute poverty.

Virtually all the available general equilibrium analyses of the distributional effects of policy changes (summarized in Dervis, de Melo, and Robinson, 1982, p. 406), which in their nature are comparative static and long-run in character, conclude that size distribution of income is remarkably stable, and thus difficult to alter through policy intervention. The composition of 'the poor,' however, is highly susceptible, in these studies, to macro-economic and policy changes. Urban unskilled workers may replace rural smallholders at the bottom end of the income distribution, or conversely, even if there is no recorded difference in the proportion living at absolute poverty levels. Despite overall stability of size distribution, the welfare of the poorest and subgroups thereof can still be altered to a degree that is highly significant *for them* by macro-economic experience and policy. For these and other reasons, there has been increasing interest in the impact of changes upon particular socio-economic groups.

Simulation of the effects of external shocks and policy responses upon income distribution and poverty using computable general equilibrium models, whatever their limitations, is still in its infancy, and remains virtually untried in the lowest-income countries. It has nevertheless clearly demonstrated that 'differences in economic environment alone suffices to make different groups gain or lose, even with the same adjustment policy. Different adjustment policies also have quite different effects on the distribution' (Dervis, de Melo, and Robinson, 1982, p. 458). The complexity of the interrelationships demands that, wherever possible, analytical approaches allow for them to be pursued. But the effort required for such exercises is considerable, and for most developing countries they remain outside the bounds of possibility for some time to come. Typically one must try to make do with much cruder and more partial approaches.

In more partial analyses, it is important to distinguish between the effects upon distribution and poverty of (i) efforts at restructuring the economy towards the production of relatively more (and the consumption of relatively less) tradable goods and services (exportables and import substitutes), principally via the rejigging of relative product and factor prices, e.g. through (real) exchange-rate devaluation, and necessary investments; (ii) macro-economic contraction or reduction in absorption, of various kinds; and (iii) changes in overall strategy that sometimes accompany stabilization and adjustment programs, e.g., financial or trade liberalization, reduction in the size of the public sector, new approaches to income distribution.

Structural adjustment programs, including those promoted by the World Bank, usually lump elements of the first two together with questions of the third type in what their advocates describe as an inseparable package. However, clarity in the analysis of short- to medium-term effects of stabilization and adjustment programs, per se, is aided by the clear separation of matters of longer-term strategy. This paper will not explore the interrelationships between longer-term strategies and distribution or poverty.

2 Stabilization and Adjustment Programs

A *Restructuring*

Efforts to restructure incentives so as to increase the production of tradables may take many forms, including various administrative devices, but typically involve attempts to alter the real exchange rate by nominal devaluation. Devaluation must have immediate distributional consequences. An IMF staff member has put the point well: 'An exchange rate action becomes a highly charged political decision precisely because it produces change in the distribution of income between producers (or potential producers) of foreign exchange and consumers of foreign exchange' (Mohammed, 1984, p. 188). In cases of severe initial imbalance, it may also 'validate' price changes that have already occurred in local markets, thereby reducing economic rents enjoyed by those previously enjoying favoured access to under-priced foreign exchange.

This is not the place for a detailed analysis of the likely impact of devaluation. But there is a rising consensus that the short-run effects will frequently be both deflationary for demand and inflationary for prices. Such demand deflation may reduce employment in the shortrun. If there is excess capacity in the tradable-goods sector, however, employment may soon rise again. Whether these employment effects translate directly into conclusions as to poverty effects depends on the nature of the economy. In some cases, the urban unemployed are not the poorest.

In the first instance, those who consume tradables will be hit the hardest by increased prices. The effects of the changing structure of prices cannot be understood without knowledge of domestic market structures, price-control systems, and the like, and the typical budgets at different income levels or in different socio-economic groups. (Strictly, one also needs information as to the substitutability of various items in consumption as relative prices alter.) If more generalized inflation results, the consequences become even harder to unravel.

The distributional implications of price inflation and financial disorder are not as simple as they are sometimes portrayed. One simply cannot generalize from the evidence of higher-income countries – to the effect that the poor are hit the hardest because 'lower-income groups tend to have the least access to assets whose values rise *pari passu* with inflation' (Johnson and Salop, 1980, p. 3). In sub-Saharan Africa those engaged primarily in subsistence activities, typically among the poorest, have been very little affected by raging inflation in the monetized sector. It has also been plausibly argued that the casual (and very poor) workers found in many of the developing countries' labour markets, through the frequency of their recontracting, have built-in resistance to the real wage deterioration that typically follows from unexpectedly high rates of price inflation in more formal labour markets (Nugent and Glezakos, 1982). However, there are both theoretical reasons and some evidence to suggest that rapid price inflation will generate faster increases in food prices than in the general price level; and this circumstance will impact disproportionately upon major poverty groups: landless rural workers, urban labour, and the urban unemployed (Killick et al., 1984, p. 47). The evidence on inflation's effects (let alone the effects of varying rates of price inflation) upon poverty and income distribution is unfortunately still quite spotty.

The restructuring, which it is the object of altered incentive structures to accomplish, will, of course, also carry distributional implications. Apart from the possibility of expanded employment through the use of previously underutilized capacity, what other overall effects upon employment, poverty, and distribution would one expect from shifts out of some productive activities (notably non-tradables) into others (tradables)? Considerable research energy has been devoted to demonstrating that manufacturing for export is likely to be more labour intensive than import-substituting manufacturing (e.g., Krueger, 1981). But rather less has been devoted to other no less interesting comparisons, e.g., the factor-intensity characteristics of import-competing food production versus various kinds of exporting; and comparisons of these and other characteristics relevant to distributional considerations of different types and patterns of export activity, e.g., smallholder agriculture, estate agriculture, other primary products, export processing zones, the use of excess capacity in what were originally import-substituting industrial establishments. Most important of all, we need to know how various categories of non-tradables typically compare with tradables in respect of these various production characteristics. The presumption must be that most non-tradables are highly labour intensive, e.g., construction, government, and other services. Indeed, 'switching from non-tradables to tradables' may sometimes be seen as little more than a euphemism for reducing wages and employment in government and the organized service sector, relative to other sectors. Clearly, much also depends on the intersectoral mobility of labour (and other resources and factors). The overall impact of restructuring upon total factor demand may thus generate redistribution at the expense of labour, particularly in the formal sectors, even when resources are shifted primarily in the direction of export activity that is labour intensive relative to most import-competing activity.

How such changes affect income distribution and poverty depends very much on the specifics of each case. Where resources are shifted from urban services to smallholder farmers to permit them either to grow more import-substituting food or export crops, as occurs in sub-Saharan Africa today, equity may increase and poverty decline. This effect is even more likely if displaced urban workers still have the option of returning to their villages. However, similar resource shifts toward estate agriculture or mining activity may, in other cases, widen income disparities and worsen the problems of urban marginal groups. In one simulation of the primary-exporting Colombian economy, the results of which are obviously dependent on the detailed assumptions of the model, subsidies to expand exports appear to increase poverty whereas import tariffs lower it (Dervis, de Melo, and Robinson, 1982).

B *Macro-economic Restraint*

Adverse external shocks of a long-run or permanent nature require restructuring towards tradables; but if this move cannot be achieved quickly and if there is inadequate offsetting expansion in external credit, external balance will require that overall spending contract. The degree to which such macroeconomic restraint is required thus depends upon both the success of internal restructuring and external circumstances over which a country has very little influence. While restructuring can itself, as has been seen, have either positive or negative effects upon the welfare of labour and the poorest (two categories which, again, are not synonymous), contraction of overall spending is almost certain to lower the well-being of both. The pursuit of poverty-related objectives, therefore, would seem to require minimizing the need for such deflationary measures, and to call for special attention to supply-side policies – encouraging investment in bottleneck-breaking and relevant restructuring activities. An appropriate incentive structure, particularly an appropriate real effective exchange rate and targeted domestic investment spending, via governmental and parastatal budgets, targeted credit, and tax-cum-subsidy arrangements, together with the necessary input of external credit, is the obvious requisite for minimizing the need for and the impact of deflation.

Faster domestic structural readjustment or greater provision of external finance to ease the adjustment process means that less consumption and income have to be cut. Econometric models that allow for production and consumption elasticities and reallocations – and, implicitly, longer time horizons – will, therefore, simulate different (less devastating) results from external adverse shocks for the welfare of the poor.

In recent years, despite significant restructuring success, inherent rigidities together with inadequate external credit have forced most of the non-oil developing countries to respond to major external shocks through severe cut-backs in overall spending. During the second major external shock of the past decade (1979–83), investment cut-backs accounted for proportionately a much larger share of these aggregate cut-backs than in 1973–5 (Helleiner, 1986a). These cut-backs in investment, made necessary by the political limits to further reductions in consumption, have themselves slowed the restructuring process and thereby created a need for even longer maintenance of restraint policies.

The roots of macro-economic imbalance may also lie in domestic 'overheating.' Macro-economic contraction in response to such domestic overabsorption may be thought normally to follow a course that simply reverses previous inappropriate expansion, and thus to reverse any associated income redistribution. But there should be no such presumption with respect to the incidence of contractionary monetary and fiscal policies. If, for example, previous over-expansion of demand was associated with attempts to improve the welfare of the poorest, it may be appropriate or even politically necessary to allow for a 'ratchet' that limits any reversal in their gains and imposes the required cut-backs somewhere else. Much may also depend upon whether cut-backs are achieved through consumption cuts (savings increases) or investment cuts. Where the adjustment mechanism primarily takes the form of domestic savings adjustment (upward) to permit continued investment at previous rates, one can expect, on Kaldorian assumptions (that capitalists save whereas wage-earners do not), that there will have to be a major redistribution of income from labour to capital or, on Keynesian ones (that, on the margin, the rich save proportionally more than the poor), from low-income earners to higher-income ones. Similarly, whether the cuts impact upon the public or the private sectors may have significant distributional implications. While there may be some exceptions, and detailed empirical analysis is rare, the usual presumption is that overall government expenditures are more equitably distributed than private ones, and that public-sector cut-backs are more likely to harm the poor than are private expenditure cut-backs of equal size. (In fact, cut-backs in public expenditure may also engender further reductions in private expenditure.)

The distributional consequences of particular fiscal and monetary policies may be quite difficult to establish. In principle, it should be relatively easy to identify ex post the losers from actual cut-backs in governmental expenditures and increases in governmental revenues by analysing their composition. As always, however, expenditure and accounting classifications are not usually those one would want for an exercise of this kind; and there remain difficult issues relating to the possibility of shifting the apparent incidence of tax and expenditure changes to others. It would be a useful exercise to seek cross-section evidence as to the 'viscosity' of different kinds of governmental expenditure in response to changing overall expenditure levels. 'Ratchet effects' that vary in intensity across categories of expenditure may make revenue or expenditure-elasticity data derived from periods of rising incomes and expenditures of limited use for the analysis of the likely composition of cut-backs. The Latin American and African experience of the past decade, and particularly the last five years, should offer plenty of scope for careful testing of the popular proposition that, whatever the composition of expenditures when they are rising, cut-backs typically impact disproportionately upon social programs and the poorest. Some (inadequately disaggregated) analysis has suggested that social sectors suffered less than others when cut-backs occurred in the 1970s (Hicks and Kubish, 1984). There is also evidence that the poorest may not be major beneficiaries of social expenditures; if this is the case, they will obviously not lose from cut-backs in them. In principle, again, at least at the technical level, it should be *possible* to target cut-backs and taxes so as to minimize the effects upon the poorest. The particular mix of revenues and expenditures actually selected in any restraint program is obviously only one of an infinite range of possibilities.

In this context, the issue with respect to food or other consumer subsidies is not so much whether they *always* raise the welfare of the poorest or how they might be constructed so as to achieve that result (Horton, 1984) as the likely effects of their removal, on fiscal policy grounds, in specific country cases. While the principal beneficiaries of such subsidies are typically urban dwellers, and these are not always the poorest, a number of careful analyses of specific country cases demonstrates that food subsidies *can* have significant poverty-alleviating effects. The Egyptian food-pricing and rationing system, for example, significantly redistributes income toward both the urban and the rural poor (Alderman and von Braun, 1984). In Thailand, raising the (artificially depressed) price of rice would have minimal effects upon rural poverty because most of the gains would be realized by large commercial farmers, while in the short-to-medium run it would noticeably reduce the incomes of the urban poor (Trairatvorakul, 1984). The restructuring of Sri Lanka's rice subsidy system in 1978-9, which assuredly saved on the government budget, appears to have had a strongly negative impact upon nutrition among the poor (Edirisinghe, 1984; Isenman, 1980, p. 240). These cases illustrate the naïvety and possible perversity of generalized advice to reduce or eliminate governmental interventions in food (or other) markets purely on stabilization and adjustment grounds. There exists a distinct possibility, contrary to much received wisdom (e.g., Finch, 1982, p. 78; Adelman and Robinson, 1978), that raising agricultural prices may actually worsen poverty problems (see also Ghai and Smith, 1983). None of this account is meant to suggest that existing subsidy schemes cannot be improved or that all ostensibly poverty-oriented market interventions achieve their objectives. The point is, rather, that each country case deserves careful analysis, that there exist governments effectively pursuing equity objectives through market intervention and even rationing measures, and that simple generalized answers to adjustment problems are of dubious value and certainly not distributionally neutral.

The analysis of the effects of generalized monetary contraction or credit ceilings upon poverty or income distribution is particularly difficult because these effects are mediated through a complex system of credit rationing and financial markets. In all economies, credit restraint and interest-rate increases hit some groups with much greater impact than others. Those who can finance themselves are least affected, and those who are most dependent upon credit, least flexible, and least influential in financial institutions are hit the hardest; but who these groups are obviously varies from place to place. 'Generalized' monetary restraint is never 'neutral' in its impact. Particularly deserving of analysis, however, are governmental attempts explicitly to influence the distribution and cost of credit to identifiable lower-income groups.

Financial liberalization and interest-rate 'reform' are matters that properly belong in the category of strategic choice. The evidence that interest rates are significantly correlated with aggregate domestic-savings rates is by no means unambiguous, and orthodox argument has gradually eased away from firm pronouncements in this regard (Giannini, 1983; Arida, 1984, pp. 26-32; Khan and Knight, 1985, p. 14). Higher interest rates are unambiguously likely to draw savings into the formal financial intermediation sector, including, in many countries, parts owned or controlled by the state, and thus to reduce 'financial repression' where it exists. In some instances – but by no means all – such a policy may also reduce capital flight abroad or even engender inflows of both previously expatriated domestic capital and fresh foreign capital. Whether redirecting savings into organized financial markets improves allocation, stability, or equity remains a matter of some dispute. It may reduce the role of efficient curb markets and even lower the total supply of loanable funds. It may also reduce the credit rationing role of the state. In both these instances the welfare of lower-income groups may suffer from the change in allocation mechanisms. It is also quite possible to overshoot, from a social standpoint, both with interest-rate increases and with financial liberalization. And such reforms can stimulate inflation. These matters are clearly *not* inherently matters purely, or even primarily, of stabilization and adjustment policy (e.g., Diaz-Alejandro, 1985; Roe, 1982; Taylor, 1983).

Whatever one may conclude about distributional effects, there must be a strong presumption that, other things being equal, macro-economic contraction will worsen poverty. While the relationship is not tight, and there is room for offsetting policies, there must also be a presumption that the greater the reduction in overall absorption, the greater the adverse impact upon poverty.

C *Strategy Change*

Changes in overall strategy may be initiated at the same time as a stabilization and adjustment program; particularly is this likely if the latter program is the product of a change of government. Pressure from international financial institutions today directs borrowing governments toward increased reliance upon market forces, trade and financial liberalization, and a reduced role for the state and state-owned enterprises. Only a few years ago the World Bank exerted pressure upon prospective borrowers to pursue policies and projects that would improve the welfare of the poorest; but this thrust has been abandoned in recent discussions of structural adjustment, at least in part because of diminished confidence that ostensibly poverty-oriented programs were actually helping the poor. It may be extremely difficult in practice to disentangle changes in overall strategy from programs of stabilization and adjustment in some countries. Indeed, proponents of the more extreme versions of current 'orthodoxy' would seem to have it that today's macro-economic imbalances usually originate primarily, or in large part, from strategic deficiencies and that adjustment *necessarily* implies a strategic (pro-market) change of direction. Recent and current macro-economic difficulties reflect, in their view, the piling of external shocks upon more deep-seated underlying problems of strategic misdirection. More plausible to most harassed decision makers in developing countries is the possibility that traditional advocates of market-oriented approaches are using the current opportunity of an unusually severe global economic environment to press their unchanged views upon countries now desperately in need of external assistance.

Issues of development strategy relating to such matters as the role of the public sector, the degree of 'openness,' and the appropriate degree of attention to be devoted to income distribution remain matters of political and professional disagreement, in which ideology and politics are at least as important as economic analysis. In principle, therefore, changes in these strategic dimensions should be analysed separately from programs of stabilization and adjustment, pure and simple, in which what is at issue is simply some combination of deflation and restructuring. Much of the Latin American stabilization debate has been confused by the consideration of cases in the Southern Cone where stabilization objectives were coupled with another, strategic, agenda (e.g., Foxley, 1981).

3 The Tanzanian Case

A proper test of the inherent interrelationship between shocks, stabilization, and poverty and income distribution requires analysis of cases in which there was no sharp break in the government regime during the period of observation. A stronger test of whether shocks and stabilization efforts must impact particularly severely (or for that matter impact at all) upon the poor is offered by analysis of cases in which governments retain clear commitments to equity objectives. Such cases are also likely to reveal equity-based sources of conflict, if they exist, between governments and the orthodoxy of the international financial institutions.

The limits to the capacity of even an unusually equity-oriented government of a low-income country to protect the welfare of the poor in the face of a deteriorating macro-economic environment are sadly evident in Tanzania. It can be argued that Tanzanian development strategy had been misguided in some of its particulars during the 1970s but, until 1978, its growth rate was well above the sub-Saharan African average (World Bank, 1981, p. 144), macro-economic management was cautious, the inflation rate was fairly modest (13 per cent), and the economy had successfully weathered the severe external shocks of 1974–5 (Green, Rwegasira, and Van Arkadie, 1981). At the same time, accomplishments in the realm of basic needs provisions were impressive. In the twenty years after independence, Tanzania raised life expectancy from 42 to 51 years, and adult literacy from 10 per cent to 79 per cent, among the very highest rates in the World Bank's 'low-income' category (World Bank, 1984). Fifty per cent of the population acquired access to potable water. Rural health centres and dispensaries greatly expanded in number as part of a general health policy emphasizing preventive medicine, though the very low starting-point still left Tanzania sadly deficient in medical facilities, by global standards.

External shocks in the form of terms of trade collapse took rising shares, averaging over 10 per cent (nearly 15 per cent in 1983), from prior levels of Tanzanian gross domestic product (GDP) during the 1979–82 period (Balassa and McCarthy, 1984, p. 83). Further blows were imparted by the costs of the 1979 Uganda war, the breakdown of the East African Community, and an unusual succession of droughts. Green estimates that Tanzania obtained no more than 15–20 per cent of the financing it would have required to offset the external blows to its current account in the 1978–84 period. Barely 1 per cent was in the form of low-conditionality finance or 'liquidity' (Green, 1984, pp. 42–3). 'Exceptional' financing in the form of supplier credits and accumulation of arrears on external payments, and, above all, massive cut-backs in import volume and thus in output were the inevitable results.

Per capita income is estimated (by the World Bank) to have dropped by between 15 and 20 per cent in 1980–2, and it probably fell by about that much again in the subsequent two years. It seems safe to assume that per capita income fell by at least 25 per cent between 1979 and 1984–5. (Green, 1984, p. 43, arrives at a comparable figure.) Whereas there was a reasonable degree of success with efforts both to stabilize and to protect the poorest in the 1974–5 period of external pressure, events this time overcame the possibilities.

The principal macro-economic policy measures employed by the Government of Tanzania during the first half of the 1980s were:
- currency devaluations – a small 'technical adjustment' in 1982, followed by two major devaluations in 1983–4, making a total of roughly 50 per cent (in terms of U.S. dollars) between 1980 and 1984;
- major real cuts and reorientation towards agriculture in the development budget;
- reductions in real public expenditures on defence and social services, and reorientation of public expenditures on the productive sectors towards rehabilitation and maintenance;
- increased taxes on beer, cigarettes, and other consumer goods;
- holding nominal wages fixed from 1981 until 1984, and then raising them

by significantly less than required to make up the effects of inflation in the interim;
- substantially raising nominal producer prices for agricultural cash crops so as at least to limit real declines.

Despite these and many other more 'structural' policy changes, for example, in marketing and distribution (reduced price controls, increased flexibility and restoration of the role of the cooperatives in agricultural marketing, concentrated efforts to raise marketing efficiency) and in governmental institutions, these measures fell far short of what was required to restore macro-economic balance. The government resorted to significant borrowing from the Central Bank with inevitable consequences for the domestic rate of price inflation. Rapid domestic inflation was less than offset by currency devaluations, so that the real effective value of the currency continued to rise. Even after the 1984 devaluation, it remained substantially over-valued relative to its level in the early 1970s (before external shocks made even that level unsustainable). Major restructuring towards increased production and reduced consumption of tradable goods was and is still required. And it is difficult to see how it can be achieved, even with further rejigging of incentives, as long as total absorption, and particularly intermediate goods imports and investment, must be so constrained by the need to maintain short-term, external balance. Only a major infusion of foreign exchange – such as might result from vigorous global recovery or from increased external assistance – seems likely to be able to break the current bottlenecks.

It is difficult to work out the details of the distribution of the effects of shock, restraint, and adjustment efforts in Tanzania. Such crucial data as those on GDP, the rate of price inflation, and informal sector and parallel market activity are among those that are either unavailable or extremely shaky. (An assessment of some of the major data limitations may be found in ILO, 1982, technical appendices.) Certainly urban real wages plunged by proportions greater than those for the economy as a whole, and the reductions were even greater for higher income earners. Official price indexes may understate the real rate of urban inflation as items in the 'basket' are frequently not available at all, and unofficial premiums may be paid above shop prices by buyers who can afford them in order to assure their supplies. As well, there has been increasing unrecorded resort to urban subsistence activity (chickens, food crops, etc.) and 'grey' activities, notably trading, on the part of urban dwellers; opportunities for these possibilities are undoubtedly greater for those at higher income levels. For what they are worth, the data on real minimum wages suggest a decline in the order of nearly 40 per cent over the 1980–4 period. (In 1980 the real minimum wage was already about 25 per cent below the level of a decade previously.) An upward adjustment of nominal wages in the mid-1984 budget was offset by simultaneous removal of the previous heavy subsidy on maize flour (*sembe*), the basic foodstuff, and other tax and price increases associated with a 26 per cent devaluation. Under the new (1984) nominal wage and tax structure, with continuing price inflation of at least 35 per cent (annual rate), the real wage probably dropped to less than half the level of 1980 in 1985. Most observers agree that the urban unskilled worker was already living at a lower level than the average subsistence farmer in the early 1980s (Green, 1984; ILO, 1982, p. 256). Employment in the formal sector was maintained (indeed, some figures suggest it even grew, though at a less rapid rate than previously); this protection of employment was obviously at the cost of significant declines in labour productivity as utilization of capacity and overall economic activity declined. The sharp drop in urban real incomes must have generated parallel reductions in the incomes of urban small and informal-sector business, and declining real wages and employment in this sector. (In a survey of firms in the Dar es Salaam informal sector in 1981 [ILO, 1982], unpaid family labour made up 50 per cent of total labour input and hired labour earned less, on average, than the minimum wage.) Government expenditures on both capital and recurrent accounts were severely cut in real terms – to the cost of the availability of services; maintenance of roads, buildings, and equipment; and the supply of crucial inputs to schools, dispensaries, and other social services. The decline in the overall quality of life in the capital city is instantly visible and much commented upon by returning visitors. Anecdotal evidence suggests that rural/urban migration has stopped, and there has probably been a reverse flow (at least from Dar es Salaam) in the last few years.

The urban formal sector is too small for even very severe cuts in its income to cushion the rest of the economy from the effects of such sharp overall decline. Real grower prices for cash crops – for both export and domestic food – dropped significantly, along with other measures of economic activity. Domestic real prices for export crops had been permitted to decline over the 1970s largely in consequence of rising domestic marketing margins but also in response to a new policy emphasis on food production (Ellis, 1982). They now dropped even further – more or less in parallel with the decline of real world prices. The real price declines for coffee shown in table 2.1 were about 45 per cent between 1969 and 1980, and another 49 per cent over the 1980–4 period. Cotton price declines, while severe, were not quite as steep. (Coffee and cotton have been the most important smallholder export crops. Similar real producer price declines occurred in other Tanzanian agricultural exports, with the single exception of cashew nuts.) The effects of these declines upon smallholder incomes were undoubtedly moderated by the opportunities for expanding both subsistence activities and sales of increasingly profitable food crops in uncontrolled or 'parallel' local markets. How much rural real incomes actually fell is therefore impossible to quantify accurately. The burden of the overall external shock seems, however, to have been borne disproportionately by urban dwellers. (The further shocks imparted by bad weather are, of course, another matter.)

It became a matter of conscious adjustment policy, beginning in 1983, to raise real producer prices for export crops (by 5 per cent per year). While in 1983-4 inflation continued slightly to outstrip nominal grower price increases, the government was now firmly committed to halting and reversing the previous downward slide in real grower prices. As has been seen, urban real incomes and incomes in the formal sector, primarily in government services, probably continued to decline.

The net effect of this 'adjustment' experience – and effective stabilization and adjustment are still far from achieved – was further to narrow intra-urban real wage differentials (though some of this effect may be offset by increased 'grey' income at the higher end); to eliminate and probably even reverse previous rural/urban unskilled labour differentials; and to reduce accessibility and quality in the previously widespread provision of health services, basic education, and water supplies. Urban poverty has certainly increased, although real declines have probably been somewhat buffered by the possibility of return migration to rural areas. Weather effects may have been just as severe as external ones in the creation of significant, though smaller, increases in rural poverty. The heaviest blows outside the capital city were probably registered by the decline and decay of public social services.

Disagreement between the Government of Tanzania and the IMF centred on the handling of agricultural prices and the exchange rate, the degree of 'shock' that the economy and polity could sustain, the role of the public sector, and the attention to be paid to income distribution. There can be no doubt that the Tanzanians erred in allowing many agricultural producer prices and the exchange rate quickly to reach inappropriate values and, subsequently, in being too slow to correct their massive currency overvaluation. But, once out of line, it is not so evident that Tanzanian advocacy of a more gradual process of price adjustment and devaluation – as opposed to the 'shock,' once-for-all attempt to restore real grower incentives and an appropriate real exchange rate through a massive nominal devaluation that the fund recommended – was incorrect.

TABLE 2.1
Indexes of real minimum wage and selected real producer prices
for export crops, Tanzania, 1969 and 1980-5

		Real producer prices[b]	
	Real minimum wage[a]	Coffee	Cotton
1969	100	100	100
1980	74	54	65
1980	100	100	100
1981	96	85	84
1982	76	80	76
1983	59	63	74
1984	63	53	72
1985	48	57	86

[a] 1969-80 data calculated from ILO, 1982, p. 268. Post-1980 wage data from official
announcements; price data were calculated from price inflation figures cited in the
Speech of the Minister for Finance to the National Assembly, 14 June 1984 (moving his
year-to-year price-change data one year forward). Inflation rate for 1984-5 has been
estimated at 30 per cent.

[b] Ellis (1982), for 1969-80. For later years, data are those of the Tanzanian Ministry of
Agriculture, converted to 1979-80 base. 1985 data estimated on basis of announced crop
prices and assumed 30 per cent inflation rate.

Inefficiencies in the public sector, particularly in the agricultural
marketing boards, which were much discussed in Fund/Bank consultations,
are matters of longer-run concern. The previous Tanzanian record of exper-
imentation, assessment, and reform suggested that they could and would, in
time, restructure their institutions if they were not effectively functioning;
and so, in substantial degree, they have done. While they certainly are relevant to future Tanzanian economic performance, these 'strategic' matters
will not be regarded here as part of the stabilization and adjustment effort.

It is not evident, in retrospect, that there were great disagreements of
distribution-related policy substance between the Fund and the Tanzanians
so much as there were differences of principles and of approach. Major differences with respect to distributional policy were not possible in the face of
such severe macro-economic constraints. The Fund's missions resolutely
refused to analyse matters of distributional equity or the broader much-
publicized aspirations (and considerable successes) of the Tanzanian
government with respect to the reduction of poverty. (The World Bank,
which had been deeply involved in the development of strategies designed to

meet basic needs in Tanzania and elsewhere, was much more sensitive at that time in these matters.) The Tanzanians insisted that they were fundamental.

Tanzania's 'social' achievements can be regarded as long-gestation-period investments that many would argue will eventually yield high returns provided they are not permitted to depreciate unduly. The World Bank, which actively encouraged a basic-needs-oriented strategy, as did many other aid donors in the 1970s, specifically warned, in its 1980 World Development Report, of the 'serious danger that economic stringency in the next few years will lead to cutbacks in human development programs, despite the importance of their contribution – often exceeding that of additional physical investment – to Africa's long-term development potential' (p. 86). For the international community now to demand severe cut-backs on the ground that Tanzania could not afford its anti-poverty programs would have seemed, at best, tactless and, quite possibly, cruelly false economy. Whatever else it may have advised, the Fund did not apparently directly target poverty-oriented programs for cuts.

One informed observer summarizes as follows:

The linked issues of absolute poverty eradication and of income distribution have certainly been ones on which Tanzania and the Fund have not seen eye to eye. However, because Tanzania's rural bias and the Fund's desire to raise the real price of exportables ran in parallel ... the actual income distribution debates have turned largely on agreeing prudent levels of export crops ... Fund missions have avoided targeting health, education and water specifically as areas for expenditure cuts ... Thus in fact income distribution and basic services have not, at least since 1979, surfaced in an overtly ideological way. (Green, 1984, p. 30)

As has been seen, changes in the structure of prices for consumed products can have profound distributional consequences and, particularly, increases in basic foodstuff prices can severely impact upon the poor. Though more difficult to measure, changes in the availability of basic consumer goods or in access to free or cheap public services may also have important effects upon poverty. The main point at which differences of approach toward distributional issues generated sharp policy disagreement between the IMF and the Government of Tanzania was on the question of the *sembe* subsidy. The IMF wanted it removed because of the substantial drain it represented on the government's recurrent budget (and, indirectly, its effect on monetary expansion). In later years, it could argue that parallel markets already so dominated urban markets that the removal of the subsidy probably would have the prime effect of eliminating economic rent (earned by the fortunate few who received *sembe* at the subsidized price and enjoyed – through resale or consumption – its full market value), and thereby could actually improve the equity of income distribution. When the argument began, however, it seemed clear that the subsidy's elimination would further reduce the welfare of urban income-earners, already hard hit by the overall macro-economic shocks, and would disproportionately affect the lowest-income urban groups whose budgets were most heavily oriented towards essential food. Although the *sembe* subsidy was not originally intended to be more than an interim measure (Green, 1984, p. 32) – a similar one introduced to offset world grain price increases in 1973–4 was subsequently removed – its retention acquired symbolic importance in the context of the dispute with the IMF. When finally eliminated in mid 1984, the resulting 160 per cent official retail price increase for maize-meal was more than compensated for, at least in the first instance, by a 35 per cent nominal increase in minimum wages (government wages and salaries increased by between 8 and 35 per cent, the smallest proportionate increases offered at the highest levels of income). *Sembe* could not have accounted for more than 20 per cent of low-income consumer budgets, and obviously much less for the better-off. (*Sembe* and rice, together, made up 21.8 per cent of the weights in the calculation of the Dar es Salaam minimum-wage-earners' price index. Food of all kinds makes up 71.4 per cent.) At least in the first instance, then, and particularly if they were already paying higher black-market prices for *sembe*, low-income workers were not made worse off by the combination of wage increase and food-subsidy elimination in mid 1984. (As has been seen, however, their real incomes probably continued steadily to decline thereafter.) Such a compensated abolition of the subsidy could have been introduced earlier, but the IMF insisted throughout, again for obvious budgetary reasons, that nominal wages should be held to increases much below anticipated major nominal price increases. In the end the Tanzanians had little option, in any case, but to eliminate the subsidy.

4 Future Directions

The analysis of interrelationships between stabilization and adjustment programs and poverty proves to be highly complex. Generalizations seem likely to be of limited value. Computable general equilibrium models, despite their inability to handle non-marginal changes, dynamic processes, and transitions between equilibria, have shed valuable light upon some of the possible longer-run effects of broad differences in adjustment policies. More work of this kind seems warranted; expense and data requirements, however, limit the range of these models' likely applicability, and there are some questions that, in any case, require more micro-level and shorter-run investigation. What seems most clearly required is more detailed analysis of specific countries' experiences with different kinds of macro-economic imbalance and different short- or medium-term policy responses. Particularly useful may be comparative empirical analyses of the composition of cutbacks in real government expenditures; the incidence of new governmental revenues; the impact of generalized inflation or particular kinds of relative price change upon the poor; and the distributional and poverty implications of alternative output-mixes, particularly allowing for differing factor intensity and other characteristics of non-tradables as against tradables, and differing characteristics of various kinds of exports. The sheer compilation of the facts with respect to the impact upon poverty of recent external shocks and policy responses remains to be done in most developing countries and is an obvious matter for research attention.

The Tanzanian case illustrates the limited range of policy alternatives that, particularly in the poorest countries, may confront even the most determined governmental protector of the most vulnerable groups. It also illustrates the difficulty of inducing from readily available data the distributional and poverty consequences of macro-economic events in a poor country. Distribution-related differences between the Government of Tanzania and the IMF seem to have been largely matters of approach and of style rather than of policy substance. Though one cannot generalize from this country's experience, it does seem that an IMF more oriented towards analysis of distributional questions may, in some instances, be received more warmly by leftist or populist governments, without any major alteration in the overall complexion of the policy package that must be agreed upon between them and the Fund. In such circumstances there seems little merit in the IMF's maintenance of a purported distributional 'neutrality' that forbids any country-level analysis of what are regarded by borrowers as crucial questions. More generally, professional analysis relating to the poverty and distributional consequences of alternative short-term policy packages (as well as long-term ones that have so far received more attention) is bound to be useful because these matters are of both national and international interest in all countries. There seems no reason why the IMF could not collaborate productively with the World Bank, the ILO, UNICEF, and others in such research and policy analysis.

On one last matter it is possible to be fairly unequivocal, and the Tanzanian case study helps to make it more concrete. The correlation between the incidence of absolute poverty and per capita income is not perfect but it is close. When equivalent external blows impact upon very low-income countries, there must be a presumption that, other things being equal (including the distribution of income), the proportion of households and people pushed over the line into 'absolute poverty' will be greater than in middle-income or better-off countries. When one adds the fact that the very low-income countries typically are less adaptable and flexible in their economic structure than are more developed countries, and are therefore likely, in response to external shocks, to have to resort to deflation to a greater degree and for longer lengths of time, this presumption increases. To make matters still worse, some of the low-income, primary exporting countries have suffered the heaviest external shocks of all in recent years; and there is every prospect of continued severe instability in real primary commodity prices. Nor can the lowest-income countries expect stabilization finance from commercial banks.

For all these reasons, international concern with global poverty ought to have led to buffering arrangements to ease the stabilization and adjustment difficulties of the poorest countries when they are hit by exogenous shocks. Unfortunately, the evolution of the international monetary and financial system has run in precisely the reverse direction in recent years, as not only aid but also both liquidity and stabilization finance for the poorest countries have actually fallen (Helleiner, 1985). There can never be total assurance that the provision of such external finance would reduce the incidence of poverty; but there is certainly a strong presumption that it could. There is evidence to suggest that in sub-Saharan Africa the provision of such stabilization finance would have increased growth rates as well (Helleiner, 1986a). Excluding China and India, the amounts required to make a significant difference to the stabilization of the low-income countries are very modest, relative to the overall activities of the IMF and World Bank. Doubling present IMF commitments to the low-income and lower-middle–income countries as a group would involve less than existing IMF commitments to Argentina alone. Reforms in this area seem the most obvious means of limiting the impact of macro-economic imbalance upon poverty.

Note

An earlier version of this paper was prepared for a conference on government policy and the poor in developing countries, co-sponsored by the Institute for Policy Analysis and the Development Studies Programme, University of Toronto, 25–26 April 1985. I am grateful to the following for comments on this earlier draft: Sidney Dell, Joan Nelson, Vito Tanzi, Rolph van der Hoeven, Frances Stewart, Steven Triantis, and participants in the conference. None bear any responsibility for the contents of the current version.

References

Addison, Tony, and Lionel Demery. 1985. 'Macro-economic Stabilization, Income Distribution and Poverty: A Preliminary Survey.' Overseas Development Institute Working Paper no. 15. London

Adelman, Irma, and Sherman Robinson. 1978. *Income Distribution Policy in Developing Countries: A Case Study of Korea.* Stanford: Stanford University Press

Ahluwalia, Montek S., and Frank J. Lysy. 1981. 'Employment, Income Distribution, and Programs to Remedy Balance-of-Payments Difficulties.' In William R. Cline and Sidney Weintraub (eds), *Economic Stabilization in Developing Countries,* pp. 149–89. Washington: The Brookings Institution

Alderman, Harold, and Joachim von Braun. 1984. 'The Effects of the Egyptian Food Ration and Subsidy System on Income Distribution and Consumption.' International Food Policy Research Institute Research Report 45. Washington

Anand, Sudhir, and S.M. Ravi Kanbur. 1986. 'Inequality and Development: A Critique.' Economic Growth Center, Yale University, Twenty-Fifth Anniversary Symposium on 'The State of Development Economics: Progress and Perspectives' (mimeo)

Arida, Persio. 1984. 'Macroeconomic Issues.' Prepared for United Nations University Conference on 'New Directions in Development Theory,' December, MIT (mimeo)

Balassa, Bela, and F. Desmond McCarthy. 1984. 'Adjustment Policies in Developing Countries, 1979–83: An Update.' World Bank Staff Working Papers, no. 675. Washington

Bruno, Michael. 1979. 'Income Distribution and the Neoclassical Paradigm.' *Journal of Development Economics* 6, no. 1: 3–10

Cornia, G.A., Richard Jolly, and Frances Stewart (eds). 1987. *Adjustment with a Human Face.* Oxford: Clarendon Press

Dervis, Kemal, Jaime de Melo and Sherman Robinson. 1982. *General Equilibrium Models for Development Policy.* A World Bank Research Publication. Cambridge: Cambridge University Press

Diaz-Alejandro, C.F. 1985. 'Goodbye Financial Repression, Hello Financial Crash.' *Journal of Development Economics* 19, nos 1–2: 1–24

Edirisinghe, Neville. 1984. 'The Implications of the Change from Ration Shops to Food Stamps in Sri Lanka for Fiscal Costs, Income Distribution, and Nutrition.' International Food Policy Research Institute, Washington (mimeo)

Ellis, Frank. 1982. 'Agricultural Price Policy in Tanzania.' *World Development* 10, no. 4: 263–83

Feinberg, Richard E. 1982. 'The International Monetary Fund and Basic Needs.' In Margaret Crahan (ed.), *Human Rights and Basic Needs in the Americas,* pp. 215–35. Washington: Georgetown University Press

Finch, C. David. 1982. 'Adjustment Policies and Conditionality.' In John Williamson (ed.), *IMF Conditionality,* pp. 75–86. Washington: Institute for International Economics and MIT Press

Foxley, Alejandro. 1981. 'Stabilization Policies and Their Effects on Employment and Income Distribution: A Latin American Perspective.' In William R. Cline and Sidney Weintraub (eds), *Economic Stabilization in Developing Countries*, pp. 191–225. Washington: The Brookings Institution

Ghai, Dharam, and Lawrence Smith. 1983. 'Food Policy and Equity in Sub-Saharan Africa.' World Employment Programme Research, Working Paper, WEP 10-6/WP 55. Geneva: International Labour Office

Giannini, A. 1983. 'The Interest Elasticity of Savings in Developing Countries.' *World Development* 11, no. 7: 601–7

Green, Reginald H. 1983. 'Political-Economic Adjustment and IMF Conditionality: Tanzania 1974–81.' In John Williamson (ed.), *IMF Conditionality*, pp. 347–80. Washington: Institute for International Economics and MIT Press

– 1984. 'Stabilisation in Sub-Saharan Africa and the IMF: A Critical Review and Prolegemonon – as Illustrated by Tanzania.' Institute of Development Studies, University of Sussex (mimeo)

Green, Reginald H., D. Rwegasira, and B. Van Arkadie. 1981. *Economic Shocks and National Policy Making: Tanzania in the 1970s*. The Hague: Institute of Social Research

Helleiner, G.K. 1985. 'Aid and Liquidity: The Neglect of Sub-Saharan Africa and Others of the Poorest in the Emerging International Monetary System.' *Journal of Development Planning* 15: 67–84

– 1986a. 'Outward Orientation, Import Instability and African Economic Growth: An Empirical Investigation.' In Sanjaya Lall and Frances Stewart (eds), *Theory and Reality in Development*, pp. 139–53. London: Macmillan

– 1986b. 'Balance of Payments Experience and Growth Prospects of Developing Countries: A Synthesis.' *World Development* 14: 877–908

Hicks, Norman, and Anne Kubisch. 1984. 'Cutting Government Expenditures in LDCs.' *Finance and Development* 21, no. 3: 37–9

Horton, Susan. 1984. 'A Survey of Food Subsidy Programs in Selected Countries.' Paper presented at a conference on consumer-oriented food subsidies, International Food Policy Research Institute, Washington

ILO. 1982. *Basic Needs in Danger: A Basic Needs Oriented Development Strategy for Tanzania*. Addis Ababa

– 1986. 'Stabilisation, Adjustment and Poverty.' WEP Z-46/WP 1. Geneva

Isenman, Paul. 1980. 'Basic Needs: The Case of Sri Lanka.' *World Development* 8: 237–58

Johnson, Omotunde, and Joanne Salop. 1980. 'Distributional Aspects of Stabilization Programs in Developing Countries.' *IMF Staff Papers* 27, no. 1: 1–23

Khan, Mohsin, and Malcolm D. Knight. 1985. 'Fund-Supported Adjustment Programs and Economic Growth.' IMF Occasional Paper 41. Washington

Killick, Tony, et al. 1984. *The Quest for Economic Stabilisation: The IMF and the Third World*. London: Heinemann

Knight, J.B. 1976. 'Devaluation and Income Distribution in Less Developed Economies.' *Oxford Economic Papers* 28, no. 12: 208–27

Krueger, Anne (ed.). 1981. *Trade and Employment in Developing Countries: Individual Studies*. National Bureau of Economic Research. Chicago: University of Chicago Press

Larosiere, J. de. 1984. 'Does the Fund Impose Austerity?' IMF brochure. Washington

Loxley, John. 1986. 'Alternative Approaches to Stabilization in Africa.' In G.K. Helleiner (ed.), *Africa and the International Monetary Fund*, pp. 117–47. Washington: IMF

Mohammed, Azizali F. 1984. 'Fund Conditionality: A View from Inside.' In Khadija Haq and Carlos Massad (eds), *Adjustment with Growth: A Search for an Equitable Solution*, pp. 180–97. Islamabad, Pakistan: North-South Roundtable

Nelson, Joan. 1984. 'The Political Economy of Stabilization: Commitment, Capacity, and Public Response.' *World Development* 12, no. 10: 983–1006

Nugent, Jeffrey B., and Constantine Glezakos. 1982. 'Phillips Curves in Developing Countries: The Latin American Case.' *Economic Development and Cultural Change* 30, no. 2: 321–34

Roe, Alan R. 1982. 'High Interest Rates: A New Conventional Wisdom for Development Policy.' *World Development* 10, no. 3: 211–22

Sisson, Charles A. 1986. 'Fund-Supported Programs and Income Distribution in LDCs.' *Finance and Development* 23, no. 1: 33–6

Stewart, Frances. 1984. 'Alternative Conditionality.' In Khadija Haq and Carlos Massad (eds), *Adjustment with Growth: A Search for an Equitable Solution*, pp. 198–216, Islamabad, Pakistan: North-South Roundtable

Streeten, Paul. 1984. 'Basic Needs: Some Unsettled Questions.' Boston University (mimeo)

Taylor, Lance. 1983. *Structuralist Macroeconomics: Applicable Models for the Third World*. New York: Basic Books

Trairatvorakul, Prasarn. 1984. 'The Effects on Income Distribution and Nutrition of Alternative Rice Price Policies in Thailand.' International Food Policy Research Institute Research Report 46. Washington

UNICEF. 1984. *The State of the World's Children, 1984*. New York: Oxford University Press

United Republic of Tanzania. 1982. *Structural Adjustment Programme for Tanzania*. Dar es Salaam

Williamson, John. 1982. 'The Lending Policies of the International Monetary Fund.' *Policy Analyses in International Economics* I. Washington: Institute for International Economics

World Bank. 1980. *World Development Report, 1980*. Washington
– 1981. *Accelerated Development in Sub-Saharan Africa: An Agenda for Action*. Washington
– 1984. *World Development Report, 1984*. Washington

Yagci, Fahrettin, Steven Kamin, and Vicki Rosenbaum. 1985. 'Structural Adjustment Lending: An Evaluation of Program Design.' World Bank Staff Working Paper no. 735. Washington

3

Taxation, Pricing, and the Poor

RICHARD M. BIRD AND BARBARA D. MILLER

... Taxes cannot make the poor richer, which is, after all, the main concern of distributional policy. Even the complete removal of all taxes on the poorest members of society would not make them much better off, simply because of the low absolute amounts of income and tax involved. Furthermore, many of the poorest people, particularly those in rural areas, take part only marginally in the economic life of the country and are thus little affected by taxes. While the regressivity of the tax system, where it exists, ought to be reduced as much as possible in order not to make things worse, it is clear that, if our main concern is with poverty as such, with the waste and misuse of human resources and the stunted opportunities in life afforded those with income below some minimum level, any fiscal corrective must be exercised primarily through the expenditure side of the budget. (Bird, 1974b, p. 4)

This statement, made over a decade ago, was substantiated by a later survey of tax-incidence studies and the poor in developing countries (McLure, 1977a). The main role for tax policy in developing countries with respect to the poor was not to make them even poorer, a task that required both the avoidance of regressivity in tax design and its reduction through tax reform. More positive policy actions to reduce poverty were to be left to government expenditure policies or to more drastic realignments of power and property through non-fiscal means. Since then, academic discussion of taxes and the poor has tended to follow similar lines. The elimination of those taxes considered to be particularly regressive has been advocated (McLure and Thirsk, 1978). The general potential of tax policies relative to expenditure policies to redistribute income in developing countries has been played down (Harberger, 1977; Goode, 1984).

Several recent developments, however, suggest that it is time to reconsider the relationship between taxes and the poor in developing countries. Developments in incidence analysis have cast doubt on the earlier consensus about the relative regressivity of various taxes (Aaron, 1975; Browning, 1978; Whalley, 1984). Some applications of those ideas to developing countries are now available (McLure, 1979; Linn, 1980a). Advances in modelling the effects of taxation have cast new light on the complex relationship between taxation and income distribution (Shoven and Whalley, 1984; Stern, 1984). New data sources have begun to be developed and exploited to explore some of these relationships in developing countries (Ahmad and Stern, 1983; Ahmad, Coady, and Stern, 1984; Ahmad, Leung, and Stern, 1984). The potential scope for tax policy to affect factor prices and hence income distribution in developing countries has recently been stressed (Bird, 1982). Moreover, scepticism has grown as to the effectiveness of public expenditure policy in reaching the very poor (Tanzi, 1974; Toye, 1981; Meerman, 1979). In any case, 'whatever experts think, policy makers will continue to attempt to use the tax system to achieve goals that they deem important' (Tanzi, 1983, p. 22). The 'good old days' of untrammelled belief in the efficacy of the tax-transfer system to achieve distributional goals are unlikely to return.[1] Nevertheless, improved income distribution continues to be an important goal of tax policy in the rhetoric of policy-makers in developing countries. For all these reasons, then, a new look at taxes and the poor in developing countries seems opportune.

The emphasis of this chapter is on the state of the relevant professional literature. The aim is to discern common threads, unresolved conflicts, and researchable lines for future investigation. The first section reviews briefly the present state of fiscal-incidence studies in developing countries: What do we know, or think we know, about how tax and pricing systems affect the poor in developing countries? For the most part, these studies suggest that the major direct impact of the government revenue system in most developing countries is on the urban poor, especially through property taxes and user charges and through indirect taxes. The next two sections of the chapter, therefore, review in more detail recent research on the distributional effects of these fiscal instruments, including preliminary results from our current analysis of the impact of indirect taxes on the poor in Jamaica. The final section contains a brief conclusion.

1 Studies of Fiscal Incidence

A decade ago, a comprehensive review of fiscal incidence studies concluded that in only two of the forty-four studies examined (covering twenty-two developing countries) was the tax system regressive in the sense that the poor, broadly defined, appeared to pay a larger proportion of their incomes in taxes than did the rich (De Wulf, 1975). In a number of other cases, however, there was evidence of some regressivity toward the bottom of the income scale. The same review found that most of the fifteen incidence studies (twelve on India alone!) that distinguished between urban and rural sectors found that taxes represented a relatively smaller share of (usually lower) incomes in the agricultural than in the non-agricultural sector. Almost no attention was paid in any of these incidence studies to the dispersion around the average of the effective tax rate within each income class. The focus of tax-incidence studies has invariably been on the *vertical* equity of taxes (do the rich pay a larger share of their income in taxes than the poor?), to the virtual neglect of the equally interesting *horizontal* equity question (do two equally poor people pay the same taxes?).

McLure (1977a) subsequently examined the results of seven of the same incidence studies – three in India and one each in Colombia, Brazil, Pakistan, Lebanon, and Jamaica – with particular attention to the poor. Although none of these studies provided sufficient data to analyse the tax burden on the poor in detail, on average it appeared that taxes took around 10 per cent of the incomes of the urban poor and a bit less of the incomes of the rural poor. Jamaica was found to be an exception in both respects, however, with taxes on the poor being close to 20 per cent of income throughout the island.

Incidence studies of any one country are, as a rule, conducted by different people, often using different assumptions, at different times. It would, therefore, not be surprising if such studies produced different results. On the whole, however, the broad pattern of results found for any country is surprisingly consistent over time. Table 3.1 shows the results of three studies of the incidence of Jamaican taxes conducted over the last twenty-five years. There are great difficulties in comparing these studies in detail, but it does not seem too misleading to characterize the results as suggesting, in general, a basically proportional incidence pattern over a fairly broad range of income, with taxes on the poor tending on the whole to be lower than those on the middle class.[2]

Both in the 1971–2 Jamaica study, where the lowest income class included 32.4 per cent of all households and the two lowest classes together included 57.5 per cent (McLure, 1977b, p. 16), and in the 1983 study, indirect taxes accounted for the bulk of the taxes paid by the poorest half of the population. The more disaggregated 1983 study found the incidence of indirect taxes to be roughly proportional (Wasylenko, 1985) among the poorer half of the Jamaican populace. Because taxes on food are low in Jamaica, and the income elasticity of non-food consumption is probably close to unity, a proportional general-consumption tax would produce more or less these results. In fact, however, as McLure (1977b, p. 56) noted, this outcome is

TABLE 3.1
The incidence of Jamaican taxes, 1958, 1971–2, and 1983
(tax as per cent of income)

Income group	1958[a]	1971–2[b]	1983[c]
1	7.7	22.3	21.4
2	7.2	17.0	21.2
3	8.7	18.4	21.7
4	8.5	17.0	24.6
5	10.1	16.4	25.1
6	8.4	18.4	27.1
7	10.5	18.3	29.6
8	15.3	20.8	33.4
9	21.2	21.0	33.3
10		22.4	23.9
11		23.6	

a Lovejoy (1963). Weekly income group in pounds, ranging from less than 2 in group 1 to over 30 in group 9.
b McLure (1977b). Dollars per year, ranging from less than J$499 in group 1 to J$5000 and over in group 11.
c Wasylenko (1985). Annual income by deciles, ranging from less than J$1846 in the first decile to over J$28,999 in the tenth decile.

the result of the complicated interplay of the effects of the quite different tax ratios that are found for different indirect taxes – some rising with income, some falling, and some remaining essentially flat. Broadly similar results, what De Wulf (1975) has called 'wandering proportionality,' have been found in many other incidence studies in developing countries.

A comprehensive recent review of urban finance in developing countries by Bahl and Linn (1985) turned up nineteen studies of the incidence of property taxes in thirteen different countries. A few of these studies – on residential property tax in Seoul, on all property taxes in Jamaica, and on the urban property tax in Bogota – have found that the burden of the property tax was distributed regressively. All the other studies, however, found the property tax to be generally progressive, or even very progressive.

As Bahl and Linn (1985) discuss in detail, this diverse group of incidence studies employs so many different and sometimes inconsistent assumptions that it is difficult to know what to make of these results. On the whole, however, the conventional view that the property tax is regressive seems less likely to be correct in developing than in developed countries, largely because the income elasticity of housing is likely to be unity or greater in developing countries.

Bahl and Linn (1985) have also reviewed carefully the scanty evidence on the incidence of the user charges levied to finance various urban services in some developing countries. In the case of water, perhaps the most important such service, both the precise nature of the rate structure employed and the physical nature of the city in question were found to affect the distributive impact of user charge systems. In Nairobi, for example, low-income areas can be supplied at lower cost, so efficient water charges would have a generally progressive incidence. The opposite, however, is true in Cali and probably in many other cities, because it is the poor who tend to live in the areas where land values are low owing to difficult access and unfavourable physical factors. On the whole, property taxes probably constitute a more progressive way to finance the expansion of basic urban services than even progressively structured service prices, essentially because housing consumption is more income-elastic than water consumption.

Most studies of the distributive effects of various tax and pricing systems in different developing countries suggest that the tax systems existing in developing countries are *not* very regressive. It is true that few of these studies focus explicitly or in much detail on the poor. It cannot be said, however, that the taxes – mostly indirect taxes – now levied on the poor in most countries are regressive, contrary to an impression that is still widespread (e.g., Chenery et al., 1974, p. 84). Almost no study pays attention to the important question of the horizontal equity of the tax system within the heterogeneous group called 'the poor,' however. The results for any country often depend on a very detailed understanding of the *precise* structure and working of the fiscal instruments in question.[3] And, finally, almost all these studies rest on questionable logical and statistical bases in the first place (Bird and De Wulf, 1973).

The incidence of the taxes studied here may constitute only one small aspect of the distributional effects of government policy as a whole, and may in a sense be swamped by the effects of inflation, trade restrictions, and the like. Nevertheless, the evidence is clearly that taxes *do* take a relatively substantial fraction of even very low incomes in most developing countries. Moreover, governments are clearly concerned with the distributional effects of taxes. There appears to be considerable interest in the scope for improving the well-being of the poorer half of the populace through appropriate redesign of taxes.

Focusing on redistributing income through the fiscal system after it has initially been distributed by the economic system may, indeed, give a misleadingly small impression of the potential of the tax system to redistribute income. The tax system, like many other aspects of government policy that affect relative prices, may also affect the initial distribution of income through its effects on, for example, the structure of industry and the demand for unskilled labour as well, in a more long-run framework, through its effects on saving, capital formation, and real wage levels. For example, the potential scope for tax policy to influence employment, the major source of income for most people, is enormous: 'Apart from the effects of taxation on capital formation itself, the proportions in which capital is combined with labour may be influenced (1) by operating on the "big" relative prices through altering the intersectoral terms of trade, the effective exchange rate, or the wage-rental ratio itself; (2) by altering the distribution of income, and hence the composition of demand; (3) by altering relative product prices; (4) by influencing the rate and nature of technological innovation; and (5) by bringing about a more unified (and price-sensitive) factor market' (Bird, 1982, p. 214). Payroll taxes and tax incentives for investment almost by definition do not impinge directly on the incomes of the poorest 40 per cent (or 60 per cent) of the population in most developing countries. Nevertheless, by tending to reduce employment in the modern sector, such fiscal measures probably mean that the poor will stay poorer longer than they would otherwise.

Similarly, as Kuznets (1966) has argued, the principal long-run redistributor of income in developing countries is almost certainly the move out of agriculture. Tax factors affecting this move may, therefore, have a much greater long-run impact on the poor than the current regressivity of tobacco taxes or whatever. Similarly, within the agricultural sector, Bird (1974a) has argued for more use of properly structured land taxes. Even though such taxes might seem at first to penalize poor peasants, they may well in the long run improve the well-being of both the rural and the urban poor through encouraging more efficient utilization of land and rural labour (particularly if coupled with appropriate land reform).

In short, tax policies that in effect encourage resources to be allocated to their 'highest and best uses' will, as a rule, tend to make the poor better off – perhaps not as obviously or immediately as would the elimination of the tax on tobacco, for example, but probably in the end more significantly. To explore such questions further, however, is beyond the scope of this chapter.[4] The balance of the chapter therefore concentrates on the question of the distributional effect of alternative indirect taxes and urban finance systems on the poor in developing countries.

2 Financing Urban Services

A striking phenomenon of recent decades is the increasing urbanization of the developing world. Average incomes are much higher in urban than in rural areas, but so is open unemployment; relatively fewer urban than rural households are poor, but the incidence of slums and squatter settlements as a proportion of urban population is often very high. The level of public utility services is much higher in urban areas, but even in the most developed parts of Latin America large numbers of urban dwellers have no access to even rudimentary services. Furthermore, there is evidence that the quality and reliability of such services has deteriorated (Linn, 1983). While there is much variation from country to country, and even from city to city within the same country, the level and nature of urban services provided often depend on the manner in which they are financed, particularly at the local level.

The subject of local government finance in developing countries has not received the attention it deserves. Two reasons for this neglect may be suggested. The first is that many people seem to think that only central governments matter financially in most developing countries. In many countries, however, local government finance is quite important. State and local governments accounted for close to one-third of the taxes collected in the non-oil developing countries in 1981 (International Monetary Fund, 1984).[5] An important local financial role does not necessarily imply any real local independence or autonomy (Bird, 1980b). Nevertheless, those interested in fiscal impacts on the poor should take a close look at the nature of urban government finances, especially in the larger cities (Smith, 1974). The urban poor *do* pay significant taxes, and many of the taxes they pay as well as service charges are levied by local governments (Linn, 1983). How local governments finance the services they provide thus has a potentially significant impact on the poor, particularly in urban areas.

A second reason for neglecting the distributional effect of local finances is the belief that distributional aims should not be explicitly pursued by local governments. Distribution policy (like stabilization policy) has traditionally been considered by public-finance analysts to be the proper concern of central governments alone. Local distributional policies would in any case be ineffective and inefficient in view of the openness of local economies (Oates, 1972).

In developing countries, however, these arguments are not very persuasive (Bird, 1980b, p. 20). In the first place, as shown above, local revenue systems *are* important in many countries. Their impact on the well-being of the poor is, therefore, a legitimate matter of concern, especially in countries in which the assumption implicit in much public finance theory that there is (or can be) a smoothly operating central government tax-transfer system that will attain any distributional policy aims is simple fantasy. Second, the very fact that the local governments in most developing countries have little autonomy – and may therefore be considered to be agents of the national government – means that local fiscal taxes and charges constitute as much a part of redistributive policy as do national taxes. The openness issue is less serious than is usually thought because what is going on is not locally differentiated redistribution but the local implementation of national policies.

A *Property Taxes*

Linn (1983) suggests three rules for those who want to alleviate urban poverty through local fiscal policy: (1) reduce regressive taxes; (2) increase progressive taxes; and (3) use benefit charges appropriately to finance urban services. The first rule relates primarily to the indirect commodity taxes levied by some local governments – the octroi in India and beer taxes in Zaire, for example (Linn, 1980b) – and is further discussed in the next section in the context of indirect tax policy as a whole. The other two 'rules' are taken up below.

Apart from the strong case that can be made for more local use of generally progressive taxes on automobile use and ownership (Smith, 1975; Linn 1979), the main progressive revenue source available to local governments in most countries is the property tax. There is increasing evidence that the property tax is, or can be, a fairly progressive way to finance urban services. As Linn (1983, p. 77) notes, however, the precise distributive effect of property taxes depends very much on the details of their structure and administration. The relative legal and administrative treatment of a rental vs owner-occupied properties, of land vs improvements, of low-value vs high-value properties, and so on, may have a profound effect upon the progressivity or otherwise of a property tax.

Higher taxes on land than on buildings, for example, would likely increase both the progressivity and the efficiency of the property tax (Holland and Follain, 1985). Because the value of landholdings generally rises with income class, a tax levied solely on land – the burden of which falls on landowners – is obviously more progressive than a tax on all real property, which in an open economy will inevitably bear more heavily on labour and on the consumption of locally produced goods than on capital. In addition, a tax on land is more neutral – less likely to deter development – than an equal-revenue tax on land and improvements (Follain and Miyake, 1984).

While there is no good distributive case for progressive *rates* of property taxation (Bird, 1974a, p. 211), there may often be substantial distributional (and administrative) benefits from combining an exemption with a flat rate. In Jamaica, the property tax is at present levied on the basis of the unimproved value of land at rates varying from 1 per cent to 4.5 per cent. Parcels valued at less than $J2000, however, pay only a flat tax of $J5. Approximately the same distributional effect could be attained with much less administrative and efficiency cost by levying a flat rate of 1.5 per cent and exempting the first $J6000 in value (Holland and Follain, 1985).

More broadly, a recent detailed study of the Jamaican property tax by Holland and Follain (1985) demonstrates that conclusions about the relative burden of different versions of property taxes on the poor can be put forward only with limited confidence.[6] Factors that make it difficult to talk about 'the' incidence of the property tax in any particular city or country, let alone in general, include the theoretical and empirical uncertainy about the incidence of the tax in the first place, the importance of detailed differences in structure in determining distributional impacts, the wide intraclass variations in such impacts depending on the distribution of land ownership and other factors, and the possibly differential effects of such administrative aspects as assessment, collection, and the appeals process. Nevertheless, despite such complexities, it seems safe to conclude in most circumstances that 'an increase in the average level of property taxation tends to be progressive in the sense that it burdens high income groups more heavily in relation to their incomes than low income groups. The progressive impact is more pronounced in the short-term than in the long-term, and more for nationwide property tax increases than for increases restricted to a particular jurisdiction' (Bahl and Linn, 1985).

In particular circumstances such features as the exemption of improvements (Holland and Follain, 1985) or the imposition of different tax rates in different locations (Holland, 1979) may provide sufficient gains in terms of both equity and efficiency to seem worthwhile. As always, however, it is a rather dangerous game to advocate undue complexity in tax design in countries in which the limits of administrative feasibility are very real (Bird, 1977).

B *User Charges and Public Services*

Complexity introduced for distributional reasons may also produce perverse results. Nominally progressive public-utility rates proved to be an inefficient technique of income distribution in Malaysia because many poor families consume more water than do rich families (Katzman, 1978). That portion of the poor population receiving services was in effect penalized by a supposedly 'pro-poor' rate structure. Similarly, in Colombia, where the subsidization of urban public services through progressive rate structures is relatively important, the benefits of this subsidy are generally *regressively* distributed within the poor population (Bahl and Linn, 1985). At the same time, the large group of the poor who receive no services have also often been burdened, through either taxes or inflation, in order to make up the deficits of public-utility enterprises.

Once again, it is very important to be clear about the details before generalizing. In some instances, for example, 'life-line' tariffs (a low tariff for an initial small block of consumption) may well provide both an efficient and an equitable way of pricing water, provided that the low rate is not below the amount appropriate to reflect the presumed external benefits from such consumption and that it is not financed by charging larger consumers at prices higher than marginal cost (Bahl and Linn, 1985). Since the income elasticity of demand for water is relatively low even in poor countries, however, and since to some extent at least household size and income may be negatively correlated, in other instances this policy may produce perverse distributional results, especially to the extent that multiple-household connections are more prevalent among low-income households.

Other water-pricing schemes besides rising block prices (progressive tariffs) are found in many countries. In Colombia, water charges are frequently related to property values in a progressive fashion. Again, however, the distributional effect of such charges depends on a wide variety of factors. In Cali, it was found that although the average price of an initial block of water rose steadily with assessed property values, the final impact of these charges was in fact regressive in terms of income (Bahl and Linn, 1985). A broader study of the incidence of the public-service charges levied in Colombian cities for residential water supply and sewerage, electricity, garbage collection, and local telephone service found, using some strong assumptions, that the incidence of these subsidies was generally progressive. But relatively few of these benefits flowed to the lowest 20–30 per cent of the population, largely because of their lack of access to services (Linn, 1980a).

It may be seriously misleading to concentrate on redistribution only within the select group of consumers receiving such services because the most important consideration may be whether the poor have *access* to services at all, not how much they have to pay for them (Selowsky, 1979; Meerman, 1979). The poor can benefit from subsidized services only when they have access to them.

In Colombia, the proportion of the urban population with access to public water supply in 1977 ranged from a high of 93 per cent in the Department of Quindio to a low of 37 per cent in the national territories (Bird, 1984, pp. 137–8). Even in the largest cities, about 25 per cent of the population had no access to services in 1974, the poorest being those most likely to do without (Linn, 1980a, p. 101). One reason for this outcome is that the poor are less able to afford the high connection and installation costs charged by the largely self-financing public enterprises responsible for providing urban services in Colombia. Because the extent of access is often related to the financial and other incentives under which service is provided, it makes little sense to discuss the distributive effects of user-charge financing of urban services without considering explicitly the precise institutional links between financing and service provision.

Another reason for lack of access may be simple political bias in favour of the better-off, the traditional and expected recipients of such services. Yet another reason may be, in contrast, that the relative insulation of the public enterprises from day-to-day political pressures may result in *reduced* access to services by the poor. The more technocratically determined investment decisions of bureaucrats, for example, may result in favoured (and usually relatively high-income) consumers receiving better services (Bird, 1980b, p. 32). The poor may thus lose out in many ways: through having to bear through taxes or inflation some of the cost of providing subsidized services to the rich, through being faced with high 'benefit' charges for a self-financing system, and through the bureaucratic and political machinations determining who gets what service in either case.

Urban transit provides another instance of the potential importance of public-service financing and pricing and the necessity of considering both the details and the broader context in order to determine the distributional impact of public-services financing. Most public mass-transit operations in developing countries are heavily subsidized and beset by management and operating problems (Bahl and Linn, 1985).

Experience suggests that the subsidization of urban mass transit is likely to be so inadequate in financially pressed developing countries that public transit systems are usually seriously underfinanced and provide correspondingly poor service.[7] The resulting problems are normally exacerbated by the political difficulty of raising fares – even though it seems likely that much of the subsidy thus extended at least nominally to the travelling poor in fact accrues to landowners or employers. It is not always clear that public-transit users are those who need subsidization most in any case. A 1978 study of Kingston, Jamaica, found that the poorest people used a higher-cost private system more than they did the public system, partly because the private service to their areas was better (Heraty, 1980).[8] This study also found that many poor people in Kingston spent a high fraction of their income on travel. More than 73 per cent of those with household incomes under $30 a week were estimated to spend over 10 per cent of their income on travel.[9]

Another aspect of the inefficient pricing of public services such as transit and water is that they encourage low-density development and urban sprawl (Downing, 1973). The waste of resources through such subsidization may initially seem distributionally worthwhile, even in poor countries with scarce public savings. Over time, however, as inflation eats away at public resources and at the effective degree of subsidization, and as more and more poor people get locked into costly and inefficient commuting and living patterns, the resulting mixture may well prove to be politically explosive.

The 'oil crisis' in recent years set off such explosions in some oil-importing countries. The poor may not drive cars, but they do ride buses and minibuses, and fuel costs account for a large and increasing proportion of transit fares. With a public bus system, fares can be held down – at the expense, of course, of an increase in operating deficits and the sorts of problems already mentioned. Jamaican experience suggests that matters may be even worse in the absence of a public transit system.

The public bus system in Kingston ceased operation early in 1984, largely as a result of pressure from international lending agencies to reduce the burden on government finance arising from public-enterprise deficits. As a result, all public road transportation in Jamaica is now in the hands of private minibus operators – a result that believers in competition and efficiency should presumably applaud.[10] In fact, however, this move to a privately run transit system may well in time result in larger rather than smaller government deficits. As Smith (1984, p. 53) has argued: 'For every dollar saved through the elimination of the publicly owned and operated bus company, more than a dollar may be lost in fuel tax revenues because of social and political pressure to keep the taxes low given the anticipated effect on public transport fares.'

In view of the attractiveness of higher fuel taxes as a generally equitable and efficient means of raising revenue, such a constraint on fuel taxes may be very costly. The demonstrations in Kingston and other parts of the island in December 1983 and January 1985 following fuel-tax increases underline both the importance of keeping fuel taxes from impacting too heavily on the poor and the difficulty of doing so when there is no public bus system to provide an administratively feasible vehicle for delivering the subsidy. The 'privatization' of public transit in Jamaica may indeed have had the promised benefits of providing transport more efficiently. But it has done so only at the expense of making it increasingly difficult to raise fuel prices to reflect the real opportunity cost of oil to Jamaica, let alone to add to scarce public-sector resources through more reliance on this most administratively feasible of progressive taxes.

3 Indirect Taxes and the Poor

On average, taxes on goods and services account for about half the total government revenue in developing countries (International Monetary Fund, 1984). The dominance of indirect consumption taxes over the more modern taxes on income and profits was long considered (Musgrave, 1969) to be little more than an unfortunate lapse arising from administrative and structural factors that would be rectified as these countries moved closer to the position of the industrial countries, where such taxes on average now provide less than one-fifth of total revenue. More recently, increasing attention has been paid even in the industrial countries to the alleged virtues of taxing consumption rather than income (see, for example, Meade et al., 1978). The theoretical and practical merits of retaining the present predominant role of consumption taxes in the developing countries have also begun to be reassessed (Tanzi, 1983). It is important, therefore, to consider carefully the implications for the poor not only of the present heavy reliance of developing countries' tax systems on indirect taxes but also of such likely changes as the rapidly spreading adoption of some form of value-added tax (Lent et al., 1973).

Indirect consumption taxes, particularly those on the traditional 'excisables,' account for most of the existing direct impact of taxes on the poor. In addition, such taxes as those on fuel may also have a substantial indirect impact on the poor through increasing transport costs.

A recent review of the incidence of different excise taxes in developing countries found the tobacco tax to be the most regressive tax in the Philippines, Guatemala, Colombia, Argentina, and Greece, among other countries (Cnossen, 1977). In Lebanon, however, the tobacco tax was actually progressive, largely because of the higher tax content of the imported cigarettes consumed by the rich (De Wulf, 1974). A similar result has also been noted in the Philippines (Asher and Booth, 1983, p. 142).

The incidence of taxes on the other important 'traditional' excise products – alcoholic beverages and hydrocarbon oils – is similarly important to the poor in many countries. As in the case of tobacco, the incidence of these levies appears to vary sharply from country to country, depending on the specifics of local consumption patterns and tax structures. Generalizations about incidence based on predetermined value judgments concerning the 'inherent' progressivity or regressivity of particular levies can be misleading. As Cnossen (1977, p. 47) notes, the income-distribution approach used in most incidence studies suppresses the potentially much more important differences between families in the same income class.

Tanzi (1974) has suggested that the dispersion around the average increases as income rises, so that estimates of average tax rates by income classes have little significance. Equally important, however, it may be argued that a given degree of dispersion has more significant equity implications at lower than at higher income levels. One early study of Guatemala, for example, suggested that heavy smokers and drinkers probably paid 3 per cent of their income in taxes while moderate consumers paid only 1 per cent (Adler et al., 1952). Differences of this magnitude at low income levels obviously raise important equity questions, particularly because the low price elasticity of demand for these products implies that it is mainly the consumption of other goods ('basic needs'?) that is necessarily reduced as a result (McLure and Thirsk, 1978).

Recent analysis also indicates that the efficiency effects of commodity taxes need to be taken much more explicitly into account in designing and reforming indirect tax systems (Stern, 1984). In particular, this analysis casts doubt on the traditional view that a uniform commodity tax such as a general sales tax is in principle better than a more differentiated set of taxes on goods and services (Due, 1970). Actually, there is substantial divergence in the literature as to whether commodity tax rates should be uniform or differentiated.

Rate differentiation of varying types has been urged on efficiency grounds, on distributional grounds, and even on stabilization grounds (Asher and Booth, 1983, p. 132). Many countries have listened to this advice, at least to the extent of having a system of progressive sales and excise tax rates intended to make the incidence of their indirect taxes progressive. However, a strong case may be made against using rate differentials in a general sales tax in order to achieve distributive ends, essentially because any equity gains from differentiation may be more than outweighed by administrative costs (Cnossen, 1982, 1984). In most developing countries, however, there are substantial differences in consumption patterns between income groups that can be differentially taxed through sales. It is not enough in such countries to say 'whatever meagre progressivity that may be achieved by a differentiated sales tax rate structure can be attained far better through a small change in the income tax' (Cnossen, 1982, p. 213). With respect to the poor, who are largely outside the income tax, this statement is not true, while with respect to the rich it assumes that the income tax is in fact an effective instrument of redistribution. This assumption is erroneous for most developing countries particularly with regard to non-wage income.

The appropriate distributional role of indirect taxes in any developing country cannot easily be decided on a priori grounds. What matters is the relative *quantitative* importance of different tax and income characteristics. Textbook advice, such as that in Chenery et al. (1974, p. 84), to discriminate between income groups through higher taxes on goods with high income elasticities and low price elasticities is as uselessly simplistic as the judgment on the same page that 'in most cases the [existing] structure of indirect taxation is markedly regressive.'

Similarly, the sweeping condemnation of sumptuary taxation of alcohol and tobacco in McLure and Thirsk (1978) offers as little guidance to what should be done in any particular developing country as does the recent evidence suggesting on grounds of efficiency that such taxes should be retained and perhaps even strengthened, at least in industrial countries (Shoup, 1983). Although, presumably, 'being poor should not entitle one to an unlimited license to create negative externalities' (Shoup, 1983, p. 262), little, if any, attention appears to have been paid to these questions in developing countries.

The sumptuary rationale appears to be important in most Asian indirect tax systems, but Asher and Booth (1983, p. 135) express substantial scepticism about the realism of this rationale given the low price elasticity of demand for such goods. They quote with approval the dictum of Due (1970, p. 63) that 'the primary argument for excises on alcoholic beverages and tobacco products is their revenue productivity.' As Shoup (1983) has noted, however, what an observed low price elasticity really shows is that the tax rate is still some distance below the maximum-revenue rate. Moreover, the observed reluctance in many countries to maintain the real level of sumptuary taxes in the face of inflation casts further doubt on the view that these levies are just a simple way to gouge the poor. Those who advocate much higher taxes on alcohol on social grounds in developing countries (Marshall, 1982) are not necessarily talking hypocritical nonsense, as McLure and Thirsk (1978) appear to suggest, especially when higher alcohol taxes would often not be regressive.[11] Once again, detailed, quantitative study, not sweeping generalization, is what is needed to advance knowledge and formulate good tax policy in this area.

What is to be taxed? At what rates? An interesting example of the sort of research needed to answer these key questions of indirect tax policy in any country is a recent series of studies of India and Pakistan produced by a group of economists at the University of Warwick. The approach in these studies derives from the general optimal commodity-tax literature, in which the aim is to raise a given revenue in such a way as to minimize the welfare loss, subject to socially determined distributional weights (Stern, 1984). This literature usually yields such vague guidelines to tax policy – 'tax products for which demand is more inelastic more heavily' – that their application to any real case is either obscure or else dependent on so many specific, quantifiable assumptions as to seem a most unpromising manual for reform in the context of a developing country. The Warwick studies, however, manage to reach some interesting, if tentative, policy conclusions.

The first step in this analysis was to calculate the effective tax rates, in itself not an easy task, particularly because the impact of taxes on intermediate goods must be traced through an input/output system in order to calculate the final tax components of different products. The taxation of inputs often produces quite a different pattern of indirect tax incidence than the nominal rate structure would suggest. Food grains, for example, are not taxed by India's central excises, but nevertheless these products were found to bear taxes ranging from 1.5 per cent to 3.6 per cent (Ahmad and Stern, 1983a). On the whole, India's indirect tax system, when the effects of all subsidies and input taxes were taken into account, was found to be progressive but rather less so than had been indicated in the major previous study (Chelliah and Lall, 1978), which followed more traditional methods.

The second stage of the Warwick group's work involves the examination and evaluation of possible alternative indirect tax structures. The major conclusion emerging from this exercise is that 'the marginal social cost of taxing different goods is quite sensitive to distributional value judgements. Cereal subsidies, for example, would be unattractive if one has little concern for inequality but more attractive otherwise' (Stern, 1984, p. 32). In the case of India, Ahmad and Stern (1983a) found that over a fairly wide range of value judgments about the importance of redistribution, reductions in fuel taxes and increases in taxes on milk products seemed indicated. A similar exercise in Pakistan suggested strongly that any concern for inequality at all made wheat and sugar poor candidates for increased taxation compared to, say, meat and eggs (Ahmad, Leung, and Stern, 1984).[12] Although this analysis can be extended only with great difficulty to non-marginal tax changes, such as the introduction of a value-added tax (VAT),[13] the study of India found that a shift to a VAT would reduce the expenditures of the poorest rural households by almost 7 per cent and of the poorest urban groups by about 5 per cent. 'The only value judgement for which it [a shift to a VAT] would be considered optimum would be that involving no concern whatsoever for income redistribution in favor of the poor' (Ahmad and Stern, 1983a, p. 105).

While there are obviously problems and limitations with studies such as these, this work has already made a contribution to our understanding of indirect tax reform in developing countries. The potential distributive importance of input taxes – stressed, for example, in Due (1970) but not discussed carefully, if at all, in most incidence analyses – has been underlined.

Small though difficult steps have been taken toward evaluating commodity-tax reforms in a much more explicit and systematic way than ever before. The inescapable extent to which judgment of particular tax changes depends on concern for the poor has been emphasized and systematically explored. And, by no means least, a step has been taken toward making optimal taxation, one of the most esoteric branches of modern public-finance theory, potentially useful to those who make policy decisions in this area.

A *A Jamaican Case Study*

Although neither the data nor the resources available in Jamaica have been adequate for an analysis as complex as that undertaken by the Warwick group, some preliminary results from ongoing work on indirect tax reform in Jamaica are reported here. An interesting feature of this work is the panel data on which it draws. As described in Miller and Stone (1985), a special survey was carried out on the expenditure patterns of 145 urban and rural low-income households over an eight-month period. The daily expenditure sheets were checked weekly by trained interviewers and supplemented by monthly questionnaires on household characteristics and economic status. While not all the data collected have yet been analysed, we have used a condensed version of the resulting extensive data set to carry out a preliminary analysis of some proposed changes in the indirect tax system. Table 3.2 shows the basic characteristics of the sample households. For purposes of preliminary analysis, this sample was divided three ways: urban and rural, female-male and female-headed households, and three expenditure classes. As shown in table 3.3, the variations in expenditure patterns between these groups are marked, suggesting that 'horizontal equity' may be an even more important consideration than 'vertical equity' in appraising alternative consumption-tax patterns.

At the present time, many consumption goods in Jamaica are subject to three separate consumption taxes with highly differentiated rate structures (Due, 1985; Cnossen, 1984). As part of a general tax reform, it has been proposed to consolidate these three levies into a uniform general-consumption tax (GCT). The impact effect on this sample of low-income households of introducing different variants of the proposed GCT was calculated, using the following simple procedure. The various expenditure items were first classified on the basis of the law and some judgment into those currently subject to the three taxes to be consolidated into the GCT and those not subject to these taxes. On average, 36 per cent of the expenditure of low-income households was found to be taxed by these levies. The variation in the proportion from household to household was very large, ranging

TABLE 3.2
Summary characteristics of the sample households, April 1984

	Urban	Rural	Total
Total population	453	493	946
Number of households	67	78	145
Average number of household members	7	6	7
Female-headed households (%)	49	38	43
Owners (%)	26	63	48
Tenants (%)	59	37	47
Squatters (%)	10	1	5
Weekly expenditures <$89 (Group 1) (%)	16	64	42
Weekly expenditures $89–189 (Group 2)(%)	55	32	43
Weekly expenditures over $189 (Group 3) (%)	28	4	15

SOURCE: Jamaica Tax Structure Examination Project (JTSFP), Low-Income Household Expenditure Survey Data, Metropolitan Studies Program, Maxwell School, Syracuse University

from a low of 15 per cent to a high of 62 per cent. Table 3.4 shows this variation in terms of the three-way classification set out earlier.[14] As this table makes clear, poorer households have more of their expenditure potentially subject to these taxes than do relatively better-off households, even within this low-income population.

The taxes paid by the different groups were then calculated on the basis of a set of assumptions that seem reasonable in the Jamaican context.[15] The results of these calculations by subgroup for the existing tax system are also shown in table 3.4. The regressivity of the existing system is apparent even in relation to *expenditure*, let alone income. The variation in taxes paid is as great as that in total expenditure, ranging across the entire sample from a low of $0.78 (or 2.4 per cent of total expenditure) for one household to a high of $9.34 (or 3.1 per cent of expenditure) for another. The importance of this variation may be underlined by noting that the highest-taxed household in the lowest income group paid an estimated $3.68 a month in consumption taxes, or 5.5 per cent of its total expenditure, compared to 2.1 per cent for the lowest-taxed household in this group, while the lowest-taxed family in the highest income group paid only $2.30 (or 1.1 per cent) compared to 3.6 per cent for the highest-taxed household in this group. In other words, the variation in effective tax rates *within* expenditure groups exceeds the variation *between* groups.

The differential impact of applying a uniform GCT rate of 20 per cent to all items that are now taxed was then calculated and compared to the

TABLE 3.3
Low-income household survey: variations in expenditure patterns (as per cent of total expenditures)

Item	Total	Urban expenditure						Rural expenditure					
		Group 1		Group 2		Group 3		Group 1		Group 2		Group 3	
		FM	F	FM	F	FM	F	FM	F	FM	F	FM	F
Number of households	145	5	6	19	18	9	10	32	18	16	9	2	1
Unprocessed food	26.2	30.6	22.5	26.8	22.3	21.4	22.3	27.7	31.7	24.6	26.6	23.8	50.1
Processed food	30.0	35.3	26.3	24.6	22.1	20.3	17.4	42.0	36.2	29.2	28.7	25.4	28.0
Subtotal food	56.2	65.9	48.8	54.4	44.4	41.7	39.7	69.7	67.9	53.8	55.3	49.2	78.1
Fuel	4.2	3.4	7.7	4.7	4.5	4.0	4.7	3.5	3.3	4.0	5.8	3.1	0.2
Tobacco	1.1	0.6	0.1	1.4	0.4	0.6	0.4	1.4	1.8	1.3	0.4	0.5	3.0
Alcohol	0.7	0.0	0.0	0.5	0.3	2.1	0.4	0.6	0.4	1.3	1.8	0.3	0.8
Dry goods	10.6	7.1	11.6	11.2	9.0	9.5	7.8	10.0	9.4	12.8	17.2	12.7	11.0
Household	6.2	4.5	5.9	9.2	9.3	6.2	11.0	3.6	4.8	2.7	7.3	9.1	3.9
Health	1.0	0.1	0.3	0.5	0.4	0.6	0.5	1.4	1.5	2.2	0.8	1.4	0.0
Transportation	6.1	4.6	7.8	7.9	6.5	10.7	8.4	4.1	3.7	6.1	6.1	9.4	0.8
Education	7.2	9.8	12.1	6.1	15.2	17.2	18.9	2.2	2.2	2.5	2.3	7.4	0.2
Entertainment	0.3	0.1	0.0	0.8	0.5	0.7	0.8	0.0	0.1	0.3	0.2	1.0	0.0
Other	5.7	4.0	4.7	5.5	8.2	5.7	6.2	3.0	4.6	13.0	2.0	1.9	1.5
Total[a]	99.3	100.1	99.0	99.2	98.7	99.0	98.8	99.5	99.7	100.0	99.2	96.0	99.5

[a] Since the figures in this table are calculated as the unweighted means of figures which are themselves unweighted means of 34 weekly observations, it is not surprising that in a few instances, particularly in the case of the smaller groups, the totals do not sum to 100. In addition, of course, small differences may arise owing to rounding.

SOURCE: JTSEP, Low-Income Household Expenditure Survey Data, Metropolitan Studies Program, Maxwell School, Syracuse University

TABLE 3.4
Low-income households: variation in consumption tax base and taxes by subgroup

	Weekly expenditure (in J$)	Taxed expenditures as per cent of total	Existing taxes (in J$)	As per cent of total expenditures
All households	113.71	33.6	3.23	2.8
Urban households	146.64	29.9	3.72	2.5
Rural households	85.44	38.9	2.81	3.3
Female/male households	119.90	32.2	3.31	2.8
Female-headed households	109.09	34.7	3.17	2.9
Total expenditure:				
Less than J$89	60.49	38.4	2.02	3.3
J$89–J$189	129.86	34.4	3.72	2.9
More than J$189	215.78	28.5	5.17	2.4

SOURCE: JTSEP Low-Income Household Expenditure Survey Data, Metropolitan Studies Program, Maxwell School, Syracuse University

existing taxes using the same assumptions. A summary of the resulting percentage changes in taxes as a proportion of total expenditures is set out as Option 1 in table 3.5. As shown there, it appears that this tax change would (1) *increase* taxes on low-income households as a group and also (2) slightly *increase* the regressivity of Jamaica's already regressive consumption tax system.[16] These results emerge both because at present many consumption items of low-income groups are taxed at rates lower than 20 per cent and because such lower-taxed items as certain processed foods constitute, on average, a slightly larger proportion of the consumption of the poorer households than of the relatively less poor households.

To assess the importance of taxing processed food in these results, calculations were done assuming that all food (and medicines) were exempt. As shown in table 3.5 (Option 2), these exemptions reverse the preceding results and lower all taxes on low-income families dramatically and in a progressive fashion. In line with a recommendation in Due (1985), we also examined the effect of taxing some items at a higher 'luxury' tax rate of 35 per cent (Option 3, table 3.5). As might be expected given the minor importance of these items in the consumption of this low-income group, the effect of this change on total tax burdens was minute. Indeed, the effect of introducing rate progression was actually to make the tax a bit more *regressive* than a uniform

TABLE 3.5
Incidence of alternative versions of the general consumption-tax packages on
low-income households (taxes as per cent of total expenditure)

Weekly expenditure class	Taxes to be replaced by GCT	Alternative GCTs			
		Option 1	Option 2	Option 3	Option 4
Less than $89	3.3	3.6	1.0	3.6	2.9
$89–$189	2.9	3.1	1.4	3.1	3.1
Over $189	2.4	2.6	1.2	2.7	2.8
Total	2.8	3.0	1.0	3.0	2.8

NOTES: 'Existing taxes' represent the effects of the consumption duties, excise duties, and
retail sales taxes that are to be replaced by the GCT on the expenditure of the low-income
household sample.
    Option 1 is a GCT levied at a rate of 20 per cent with only unprocessed food exempt.
    Option 2 is a GCT levied at a rate of 20 per cent with all food exempt.
    Option 3 is a GCT levied at a basic rate of 20 per cent, with a supplementary rate of 35
per cent on 'luxury' consumption; only unprocessed food is exempted.
    Option 4 is a GCT levied at a rate of 25 per cent with unprocessed food and a limited
range of the basic food items exempted.

tax because the very poorest people in the sample actually spend a bit more
on 'luxury' cosmetics than the others!

    This last observation suggests the danger of imposing predetermined
judgments about what is and is not a 'luxury' so far as low-income people
are concerned.[17] Attempting to make sales taxes more progressive by imposing 'luxury' rates on arbitrarily selected items is at best a very crude tool for
redistribution. And at worst, as in the present instance, it is a tool that may
have perverse results, quite apart from the obvious horizontal equity problems with this approach.

    While a similar caution about within-group redistribution is warranted,
the exercise described above suggests strongly that at least some additional
exemptions from the GCT beyond unprocessed foods (and services) may be
warranted on distributional grounds. Closer examination of the data underlying table 3.5 indicates that exempting just five products – flour, cooking
oil, condensed milk, sugar, and butter/margarine – would eliminate almost
all of the regressivity from taxing processed food under the GCT. These five
products account for 83 per cent of the total tax reduction shown in table
3.5 under Option 2 for all households, and for 84 per cent of the reduction
for the lowest-income group, 80 per cent for the second group, and only 70
per cent for the highest of the three groups distinguished there. Option 4 in

table 3.5 shows that the result of exempting these five additional products, while adjusting the GCT rate to 25 per cent to hold revenue constant, would be to make the incidence of the GCT roughly proportional to expenditure, compared to the strong regressivity exhibited by the existing taxes that would be replaced by the GCT.

Although for the group as a whole each of the five items mentioned above is roughly equal in importance, it is interesting to note that by far the most regressive tax on food items is that on sugar. This finding once again suggests the danger of imposing a priori views of what is, or is not, a 'basic' necessity for the poor! In contrast to Due (1985, p. 36), who explicitly singles out sugar for taxation at 20 per cent, these results suggest that even the existing 5 per cent levy should be removed.[18]

The conclusion of this preliminary analysis is that there is a very good case on distributional grounds for exempting at least a select list of basic food items from the GCT in order to avoid increasing unduly the regressivity of the already regressive consumption-tax system in Jamaica. In particular, in addition to exempting all unprocessed foods (fresh meat, fresh fish, milk, eggs, fruit, and vegetables), it seems desirable to exempt flour, condensed milk, butter and margarine, cooking oil, and sugar from the tax. Contrary to the recommendations in Due (1985), however, there seems no reason, at least in terms of income effects on low-income households, to exempt other processed foods products (such as baby food) or medications. Nor does there seem much, if any, case for the 'luxury' tax rates he proposed on a large group of products (e.g., cosmetics, jewellery). Further detailed attempts to 'fine tune' the rate and exemption structure of the GCT seem more likely to destroy the integrity of the new tax than to make it serve better any distributional goals.

Much more will be done with this data base to explore the effects of alternative tax patterns on households of different sizes and compositions.[19] Dwyer (1983), for example, has suggested that female-headed households tend to allocate income differently than female-male households, 'more productively' she asserts (p. 20), with more going to food, health, and clothing and less (presumably) to alcohol and tobacco. The data in table 3.3 suggest, however, that female-headed households in Jamaica actually spend a lower percentage on food, particularly in urban households. However, female-headed households appear to spend more on education, again particularly in urban households.

Similarly the data need to be converted to a 'consumer-equivalent' basis for comparative purposes. Espuet (1984) has made a preliminary effort along these lines in his study of a rural Jamaican community, but much more can be done, as discussed in Blokland (1976) and Lazear and Michael

(1980). The longitudinal nature of the data will also be utilized to analyse demand responses to changing prices during the rapid inflation occurring over the study period. The analysis obviously needs to be extended to the other very important indirect taxes in Jamaica (Bird and Miller, 1985).

Nevertheless, as Fass (1980, p. 133) said of an earlier study of poverty in Haiti, in work such as this 'it seems inappropriate to seek out absolute accuracy. What really is necessary is that data stay within the bounds of reason and provide interpretation and results that are meaningful.' By this test, we think that even these preliminary results provide strong evidence of the potential impact on the poor of particular changes in the design of indirect taxes. In the face of the apparent strong direct impact on the poor of taxes on basic foodstuffs, for example, it would take a very low inequality aversion coefficient indeed not to recommend their exemption.[20] Similarly, the perverse distributive effect of some avowedly 'progressive' rates (e.g., on cosmetics) should also, we believe, carry some weight in designing consumption tax structures in countries like Jamaica, particularly given the high administrative costs associated with such rate differentiation. As has been noted time and again in this paper, detailed expenditure data and close attention to the details of tax structure are needed to reach conclusions such as these.

B *Microlevel Data Sets and Fiscal Incidence*

As the Jamaican example suggests, the most useful data sets for the analysis of indirect taxes will include several features: longitudinal data on expenditures so that changes over time can be analysed; expenditure categories that are sufficiently fine-tuned so that the details of the tax ratio can be examined; actual price data rather than imputed prices; and demographic information on the population surveyed. Such features are basic to the endeavour, yet are rarely found in any study in the literature on indirect tax incidence.

For an even better understanding of fiscal impacts, still other information is needed. For example, beyond the bare facts of household composition such as number of household members and their age and sex, it is important to try to find out both who is the 'household head' (not always an easy question) and the number of income earners in the household. Such factors may affect substantially the pattern of expenditures and consequently the effects of tax changes (Dwyer, 1983).[21] Household characteristics greatly influence the nature of consumption patterns (Strauss, 1982; Kelley, 1981). An obvious example is one cited by Brown and Deaton (1972) in which a household with beer-consuming adults but no children will have a higher per capita consumption rate than a household with beer-consuming adults and children. We must be able to separate adults from children in order to see clearly the incidence of a tax on beer in this case.

The conventional analysis of tax incidence in effect assumes that the family is a sort of 'black box.' If one tax on a family is reduced and another increased by the same amount, it is assumed that there will be no net effect on the family. But what if the tax reduced is on beer consumed by the husband and the tax increased is on condensed milk consumed by the children? Would the effects be different if the increases and reductions were reversed? Households organize their finances in many ways, and there is no certainty that the effect on expenditure patterns will be the same in all cases (Pahl, 1980, 1983).

Even more ideally, and to our knowledge non-existent in the fiscal-incidence literature, would be a data set that would combine the features on the 'whole consumption/production vector' (Behrman and Deolalikar, 1985) and so allow us to learn how consumption would be altered, within the household and among households, by changing prices, how such changes would affect nutrient intake, and how changes in nutrient intake would affect productivity.[22] Studies that could incorporate such data would greatly advance our knowledge of current tax incidence, changes in incidence over time, and how such changes alter consumption, nutritional status, and productivity. All these processes must be eventually taken into account if we are to place taxation in the wider context of how the poor will fare in the course of development.

4 Issues for Future Research

The first, and perhaps the most important, conclusion of this chapter is simply that the issue of fiscal incidence and the poor matters. The tax system in most developing countries impinges on the lives of many poor people in potentially important ways. The poor, especially the urban poor, *do* pay substantial taxes. The extent, nature, and perhaps duration of their poverty *are* affected in many ways by the characteristics and operation of the tax system. Both governments and researchers concerned with poverty in developing countries should, therefore, be aware of these effects. The interaction of taxation and poverty is thus an important subject for research.

A second conclusion is that unfortunately this interaction is a very difficult subject to study. Not only are the underlying theoretical issues inherently complex and the needed facts hard to find, but it is essential to understand the detailed reality of the fiscal instruments under examination and to ground that understanding firmly in the relevant broad policy context. Such generalizations as 'income taxes are better than sales taxes' or 'beer taxes are always regressive' are useless guides to designing or reforming tax policy in any particular country.

New data and techniques may make it possible in the future to refine answers to meaningful old questions (will the substitution of a general sales tax for a set of excise taxes be progressive or regressive?) and to answer important new questions (will an increase in tobacco taxes impact differently on children in female-headed households?). There is still a long way to go in the analysis of the distributional effects of taxes.[23] But it is gradually becoming possible to carry out serious studies in a field that has far too long been dominated by misleadingly overly simplistic quantifications of untested, and too often ad hoc, hypotheses.

The set of those who can simultaneously deal with complex theoretical issues, with primary data-grubbing, with institutional realities, and with broad economic policy concerns is probably almost an empty one. In the future, there must probably be more 'team research' along the lines of the Warwick and Jamaican studies cited earlier. But however such research is carried out, a final conclusion suggested by this chapter is that much more attention should be paid to collecting and analysing data bearing on these matters, with particular emphasis on trying to obtain a better understanding of the extent and nature of the variations among the poor. It may be useful for many purposes to seize upon the simple lack of command over economic resources of the poor as their dominant and most important characteristic. What has been too often neglected, however, are the very great differences *within* those classed as 'the poor': between urban and rural; between employed and unemployed; between those in male-headed and female-headed families; between those with and without children; between smokers and drinkers and the abstemious; and so on.

Yet if we know anything about the effects of taxation on the poor in developing countries, we know that these effects often vary more with such characteristics than they do with any measure of total income or expenditure. Beyond gathering more detailed data in order to be able to depict more accurately the impact of taxation on the poor, we also need a much clearer idea of the normative and positive relevance of the observed deviations among different groups of poor people. Do the non-smoking poor care that their addicted colleagues pay heavy taxes? Should they? Do their colleagues care? Should anyone care?[24]

We do not, as yet, *know* much about either the short-run or the long-run impact of taxes on the poor in developing countries. But we are perhaps approaching a point where the economist's increasing understanding of the implicit models underlying incidence analysis and the increasing availability of relevant data are, despite a continued lag on the data side, better matched than ever before. We are able, at last, to begin to respond to the oft-expressed concerns of policy-makers with respect to the distributional impact of revenue measures with something other than qualitative bromides or quantitative exercises in sleight of hand. With luck, and even more with perseverance, a similar survey a decade hence may be able to report not just promising beginnings but firm results.

Notes

1 A decade ago, for example, the Organization of American States, like many economists of the day, blithely characterized the tax system as the 'supreme equalizer' (Organización de los Estados Americanos, 1973, p. 348).
2 The considerable differences in tax levels apparent in table 3.1, particularly in the upper-income groups, are attributable to differences in time period, tax coverage, income concept, and incidence assumptions. These differences are not discussed further here. It should be emphasized, however, that *all* the studies of tax incidence in developing countries reviewed here assume that sales and excise taxes are fully shifted forward. For a contrary argument in the context of the United States, see Browning (1978). The validity of this assumption in developing countries with substantial trade restrictions is also open to question (Bird and De Wulf, 1973), but this point is not further discussed here.
3 See, e.g., Bahl and Linn (1985), on the effects on property tax incidence of different administrative systems.
4 Some useful appraisals along general equilibrium lines have been carried out in developing countries with respect to particular fiscal policy issues (Minford, 1970; Berry, 1972; Thirsk, 1980). Data limitations have so far generally rendered impossible the application of even such simplified versions of reality as a computable general equilibrium model (Shoven and Whalley, 1984) to tax policy in such countries, however.
5 In contrast, the same source shows that in thirty-eight of the fifty-five non-oil developing countries for which data are available, central governments account for 95 percent or more of all tax revenue, and in only nine of the fifty-five is this proportion less than 90 per cent. The explanation for this apparent difference is that some of the larger developing countries are most decentralized. In Brazil, for example, subnational governments collected 24 per cent of all taxes in 1982, while in India, the comparable figure was 30 per cent.
6 It is interesting to note that the Jamaican property tax was held up by Linn (1983, p. 78) as an example to other developing countries.
7 As is well known, such subsidization is in any case definitely a second-best alternative to congestion pricing (Churchill, 1972).
8 At the time, a large subsidized urban public bus company provided most transit services, with the balance provided by a variety of private mini-buses, often operating illegally.

9 'For many of these low income households, transport costs were higher than the rent, but the fares to and from work were regarded as a necessary part of enjoying a job income (rather like at-source deductions). Some of them regularly ran out of cash by Thursday and would walk to work or try to obtain a lift part way from a friend who had some means of transport, either privately owned or as part of his work. Few could aspire to any form of private transport of their own, even a bicycle' (Heraty, 1980, p. 14). Similar results are common in other countries (Linn, 1983, p. 105).

10 'There exists ample evidence that cities which are served by privately operated buses tend to have better transit service at substantially lower costs to transit users and to the governments alike than do cities served by public bus undertakings' (Bahl and Linn, 1985, pp. 1–34).

11 See, for example, the case of Papua New Guinea discussed in Bird (1983).

12 As emphasized repeatedly in the Warwick studies, such specific results are – as is common with optimal tax work – quite sensitive to the functional forms used in estimation. Moreover, their analysis to date has largely ignored the effects of taxes on incomes (the sources side).

13 In addition to serious conceptual problems, the analysis does not take into account the implications or costs of the significant administrative changes inherent in such a reform.

14 Some figures in table 3.4 vary slightly from those in the text because the former are weighted means and the latter unweighted means. (See also note to table 3.3.)

15 For a full description of the methodology, see Bird and Miller (1985).

16 Note that these figures do *not* include the almost invariably regressive sumptuary items. For a full discussion of the incidence of all indirect taxes on low-income households in Jamaica, see Bird and Miller (1985).

17 Much the same result, for example, emerged in Bird's earlier (unpublished) study of a similar point in the Philippines, where it was found that hair oil – an obvious 'luxury' – was in fact a basic consumption item for even the lowest income groups. The Philippine example also points up the rather odd results that may emerge if tax-rate classifications are determined on the basis of household surveys, which classify as 'essential' the most widely used goods – a practice commended by both Due (1970) and Asher and Booth (1983).

18 Recall the similar results for Pakistan mentioned earlier in this chapter.

19 For further analysis of the existing indirect tax system and GCT in Jamaica, see Bird (1985).

20 It should also be recognized that since most such foodstuffs are *not* consumed by the poor, exemption is not a particularly efficient way to help the poor. In the absence of an efficient transfer system, however, it is much better than nothing.

21 See Folbre (1984) for a critique of the use of a joint utility function for the household.

22 Behrman and Deolalikar (1985) do an excellent job of bringing the consumption/production function together in an analysis of data from rural southern India. Taxation, however, is not a concern of their study.

23 Many common layman's questions on incidence ('is the tax system as a whole progressive?') can probably never be answered satisfactorily (Bird, 1980a). But increasing familiarity with general equilibrium and other modelling techniques

has made clearer how dependent the results of incidence studies are not only on data but also on our implicit models; e.g., assuming the forward shifting of excise taxes in the face of trade restrictions, as has been done in all studies cited here, requires some strong, and rather strange, assumptions.
24 Some arguments suggest no one cares – or should (Buchanan, 1969).

References

Aaron, H.J. 1975. *Who Pays the Property Tax? A New View*. Washington: The Brookings Institution

Adler, J., E.R. Schlesinger, and E.C. Olson. 1952. *Public Finance and Economic Development in Guatemala*. Stanford: Stanford University Press

Ahmad, E., and N. Stern. 1983. 'Effective Taxes and Tax Reform in India.' Discussion Paper 25, Development Economic Research Centre, University of Warwick

Ahmad, E., D. Coady, and N. Stern. 1984. 'Tax Reform, Shadow Prices and Effective Taxes: Illustrations for Pakistan for 1975/76.' Discussion Paper 48, Development Economics Research Centre, University of Warwick

Ahmad, E., H-M Leung, and N. Stern. 1984. 'Demand Response and the Reform of Indirect Taxes in Pakistan.' Discussion Paper 50, Development Economics Research Centre, University of Warwick

Asher, M.G., and A. Booth. 1983. *Indirect Taxation in Asean*. Singapore: Singapore University Press

Bahl, R., and J. Linn. 1985. 'Urban Public Finance and Administration in Developing Countries.' World Bank draft. Washington (mimeo)

Behrman, J.R., and A.D. Deolalikar. 1985. 'How do Food and Product Prices Affect Nutrient Intakes, Health and Labor Force Behavior for Different Family Members in Rural India?' Paper presented at the meeting of the Population Association of America, March, Boston

Berry, R.A. 1972. 'Presumptive Income Tax on Agricultural Land: The Case of Colombia.' *National Tax Journal* 25: 169–82

Berry, R.A., and R. Soligo (eds). 1980. *Economic Policy and Income Distribution in Colombia*. Boulder, CO: Westview Press

Bird, R.M. 1974a. *Taxing Agricultural Land in Developing Countries*. Cambridge, MA: Harvard University Press

– 1974b. 'Public Finance and Inequality.' *Finance and Development* 11: 2–4

– 1977. 'Tax Reform and Tax Design in Developing Countries.' *Revista di diretto finanziario e scienza delle finanze* 36, no. 2: 297–306

– 1980a. 'Income Redistribution through the Fiscal System: the Limits of Knowledge.' *American Economic Review Papers and Proceedings* 70: 77–81

– 1980b. *Central-Local Fiscal Relations and the Provision of Urban Public Services*. Canberra: Centre for Research on Federal Financial Relations, Australian National University

– 1982. 'Taxation and Employment in Developing Countries.' *Finanzarchiv* 40, no. 2: 211–39

– 1983. *The Allocation of Taxing Powers in Papua New Guinea*. Port Moresby: Institute of National Affairs

- 1984. *Intergovernmental Finance in Colombia*. Cambridge, MA: International Tax Program, Harvard Law School
- 1985. 'The Impact of the Proposed General Consumption on Low-Income Households.' Syracuse University (mimeo)
Bird, R.M., and L. De Wulf. 1973. 'Taxation and Income Distribution in Latin America; A Critical Review of Empirical Studies.' *International Monetary Fund Staff Papers* 10: 639-82
Bird, R.M., and B. Miller. 1985. 'The Incidence of Indirect Taxes on Low-Income Households in Jamaica.' Syracuse University (mimeo)
Blokland, J. 1976. *Continuous Consumer Equivalence Scales*. The Hague: Martinus Nijhoff
Brown, A., and A. Deaton. 1972. 'Surveys in Applied Economics: Models of Consumer Behavior.' *Economic Journal* 82: 1145-1236
Browning, E.K. 1978. 'The Burden of Taxation.' *Journal of Political Economy* 86: 649-71
Buchanan, J.M. 1969. *Cost and Choice*. Chicago: Markham Publishing Company
Chelliah, R.J., and R.N. Lall. 1978. *Incidence of Indirect Taxation in India 1973-74*. New Delhi: National Institute of Public Finance and Policy
Chenery, H., et al. 1974. *Redistribution with Growth*. London: Published for the World Bank and the Institute of Development Studies by Oxford University Press
Churchill, A. 1972. 'Road User Charges in Central America.' World Bank Staff Occasional Paper number 15. Washington
Cnossen, S. 1977. *Excise Systems: A Global Study of the Selective Taxation of Goods and Services*. Baltimore: Johns Hopkins Press
- 1982. 'What Rate Structure for a Value-Added Tax.' *National Tax Journal* 35: 205-14
- 1984. 'Jamaica's Indirect Tax System: The Administration and Reform of Excise Taxes.' Staff Paper no. 8, Jamaica Tax Structure Examination Project, Metropolitan Studies Program. Maxwell School, Syracuse University
De Wulf, L. 1974. 'Taxation and Income Distribution in Lebanon.' *Bulletin for International Fiscal Documentation* 28: 151-9
- 1975. 'Fiscal Incidence Studies in Developing Countries: Survey and Critique.' *International Monetary Fund Staff Papers* 22: 61-131
Downing, P.R. 1973. 'User Charges and the Development of Urban Land.' *National Tax Journal* 26: 631-7
Due, J.F. 1970. *Indirect Taxation in Developing Countries*. Baltimore: Johns Hopkins Press
- 1985. 'Revision of the Indirect Tax Structure in Jamaica: A Proposal for a General Consumption Tax.' Staff Paper no. 6 (revised), Jamaica Tax Structure Examination Project, Metropolitan Studies Program, Maxwell School, Syracuse University
Dwyer, D.H. 1983. 'Women and Income in the Third World: Implications for Policy.' Working Paper no. 18, Population Council. New York
Espuet, P. 1984. 'Poverty in a Rural Jamaica Community.' Unpublished thesis, University of the West Indies, Jamaica
Fass, S. 1980. *The Economics of Survival: A Study of Poverty and Planning in Haiti*. Washington: Agency for International Development

Folbre, N. 1984. 'Household Production in the Philippines: A Non-Neoclassical Approach.' *Economic Development and Cultural Change* 32: 303–30

Follain, J., and E. Miyake. 1984. 'Land versus Property Taxation: A General Equilibrium Analysis.' Staff Paper no. 13, Jamaica Tax Structure Examination Project, Metropolitan Studies Program, Maxwell School, Syracuse University

Frank, C.R., Jr, and R.C. Webb (eds). 1977. *Income Distribution and Growth in the Less-Developed Countries.* Washington: The Brookings Institution

Goode, R. 1984. *Government Finance in Developing Countries.* Washington: The Brookings Institution

Harberger, A.C. 1977. 'Fiscal Policy and Income Distribution.' In Frank and Webb, 1977, pp. 459–80

Heraty, M.J. 1980. *Public Transport in Kingston, Jamaica and Its Relation to Low Income Households.* Crowthorn, Berkshire: Overseas Unit, Transport and Road Research Laboratory

Holland, D.M. 1979. 'Adjusting the Property Tax for Growth, Equity and Administrative Simplicity: A Proposal for La Paz, Bolivia.' In Roy W. Bahl (ed.), *The Taxation of Urban Property in Less Developed Countries,* pp. 119–34. Madison: University of Wisconsin Press

Holland, D., and J. Follain. 1985. 'The Property Tax in Jamaica.' Staff Paper no. 16, Jamaica Tax Structure Examination Project, Metropolitan Studies Program, Maxwell School, Syracuse University

International Monetary Fund. 1984. *Government Finance Statistics Yearbook,* vol. 8. Washington

Katzman, M.T. 1978. 'Progressive Public Utility Rates as an Income Redistribution Device in Developing Countries: The Case of Municipal Water.' In J.F.J. Toye (ed.), *Taxation and Economic Development,* pp. 174–92. London: Frank Cass

Kelley, A. 1981. 'Demographic Impacts on Demand Patterns in the Low-Income Setting.' *Economic Development and Cultural Change* 30: 1–16

Kuznets, S. 1966. *Modern Economic Growth.* New Haven: Yale University Press

Lazear, E., and R.T. Michael. 1980. 'Family Size and the Distribution of Real Per Capita Income.' *American Economic Review* 70: 91–107

Lent, G.E., M. Casanegra, and M. Guerard. 1973. 'The Value-Added Tax in Developing Countries.' *International Monetary Fund Staff Papers* 20: 318–78

Linn, J.F. 1979. 'Automotive Taxation in the Cities of Developing Countries.' *Nagerlok* 11: 1–23

– 1980a. 'The Distributive Effects of Local Government Finances in Colombia: A Review of the Evidence.' In Berry and Soligo, 1980, pp. 69–111

– 1980b. 'Urban Finances in Developing Countries.' In Roy Bahl (ed.), *Urban Government Finance: Emerging Trends,* 245–83. Urban Affairs Annual Reviews, vol. 20. Beverly Hills: Sage

– 1983. *Cities in the Developing World.* New York: Published for the World Bank by Oxford University Press

Lovejoy, R.M. 1963. 'The Burden of Jamaican Taxation, 1985,' *Social and Economic Studies* 12: 442–58

Marshall, M. (ed.). 1982. *Through a Glass Darkly: Beer and Modernization in Papua New Guinea.* Monograph 18, Institute of Applied Social and Economic Research. Boroko, Papua New Guinea

McLure, C.E., Jr. 1977a. 'Taxation and the Urban Poor in Developing Countries.' *World Development* 5: 169–88

- 1977b. 'The Incidence of Jamaican Taxes, 1971-1972.' Working Paper no. 16, Institute of Social and Economic Research, University of the West Indies, Mona, Jamaica
- 1979. 'The Relevance of the New View of the Incidence of the Property Tax in Less Developed Countries.' In Roy W. Bahl (ed.), *The Taxation of Urban Property in Less Developed Countries*, pp. 51-76. Madison: University of Wisconsin Press
McLure, C.E., Jr, and W.R. Thirsk. 1978. 'The Inequity of Taxing Inequity: A Plan for Reduced Sumptuary Taxes in Developing Countries.' *Economic Development and Cultural Change* 26: 487-503
Meade, J.E., et al. 1978. *The Structure and Reform of Direct Taxation*. London: George Allen and Unwin
Meerman, J. 1979. *Public Expenditure in Malaysia: Who Benefits and Why*. New York: Published for the World Bank by Oxford University Press
Miller, B.D., and C. Stone. 1985. 'The Low-Income Household Survey: Description and Analysis.' Syracuse University (mimeo)
Minford, A.P.L. 1970. 'A Model of Tax Incidence for Malawi.' In Centre of African Studies, *African Public Sector Economics*, pp. 67-93. Edinburgh
Musgrave, R.A. 1969. *Fiscal Systems*. New Haven: Yale University Press
Oates, W.E. 1972. *Fiscal Federalism*. New York: Harcourt Brace Jovanovich
Organización de los Estados Americanos. 1973. *La Política Tributaria como Instrumento de Desarrollo*. Washington
Pahl, J. 1980. 'Patterns of Money Management within Marriage.' *Journal of Social Policy* 9: 313-35
- 1983. 'The Allocation of Money and the Structuring of Inequality within Marriage.' *Sociological Review* 31: 237-62
Selowsky, M. 1979. *Who Benefits from Government Expenditure? A Case Study of Colombia*. New York: Published for the World Bank by Oxford University Press
Shoup, C.S. 1983. 'Current Trends in Excise Taxation.' In Sijbren Cnossen (ed.), *Comparative Tax Studies*, pp. 257-75. Amsterdam: North-Holland Publishing Company
Shoven, J., and J. Whalley. 1984. 'Applied General Equilibrium Models of Taxation and International Trade: An Introduction and Survey.' *Journal of Economic Literature* 22: 1007-51
Smith, R.S. 1974. 'Financing Cities in Developing Countries.' *International Monetary Fund Staff Papers* 21: 329-88
- 1975. 'Highway Pricing and Motor Vehicle Taxation in Developing Countries: Theory and Practice.' *Finanzarchiv* 33: 451-74
- 1984. 'Motor Vehicle Taxation in Jamaica.' Staff Paper no. 10, Jamaica Tax Structure Examination Project, Metropolitan Studies Program, Maxwell School, Syracuse University
Stern, N. 1984. 'Optimum Taxation and Tax Policy.' DM/84/9, Fiscal Affairs Department, International Monetary Fund, Washington
Strauss, J. 1982. 'Determinants of Food Consumption in Rural Sierra Leone: Application of the Quadratic Expenditure System to the Consumption-Leisure Component of a Household-Firm Model.' *Journal of Development Economics* 11: 327-53

80 Richard M. Bird and Barbara D. Miller

Tanzi, V. 1974. 'Redistributing Income through the Budget in Latin America.'
  Banca Nazionale del Lavoro Quarterly Review 17: 65–87
– 1983. 'Tax Systems and Policy Objectives in Developing Countries: General
  Principles and Diagnostic Tests.' DM/83/78, Fiscal Affairs Department, Inter-
  national Monetary Fund, Washington
Thirsk, W.R. 1980. 'A General Equilibrium Analysis of the Effects of Subsidized
  Farm Mechanization on Output and Income Distribution in Colombia.' In
  Berry and Soligo, 1980, pp. 177–201
Toye, J. 1981. *Public Expenditure and Indian Development Policy 1960–1970.*
  Cambridge: Cambridge University Press
Wasylenko, M. 1985. 'The Distribution of Tax Burdens in Jamaica.' Syracuse
  University (mimeo)
Whalley, J. 1984. 'Regression or Progression: The Taxing Question of Incidence
  Analysis.' *Canadian Journal of Economics* 17: 654–82

4

Public Subsidies in the Social Sector: Equity and Efficiency

EMMANUEL JIMENEZ

The public sector in developing countries has traditionally played an important role in the financing of social services. In education, the most accurate available indicator is the percentage of students who are enrolled in public school.[1] In 1975 the ranges were 82-87 per cent at the primary levels in Latin America, Asia, and West Africa and 67-71 per cent at the secondary levels (table 4.1). The proportions at the university levels are also substantial (World Bank, 1980). These enrolment figures have important implications for government expenditures, since tuition and fees recover very little of the costs in public institutions.[2] Moreover, large bursaries to students to cover living and other expenses, and transfers to subsidized private schools, add large amounts to the fiscal burden. The share of education in the government budget hovers around 16 per cent for all developing countries. However, the figure goes to 23 per cent for francophone countries in sub-Saharan Africa (table 4.2).

In health, the figures vary more widely across countries for definitional reasons. However, gross estimates of public as a per cent of total health expenditures indicate averages of about 63 per cent in Africa, 48 per cent in Latin America and the Caribbean, and 30 per cent in Asia (table 4.1). The percentage share of health expenditures in the government budget is about 3 per cent for low-income countries and 5-6 per cent for middle-income countries (table 4.2).

The extent of public intervention in the social sectors has been justified on equity grounds. One argument is that public expenditures on social ser-

The World Bank does not accept responsibility for the views expressed herein, which are those of the author and should not be attributed to the World Bank or its affiliated organizations.

TABLE 4.1
Share of the public sector in health and education

| | Per cent of students in public schools 1975[a] | | Private as per cent of total health expenditure (1975–80)[b] |
	Primary	Secondary	
Africa			38.3
East	57	55	
West	82	70	
Asia	87	71	70.1
Latin America and Caribbean	87	67	49.4
Europe, Middle East, and North Africa	94	92	42.7

[a] Tan (1985a) and World Bank estimates
[b] De Ferranti (1985)

vices can be used as an effective method of income redistribution, particularly if they are financed out of progressively collected revenue sources. Another is that health and education should be considered as 'basic human needs,' to which the public sector should guarantee access to some minimum threshold amount. Widely accepted campaigns for universal primary education and 'health for all by the year 2000' (WHO, 1981) are examples of the basic needs view.

The other justification for heavy public subsidization has been on efficiency grounds, based on traditional public-finance arguments. A completely private system would lead to sub-optimal levels of consumption of the public service for a number of reasons. Because of externalities, individual consumers would undervalue the consumption of a particular service. Because of scale economies, providers would charge a price that would be too high relative to that which is socially optimal. Because of failure in related markets, such as that for credit, individuals could not generate requisite resources to consume the desired amounts.

In recent years, many developing countries have confronted tightening budget constraints. Country conditions have changed substantially because policies regarding the financing of education and health were developed. Thus, it is time to investigate the record of public investments in meeting their goals regarding equity and efficiency. This review shows that there is substantial room for improvement in both areas. As a result of the re-

TABLE 4.2
Public expenditure on education and health, major world regions, 1980

	Expenditure on education as per cent of state budget	Expenditure on health as per cent of state budget
Africa		
East	11.1	5.3
West	14.9	4.7
Asia		
East Asia and Pacific	13.4	5.1
South Asia	14.6	3.7
Latin America	15.6	8.2
East and North Africa	15.8	4.2
Developing countries	14.5	5.4

SOURCE: UNESCO, *Statistical Yearbook*, various issues; De Ferranti (1985a)

examination of the traditional assumptions that justified public intervention, this chapter concludes that, perhaps, a return to some form of private participation is warranted.

1 Equity in the Distribution of Public Social Expenditures

A *Patterns of Distribution*

Despite the policy of free provision, the distribution of public resources devoted to education is not progressive with respect to current household income. The rich get more of the subsidy because of their enrolment ratios, particularly at those educational levels where subsidies are highest. The total monetary effect for various world regions has recently been estimated in a World Bank study by Mingat and Tan (1986b). Table 4.3 shows the proportion of total public resources appropriated by different socio-economic groups. Because of the paucity of income data in developing countries, the distribution figures are categorized on the basis of occupational rather than income categories.[3] The figures take into account the cumulative effects of subsidies obtained at previous levels of education. A comparison of the share of resources received by three socio-economic groups with their share of the total population of school-age children provides a measure of the benefit that each socio-economic group derives from education subsidies. This is termed the subsidy-benefit ratio. The data show

TABLE 4.3

Share of public resources appropriated by different socio-economic groups in education in the major regions of the world, 1980

Region	Proportion in the population (%) (1)			Proportion of public school resources (%) (2)			Ratio of proportion of resources and population (2)/(1)				
		Manual workers & traders	White collar		Manual workers & traders	White collar		Manual workers & traders		White collar	
	Farmers			Farmers			Farmers	Absolute	Relative to farmers	Absolute	Relative to farmers
Africa											
anglophone	76	18	6	56	21	23	0.73	1.19	1.6	3.78	5.2
francophone	76	18	6	44	21	36	0.58	1.15	2.0	5.93	10.3
Asia	58	32	10	34	38	28	0.59	1.19	2.0	2.79	4.8
Latin America	36	49	15	18	51	31	0.49	1.04	2.1	2.03	4.3
Middle East and North Africa	42	48	10	25	46	29	0.60	0.35	1.6	2.87	4.8
OECD	12	53	35	11	46	42	0.95	0.87	0.9	1.2	1.3

SOURCE: Mingat and Tan (1986b)

that it is much higher for the white-collar group than for the other groups, indicating that this group enjoys a more-than-proportionate share of all education subsidies. In most developing country regions, the children of white-collar workers gain nearly six times as much benefit from public education subsidies as the children of farmers. In francophone Africa, the contrast is even more marked: children from white-collar families gain over ten times as much from subsidies as farmers' children. Thus, the 'provision of free or heavily subsidized education does not ensure equity in the distribution of public resources' (Mingat and Tan, 1985b).

Information on the distribution of public-health subsidies by income class is more difficult to compile. Table 4.4 summarizes the distribution of overall public-health subsidies for a number of countries. The evidence is that this distribution is not as regressive as that for educational subsidies. However, neither is it progressive (with the possible exception of pre-revolutionary Iran). The poorest 40 per cent in Colombia, Malaysia, and Sir Lanka receive, respectively, 41, 47, and 46 per cent of the public subsidy for health. This distribution is mostly a result of the progressive incidence of public expenditures on rural health care. The distribution is more regressive in Indonesia and the Philippines, where the poorest 40 per cent receive only 19 and 27 per cent, respectively, of the subsidies from public-health centres and hospitals.

These numbers are made even more dramatic when one considers the relative needs of income groups. Although space does not permit a thorough review, the bias against lower-income groups in the distribution of public education and health expenditures is more pronounced when one considers the large number of school-age children and the incidence of disease for the poorer household.

In summary, the distributions of government subsidies in health and education are, at best, neutral with respect to household income. Indeed, for most types of education, the distribution is highly regressive. Thus, present policies regarding the public provision of educational and health services have not succeeded in substantially improving the national distribution of resources.

This result is preserved even when the financial contribution of richer households to public revenue is taken into account. It is sometimes argued that because most public subsidies to education and health are drawn from general revenues, which are financed by a progressive tax system, the regressive distribution of these subsidies may be mitigated. The evidence indicates otherwise. While revenue from income taxation may be based on a progressive schedule, a large proportion of central government revenue, which funds most health and educational expenditures in highly centralized

86 Emmanuel Jimenez

TABLE 4.4
Percentage share of public-health subsidies by income group

Country (source)	Year of data	Type of health subsidy	Poorest 20%	20-40%	40-60%	60-80%	80-100%
Chile (Foxley et al. 1979)	1969	Public health	31 (poorest 30%)		35 (40-60%)		35 (70-100%)
Colombia (Selowsky 1979)	1974	NHS hospital[b]	30	23	20	18	12
		SSS hospital[b]	8	15	29	24	23
		Health centre	25	29	23	15	8
		Overall public	20	21	20	20	20
Indonesia (Meesook 1984)	1980	Overall public	19 (poorest 40%)		3 (40-70%)		45 (70-100%)
Iran (Richards 1982)	1977[c]	Overall public	30	21	19	18	13
Malaysia (Meerman 1979)	1974	Inpat. hospital	19	27	10	24	20
		Outpat. hospital	22	20	23	14	6
		Rural clinic	28	27	19	19	8
		Overall public	21	26	15	22	17
Philippines (Richards 1982)	1975[c]	Overall public	14	13	15	18	40
Sri Lanka (Richards 1982)	1978[c]	Overall public	25	21	20	19	14

[a] All rows sum to 100%.
[b] NHS = National Health Service; SSS = Social Security System.
[c] These figures are from an ILO review (Richards, 1982). The data are from restricted ILO documents. The years quoted are the dates of the original studies.

developing countries, is raised through indirect taxation. Thus, when all sources of tax revenue are taken into account, the tax systems in these countries are not strongly progressive and may even be regressive (see table 4.5).

B *Reasons for the Distribution*

Under present financial arrangements, richer households have greater access to public subsidies in education and health services than do poorer households. First, the presence of private costs implies that income constraints bound consumption choices, even if the public authorities do not charge for the services. Second, for any given type of service, but especially

TABLE 4.5
The incidence of taxation by income group, selected countries

Country	Per cent of income paid in taxes		
	Lowest income	Middle income	Highest income
Argentina	17.2	19.8	21.4
Brazil	5.2	14.3	14.8
Chile	18.5	16.2	26.7
Colombia	17.1	13.1	29.9
Kenya	11.5	8.8	12.7
Korea	16.4	15.7	21.6
Lebanon	8.4	20.2	20.3
Malaysia	17.7	16.5	42.1
Mexico	40.2	22.7	14.9
Pakistan	15.0	9.6	25.3
Peru	4.8	17.4	26.6
Philippines	23.0	16.9	33.5

NOTE: Figures include direct and indirect taxes.
SOURCE: De Wulf (1975); Foxley et al. (1979); Mann (1982); Heller (1981); and Gillis and McLure (1978)

for education, the private costs of using publicly subsidized health and educational services are positively related to household income. It is also possible to argue that private benefits are negatively related to income. Third, governments tend to subsidize relatively more (in relation to private cost) those types of social services that have the lowest private returns for indigent families. This effect reinforces the first in biasing the participation rate towards richer families. Finally, among those who are induced to seek the subsidy services, there is excess demand. The method of rationing scarce services is biased towards richer demanders.

(i) Presence of Private Costs
Fees are not the only costs of consumption. Free provision is not free consumption. Other costs, such as transport, the purchase of auxiliary complementary services, and the opportunity cost of the consumer's time, are real constraints to poor households and constitute a major component of the cost of consumption.

Table 4.6 presents some indicators of the magnitude of non-fee costs for education for selected countries. Important components of these indirect costs are for transport; auxiliary materials such as books, school supplies, and uniforms; board and lodging, where they are available (although some of these costs are living costs that households may have had to incur anyway, had the student not gone to school).

Although more difficult to estimate directly, the largest non-fee cost, particularly for secondary and higher levels of education, is that of the opportunity cost of the student's time. This factor is particularly important for education. Many poor households require substantial contributions from children to augment total family resources, especially if work activity is defined as including market work, home production, and housework. For example, the Malaysian evidence indicates that the proportion of children in a family participating in work activity rises from 0.31, for Malay girls aged 5–6, to 0.99 for those aged 15–19; and 0.17 to 0.92, respectively, for Malay boys of the same age groups (De Tray, 1984).[4]

Similar costs can be documented for any given type of health-care service. For example, physician services in the form of government-run clinics may be free. However, transport costs would still have to be incurred. Also, drugs may not be subsidized to the same extent (De Ferranti, 1983; Musgrove, 1983).

The presence of these costs would lead poorer families to demand less of health and education services than richer households in developing countries. (If they were truly free, and benefits were distributed to all, this demand should be relatively insensitive to income). Musgrove, for example, estimates income elasticities greater than unity in the demand for health services. And the poorest households may not participate at all. This is particularly true for services not deemed essential for immediate survival, such as education.

(ii) Differential Costs and Benefits

It is likely that the costs of consuming any given type of educational or health service are greater and the perceived benefits may be less for lower-income households. Costs tend to be higher in serving the poorest segments of the population because these households live in rural areas, where they are more dispersed. Most of these transport costs are borne by the user, particularly for primary education and primary health care (Jimenez, 1987). They are far from trivial for the poorest segments of the population, and, in some instances, board and lodging costs may have to be incurred as well. Household income is greater in urban areas and the result is that demand would be greater for richer income groups.

Another source of greater cost is the lack of access to financial markets. For example, the lack of educational credit markets does not enable the poorest household to borrow needed funds. Households are then con-

TABLE 4.6
The private costs of publicly provided educational services
(all figures in current u.s. dollars)

Country	Survey year	Per capita income	Type of service	Average bursary provided	Average household expenses per student		
					Fees	Indirect costs[a]	Opportunity costs
Malaysia	1974	680	Primary	1	2	51	–
			Secondary	5	30	123	–
			Post-secondary	7	141	235	–
Tanzania	1981	280	Secondary	0	0	137	1,115[b]
Malawi	1983	210	Std. 8	0	5	34	–
			Secondary	–	86	126	–
Mali	1981	190	Rural primary	0	2	5	0

[a] Includes books, transport, room, board, supplies, uniforms, etc.
[b] As perceived by the student. A dash means not available.
SOURCE: Meerman (1979) for Malaysia; Tan et al. (1984) for Malawi; Tan (1985b) for Tanzania; Birdsall (1983b) for Mali. Per capita income from World Bank

fronted with a choice between savings and present consumption. This choice has been posited as one explanation why the average propensity to save rises with income – because at low income levels, survival is threatened below some minimum consumption threshold (Gersovitz, 1983).

Not only are costs expected to be greater for lower-income households. The perceived benefits of receiving the social service may be less as well. Households in higher socio-economic strata may simply be more aware of the benefits of health and nutrition, as well as of the greater opportunities that are opened by education. For educational services, there are a number of other reasons. First, higher-income households tend to provide a better environment for studying, including parental help, and thus increasing the returns to education. Second, these households require a vent for investment of their assets in economies where capital markets are constrained and may simply substitute human for physical capital in their investment portfolio. Third, in non-competitive job markets, where whom one knows is as important as what one knows, the elite once again have an advantage.

(iii) Patterns of Government Expenditure
The choice of which service to subsidize has a profound impact on the distribution of public resources. The evidence is that the public sector in

many countries subsidizes those types of health and education services to which access is severely limited and for which the benefit/cost ratio is higher for higher-income groups.

The difference in the benefit/cost ratio between richer and poorer income groups is likely to be greater for higher education than for primary education. The most important reason for this result is the opportunity cost. Yet, a great proportion of government subsidies is direct at higher levels. Table 4.7 shows the proportion of the world regional populations with no education or only primary schooling as compared to the proportion with higher education. It further compares the share of government educational resources that these two groups receive. The figures take account of the subsidies received by those in higher education throughout their school career, including subsidies at the primary and secondary levels. In developing countries as a whole, on average, 71 per cent of the population in each generation receive none or only primary schooling and obtain only 22 per cent of the resources devoted to education. In contrast, the proportion who attain higher education is only 6 per cent, but this minority obtains 39 per cent of total resources. The most skewed distribution is in Africa: in francophone Africa, 2 per cent of each cohort in the population attain higher education and receive 40 per cent of the public resources devoted to education; in anglophone Africa, 1 per cent of the cohort receives more than one-quarter of all public education resources available to that cohort. The primary reason is the large public reimbursements for out-of-pocket personal costs, such as transport and books (Eicher, 1984; Hinchliffe, 1984; Mingat and Psacharopoulos, 1985). In anglophone Africa, 'student subsidies represent 14% [of total subsidies] at secondary and higher education levels, while in francophone Africa the figures are much higher, 23 and 43% respectively. In countries like the Congo, the Central African Republic and Ivory Coast, scholarships ... even exceed teaching expenditures at the higher level' (Mingat and Psacharopoulos, 1985). To put these numbers into perspective, per student scholarships as a percentage of per capita GNP are: 120 per cent in the Ivory Coast, 160 per cent in Senegal, 700 per cent in Mali, and 800 per cent in Niger and Burkina Faso.

Another government policy that induces inequitable distribution is that spending for given types of urban schools far outstrips spending for rural schools. Table 4.8 is indicative of this trend, which is most pronounced for post-primary education in some countries. In Colombia, secondary education in rural areas, where 32 per cent of the school-age population resides, receives 19 per cent of total government resources. In Indonesia, upper secondary education in rural areas, where 76 per cent of the school-age population resides, received 50 per cent of the government subsidies.

TABLE 4.7
Distribution of total educational resources and population by terminal level of schooling, major world regions, 1980

Region	Primary or less		Higher education	
	% population	% resources	% population	% resources
Africa				
francophone	86	16	2	40
anglophone	83	39	1	26
Latin America	56	16	12	42
Asia				
East Asia and Pacific	57	19	9	40
South Asia	81	23	4	39
Middle East and				
North Africa	64	19	9	45
Developing countries	71	22	6	39
Developed countries	20	8	21	37

SOURCE: Mingat and Tan (1985a)

Similar considerations apply to the health sector. Table 4.9 shows that the rural populations in Colombia obtain 19 per cent of government subsidies but account for 38 per cent of the total population. One of the most skewed rural/urban differentials in health spending is in China. Rural households, which make up 79 per cent of all households, receive 29 per cent of all government subsidies. In Brazil, coverage of the public social-security system (INAMPS) is more complete in urban areas. Musgrove (1983) finds that in metropolitan areas 'most health care is provided directly, with little or no out-of-pocket cost to the consumer, whereas in smaller cities and rural areas INAMPS often reimburses consumers for private expenditures, as well as paying other public sector institutions for the services provided' (p. 254).

(iv) Rationing Criteria
There is excess demand for most subsidized social services. The distribution of public resources devoted to these services thus depends not only on which types of households want them, but also on how the public authority decides to allocate the scarce school places or hospital beds. It can be argued that, at least for education services, the allocation mechanisms tend to be regressive.

The most popular system of rationing scarce educational places is to use performance in school or in entrance examinations. Those who score the

TABLE 4.8
Distribution of government educational subsidy by type of education and location

Country	Year	Type of schooling	Share of educational subsidy (%)		Share of school-age cohort (%)	
			Rural	Urban	Rural	Urban
Indonesia	1982	Primary	83	17	84	16
		Upper secondary	71	29	80	20
		Lower secondary	50	50	76	23
		University	21	79	78	22
		All levels	76	24	83	17
Malaysia[a]	1974	Primary	52	48	–	–
		Secondary	50	50	–	–
		Post-secondary	37	63	–	–
		All	–	–	56	44
Colombia	1974	Primary	35	65	35	65
		Secondary	19	81	32	68
Kenya[b]	1976	Secondary	87	13	95	5

[a] Shares are estimated from enrolment in public institutions. Shares of school-age cohort are assumed to be equivalent to population shares. Dash means not available.
[b] Urban shares as from enrolment data in Nairobi assisted schools
SOURCE: Meesook (1984) for Indonesia; Meerman (1979) for Malaysia; Selowsky (1979) for Colombia; Bertrand and Griffin (1984) for Kenya. For each row, adding rural and urban would total 100 per cent

highest are allowed to enter. Whatever the efficiency implications of this system (they are discussed below) the impact on equity is not neutral, even if it is assumed that innate ability is randomly distributed throughout the population.

There are several reasons why children from richer households can be expected to perform better than those from poorer households on the basis of the above selection criteria. First, richer households have more of their own funds to invest in private tutoring or in the purchase of books. This asset may give their children a comparative advantage in entrance examinations. Second, richer households may be better aware of the benefits of schooling. Consequently, they cultivate a milieu that is conducive to studying and where scholarly activity is not disparaged. The result is often better performance.[5] Third, the need to acquire good grades or to pass competitive tests often leads to repetition in primary or secondary schooling, and poorer households may be unable to finance extended primary or secondary schooling. Thus, even a system of free secondary or higher education that

TABLE 4.9
Distribution of government health subsidy by type of service and by location

Country	Year	Type of schooling	Share of educational subsidy (%)		Proportion of population	
			Rural	Urban	Rural	Urban
Indonesia[b]	1983	All public (Java)[c]	50	16	55	11
		All public (Outer)[c]	27	6	28	6
		All public (Indon.)	77	23	83	17
Malaysia[b]	1974	All public[d]	57	43	60	40
Senegal	1981/82	All public[h]	57	43	81	19
Colombia	1974	NHS hospitals[e]	39	61	–	–
		SS hospitals[e]	2	98	–	–
		Health clinics	23	77	–	–
		All public	19	81	38	62
China	1981	Hospitals[f]	25	75	–	–
		Other MOPH acts.	84	16	–	–
		Med. insurance[g]	0	100	–	–
		All public	29	71	79	21

[a] Subsidies are government expenditures net of any fees received.
[b] Services include government hospitals, public-health centres, and community-health volunteers.
[c] These are percentages of all (Indonesia) subsidies.
[d] Includes rural outpatient clinics, district hospitals, and general hospitals.
[e] National Health Services (NHS) and Social Security (SS) hospitals.
[f] These are expenditures by the Ministry of Public Health and include hospitals of traditional medicine, commune health centres, anti-epidemic activities.
[g] Health insurance to provide free health care is an expenditure by the Ministry of Finance.
[h] Urban = Cap Vert region (Dakar).
SOURCE: Meesook (1984) for Indonesia; Meerman (1979) for Malaysia; Selowsky (1979) for Colombia; Prescott and Jamison (1983) for China; De Ferranti (1983) for all others. Dash means not available.

depends entirely on competitive examinations to select students may in fact discriminate against those who have high ability but insufficient current income to finance the indirect costs of schooling.

This effect is exacerbated because the bulk of the subsidies in education is concentrated on higher education, where the selectivity criteria are the most stringent. The poorer income groups are underrepresented not only because they must be selected from the pool of secondary-school graduates, but also because they are already underrepresented in that qualifying pool.

The selection processes in the health sector vary considerably by type of service. When publicly provided curative care is in excess demand, the most popular allocation mechanism seems to be the queue. The distributional impact of this type of rationing is unclear. If opportunity costs are lower for poorer households, then it may be progressive. Although it was argued above that for the poorest the opportunity cost of seeking public services such as education or preventive health care may be survival in terms of nutrition (time off work), it may also be the opportunity cost of not obtaining curative care.

2 Efficiency of Public Subsidization

The extent and nature of public subsidization of educational and health services have been characterized by inefficiencies that inhibit further expansion and improvements of these sectors in relation to other sectors. Moreover, the distribution of public subsidies among types of institutions within the education and health sectors has resulted in the misallocation of the scarce resources.

A *Underinvestment in Education and Health*

The ability of many governments to mobilize resources to meet the public-service needs of growing populations has been restricted by the recent world-wide recession. Average per capita growth rates in 1970–80 have fallen in the thirty-three countries with the lowest per capita income (excluding China and India) by over 50 per cent (from 2 per cent per annum to 0.9 per cent) of rate of the previous decade (World Bank, 1982).

The impact on government budgets has been immediate (for a more detailed discussion, see Jimenez, 1987). As a result, the gap between governments' goals regarding the provision of public services, particularly health and education, and the resources required to finance them has been widening. Between 1973 and 1980, the share of education and health services in government expenditures fell 11 and 13 per cent, respectively, for non-oil developing countries as a group. The decline is particularly pronounced for the African countries where, for example, the share of health in total government expenditures fell, on average, 20 per cent.[6] One estimate of the cost of financing a so-called basic human development package of education and health related services implies budget shortfalls, for the average developing country, as high as 17 per cent of gross national product (GNP) (Meerman, 1979).

There is also evidence that some governments, in adjusting to the tighter budgetary restraints, have opted to lower per capita recurrent subsidies rather than sacrifice coverage. While politically more palatable, this action has led to the so-called recurrent cost problem: i.e., investment projects are not being fully funded with the resources required to run and maintain them as designed (see Heller, 1979, for a detailed definition). The relatively high proportion of recurrent costs in social expenditures makes them more vulnerable to such budgetary restrictions. For example, a recent cross-section time-series study of twenty-eight developing countries concludes that the public-sector response to tightening fiscal pressures on education over the last decade has been to squeeze recurrent non-wage expenditure per student (Heller and Cheasty, 1983). Such policies have led to shortages in books and teaching materials but not in classrooms in Mali (Birdsall, 1985). One example where the ratio of public-health recurrent expenditures to capital expenditures has been steadily falling is Botswana (Jimenez, 1987).

B *Resource Misallocations within Education and Health*

Another source of inefficiency can be traced to intra-sectoral sources. The distribution of public subsidies among types of educational, and perhaps health, services as well as the access to those services among individuals tends to be distorted. These misallocations have persisted primarily because of the failure of government policies – which might have been justifiable in the period when newly emergent nations were trying to consolidate their gains – to adjust to changing circumstances.

(i) Misallocations among Types of Social Services
At least for education, there is evidence that public subsidization needs to be refocused. Not all types of educational investment are equally profitable. Table 4.10 indicates that the social rates of return to primary education are much higher than those to post-primary education for the developing countries. Within the developing country group, the differences are largest for the African countries. These rates of return compare the benefits to education, as measured by the additional income from completing more schooling, with the costs of education, as measured by opportunity costs in terms of forgone earnings and the cost of providing the education, regardless of who pays for them. Since the non-monetary benefits of education, such as the gain to society over and above those that accrue to individuals from good citizenship and having a literate and numerate population, are likely to be larger for lower levels of education, at least for the poorest countries, taking them into account in these calculations could accentuate the result.

TABLE 4.10
The rates of return to investment in education by level, country, type, and region (percentages)

Country type/ region	Social rate of return			Private rate of return		
	Primary	Secondary	Higher	Primary	Secondary	Higher
Developing						
Africa	28	17	13	45	26	32
Asia	27	15	13	31	15	18
Latin America	26	18	16	32	23	23
Intermediate	13	10	8	17	13	13
Advanced	–	11	9	–	12	12

NOTE: Dash means not available because of lack of a control group, namely those with no schooling.
SOURCE: Psacharopoulos (1985), table 1

Yet the present pattern of public education investment does not appear to be aimed at equalizing the social rates of return described above. Post-primary education, and particularly university education, is relatively more heavily subsidized than primary education, in comparison to the costs that have to be incurred by private individuals. A comparison of private rates of return in table 4.10 with the social rates of return is a measure of the degree of relative subsidization of each level of education. For all three country groups, the ratio of private to social rates of return is greater for higher education than for secondary education. For the African countries, the ratio is higher even when compared with primary education. These results are not surprising when one considers the subsidization schemes documented earlier.

The potential gains in redirecting investments from activities with lower rates of return (e.g., higher education) to those with higher rates of return (e.g., primary education) can be substantial. These calculations are rough, but indicative. If the magnitude of the shift in investments were such as to equalize rates of return across levels of education, the gains in allocative efficiency would amount to 2.6 per cent of the gross domestic product (GDP), or almost the entire education budget in five African countries for which data are available (Dougherty and Psacharopoulos, 1977). The figures for the four Latin American countries are even more dramatic.

(ii) Misallocation within Types of Social Services
Heavy public subsidization also has implications in the way that resources are allocated within institutions. One aspect is that the reliance on public

provision of educational and health services has led to inefficiencies because public-sector managers have less incentive to minimize cost than their private-sector counterparts.[7] Very few comparisons have been made of the efficiency of public- versus private-sector provision of educational and health services. The difficulty is in ensuring that in cost comparisons output is held constant in terms of both quantity and quality.

A related aspect of efficiency within institutions is whether publicly subsidized health and educational services allocate access according to those consumers who have the 'highest return.' In health services, this means that those who have the most to gain from being well or those who are sickest are given priority. In effect, the issue is whether the methods of quantity-rationing of publicly subsidized services are efficient, since these services are supposedly not rationed by willingness to pay.

A full analysis of the efficiency of alternative access methods is complex because much depends on the existence of related markets, such as those for educational credit and health insurance. Such a discussion would be beyond the scope of this paper. However, it is worthwhile to emphasize that rationing schemes that seem, at first blush, to be relatively efficient methods of allocation may not be so.

For example, the most popular method of allocating scarce public-school places is by performance in entrance examinations or in school. Although this method may appear to sort students solely on the basis of ability, in practice it leads to sorting on the basis of willingness to pay. Richer households have more resources to invest in tutoring or in materials to assist their children to enter. There is even evidence from African countries like Mauritius (see Woodhall, 1983) that students are kept in school longer (through repetition) for the sole purpose of enhancing progression to higher levels. The result is a greater representation of richer households in the rationed school level than is warranted.[8] There will be excess investment in types of schooling inputs that are socially costly and only marginally beneficial in terms of raising productivity – an argument for improved educational credit schemes.

In the health sector, the most popular quantity-rationing device appears to be the queue. Although hard evidence is not available, various field reports are replete with examples of overcrowding in health centers (Jimenez, 1987). Queuing may be efficient for in-patient care, where physicians have an opportunity to assess needs and grant entry accordingly. For other types of health care, such as out-patient services, reasonably efficient allocation mechanisms are not as forthcoming. Although a portion of health-care demand is randomly determined, a great deal of it is endogenous to individual behaviour. Queues do not provide inducements for individuals to engage in preventive care.

3 Directions for Policy Change: Selective User Charges

It is useful to summarize the evidence reviewed so far. The distribution of government subsidies for health and education is not progressive. In fact, for education it is strongly regressive. The reasons are:

a Free provision does not mean free consumption. So, we would expect income to still determine consumption, even if no charges are levied by the public sector.

b Costs are higher for poorer income groups because they lack access to credit markets and insurance markets, and because they live in remote areas.

c Subsidies are highest for the types of public services that are consumed by richer income groups (higher education, private rooms in hospital care).

d Quantity-rationing depends on willingness to pay.

Public-sector financial involvement has contributed to inefficiency. The reasons are:

a It has led to underinvestment in social sectors as a whole. Recent constraints on public investment, combined with restrictions on private-sector involvement, have led to this result.

b There is misallocation of resources among types of education and, perhaps, health services. In education, there is overemphasis on higher as compared to primary education. In health, there is not enough done for preventive care and too much for high-cost in-patient curative care.

c There is misallocation of resources within social services. First, the wrong students or patients may be chosen. Second, there are not enough managers to minimize cost.

How should the public sector respond? The idea is to generate resources without relying on traditional resources (i.e., tax revenue)? and also to improve equity and internal efficiency. One option is to relax some of the constraints that prevent the private sector from responding, at least from the financial side. This option implies a selection lowering of subsidies through a combination of user fees and lower allowances. It must be selective, at least by type of service. Subsidies should be decreased for those services that exhibit fewer externalities and to which access is biased towards richer income groups. Because there is frequently excess demand for these services, more resources will be generated for the sector – to be invested where they are most socially productive (see Jimenez, 1987, for a technical discussion).

On the basis of the above criteria, there is a strong case in education for raising user charges in publicly provided higher education and using the freed budgetary allocations to expand lower levels, particularly primary.

Externalities in education are likely to be exhausted beyond literacy and numeracy.[9] The excess demand for university places, as reflected in acceptance ratios, is one indicator that the willingness to pay is likely to be non-zero. Finally, it has already been demonstrated that the richer income groups are grossly overrepresented in publicly subsidized higher education. A series of steps could be the following: (1) eliminate living allowances that are often higher than the opportunity cost of schooling; (2) introduce fees for boarding and other services; (3) introduce fees for tuition to recover a larger percentage of the cost. Accompanying these steps should be the development of student loan schemes and access to credit. To the extent that some subsidies remain, they should be more geared to income rather than distributed uniformly.

Where should the revenues generated go? To primary education, if possible, because social rates of return are highest there. A recently completed case study of nine African countries concluded that even a modest reallocation of resources through the above policy can have a significant impact. The effects of withdrawing all public subsidies for (a) students' living expenses, by abolishing scholarships, and (b) tuition costs, by introducing fees, are shown in table 4.11. In Niger and Burkina Faso, the gain in terms of additional primary enrolments would be modest because of the small current enrolments in higher education; but in Malawi and Senegal, the primary enrolment rate could almost double, if all subsidies to higher education were reallocated to primary schooling.

It has been suggested that the wider array of health services can be categorized into three groups for the purposes of determining the applicability of user charge policies (table 4.12). For curative services, except for those that are referred (all in-patient and some out-patient care), 'fees ... undoubtedly should be increased above the current very low (or zero) levels in many cases' (De Ferranti, 1985). The funds can then be used to expand services in overcrowded facilities. For patient-related preventive services, the case is not as strong because of externalities and lack of information on the part of patients. However, some anecdotal evidence does exist to indicate that willingness to pay is non-zero so that, with an appropriate information campaign, some charging may be warranted. For non-patient-related preventive services, the extent of externalities, exclusivity, and the merit-goods argument preclude the imposition of user charges.

One sequence of events if there are no insurance markets or if they are small and confined to urban salaried households (as they are now) would be the following, in order of ease of administration: (1) institute hospital charges for private patients; (2) provide for greater cost recovery, including user charges plus premiums, for hospital charges of the insured; (3) bypass

TABLE 4.11
Actual and potential enrolment ratio at the primary level in selected African countries

Country	Actual primary enrolment ratio	Potential primary enrolment ratio if higher education students bear entire cost of		
		Living expenses	Operating costs	Both
Central African Republic	68	76	71	80
Ivory Coast[a]	76	94	91	100
Mali	27	33	29	35
Niger	23	25	24	26
Senegal	48	58	61	71
Togo[a]	100	100	100	100
Burkina Faso	20	24	22	26
Malawi	59	64	86	91
Tanzania[a]	100	100	100	100

[a] For these countries, the shift in resources will release more than sufficient resources to provide universal primary education at the existing unit costs; hence the resources could be used for other purposes, such as improving school quality.
SOURCE: Mingat and Tan (1985b)

fees in countries where a referral system exists; (4) institute other in-patient charges (meals, charges for visitors); (5) introduce out-patient fees (Birdsall, 1985). If possible, there should also be an introduction of insurance markets to cover a wider array of people. However, at the same time it would be important to try to ensure that services or insurance coverage continued to be available to the poorest, and that user fees did not restrict this group's access to care. Many countries have successfully implemented such schemes (Zschock, 1983).

Finally, another possible government response to meeting the social-service needs of its population under constraints would be to lift outright prohibitions (if any) on private providers and, in certain instances, relax the constraints under which they operate.[10] The private sector already responds in meeting the excess demand for public education in many countries (Tan, 1985a). One example for education is Kenya's *harambee* system (Armitage and Sabot, 1987; Bertrand and Griffin, 1984). The private sector in health has traditionally been large (De Ferranti, 1985). Lifting the excessive regulations under which the private sector operates may allow social-sector expansion without reliance on additional government subsidies. This type of

---

TABLE 4.12
Health services: categories for user charge policies

I *Curative care*
Includes personal services (care of patients) by health facilities and independent providers, including traditional practitioners; and purchases by users of medicines. Can be subdivided into (i) 'first-contact' services (all outpatient); (ii) referral services (in-patient and some out-patient).

II *Preventive care: patient-related*
Includes services to well patients, particularly infants, mothers, and pregnant women; also oral rehydration therapy (see note in table 4.4) and hypertension control. Delivered through maternal and child health clinics at health facilities and community health programs. Typical services are immunization, growth monitoring, and instruction on improved breast-feeding and weaning practices.

III *Preventive care: non-patient-related*
Includes disease control (both vector control and mass campaigns), sanitation, education and promotion of health and hygiene, control of pests and zoonotic diseases, and monitoring of disease patients.

SOURCE: De Ferranti (1985)

reform requires some care so that the private sector does not end up pre-empting public-sector resources (e.g., public subsidy of training doctors). There are also lessons to be learned from mixed public and private provision of health in the United Kingdom and the United States, for example, where the end result is two classes of service with services for the poor being markedly inferior.

However, removing the constraints on the private sector should be used, to the extent possible, to direct government subsidies toward providing adequate health and educational services to the relatively poor. Strained public resources need not be used to subsidize the rich, who should nonetheless be allowed to satisfy more of their demands with their own private resources.

Notes

Part of the research in this paper was conducted while the author was a consultant to the Resource Mobilization and Public Management Division, Country Policy Department, the World Bank, Washington. The paper also draws on recent work in collaboration with George Psacharopoulos and Jee-Peng Tan. Any remaining errors in this particular paper, however, are the author's, as are the views expressed herein. The latter should not be attributed to the World Bank or its affiliates. A version of this paper was published in the

World Bank Research Observer as 'The Public Subsidization of Education and Health in Developing Countries: A Review of Equity and Efficiency,' vol. 1, no. 1 (January 1986).

1 Indicators on the basis of public versus private educational expenditures are available but might be misleading because of the way they are aggregated – for example, from national accounts data, one can calculate the share of public in total national expenditure on recreation, entertainment, education, and cultural services, but not on education alone. Tan (1985a) shows expenditure shares to range from 89 to 45 per cent in Africa, 84–12 per cent in Asia. However, these are likely to be underestimates because of the definition of the category.

2 The degrees of cost recovery in public education vary by regional grouping and by level of education. Data for twenty-five developing countries were recently compiled and reveal that, around 1980, the per cent of unit public costs covered by fees amounts to: 5.7 (primary), 11.4 (secondary), and 1.9 (higher) in Africa; 1.7 (primary, 15.6 (secondary), and 8.5 (higher) in Asia; 0.9 (primary), 1.7 (secondary), and 6.6 (higher) in Latin America. These numbers are compiled from Wolff (1984), Ainsworth (1984), Jimenez (1987), Schiefelbein (1985).

3 Fields (1980) surveys some evidence on the distribution of enrolment ratios for developing countries. Some recent contributions, which confirm the earlier findings, include those of Mingat and Tan (1986a) for Malaysia, Meesook (1984) for Indonesia, Birdsall (1983a) for rural Mali.

4 De Tray (1984) uses these data to conclude that, on the basis of a multivariate regression, income is unrelated to children's work activities. However, both household income and parents' education are included in the equation and it is likely that the income effect is captured by parental status variables. Indeed, parents' education is significantly negatively correlated with children's work activities.

5 The impact of socio-economic characteristics on school achievement is well documented. See, for example, Heyneman and Loxley (1983).

6 These figures, quoted in Jimenez (1987), are taken from IMF, Government Finance Statistics.

7 Some analysts would argue that even conscientious public-sector reform would only lead to temporary improvements. The reason is that the members of society, as co-owners of a public enterprise, have less incentive to monitor its output (given that this is even possible) than do the owners of a private enterprise because the former do not have full property rights. That is, the general taxpayer cannot sell his/her share of the enterprise so that he/she has less incentive at the margin to ensure its success.

8 The efficiency loss is substantial. Pinera and Selowsky (1981) estimate that if the allocation of school places were based more on ability and if all the most able students were given the opportunity to benefit from secondary and higher education, the efficiency gains would amount to 5 per cent of GDP in Latin America, Africa, and the less-developed countries of Asia.

9 In fact, overly inflated public-sector wage scales in some African countries may make these externalities negative for higher education because a greater proportion of graduates go into the public sector.

10 See Cameron and Hurst (1983) and Cowen and McLean (1984) for a review of the restrictions on public providers.

References

Ainsworth, M. 1984. 'User Charges for Cost Recovery in the Social Sectors: Current Practices.' Country Policy Department, World Bank Discussion Paper no. 184. Washington

Akin, J., C. Griffin, D. Guilkey, and P. Popkin. 1982. 'The Demand for Primary Health Care in the Bicol Region of the Philippines.' Paper presented at the National Council for International Health Conference, 14–16 June, Washington

Armitage, J., and R. Sabot. 1987. 'Efficiency and Equity Implications of Subsidies of Secondary Education in Kenya.' In D. Newbery and N. Stern (eds), *Modern Tax Theory for Developing Countries*, pp. 589–614. New York: Oxford University Press

Bertrand, T., and R. Griffin. 1984. 'Financing Education in Kenya.' Country Policy Department, World Bank Discussion Paper. Washington

Birdsall, N. 1983a. 'Demand for Primary Schooling in Rural Mali: Should User Fees Be Increased?' Country Policy Department, World Bank Discussion Paper no. 1983-8. Washington

– 1983b. 'Strategies for Analyzing Effects of User Charges in the Social Sectors' (draft). Country Policy Department, World Bank Discussion Paper no. 1983-9. Washington

– 1985. 'Cost Recovery in Health and Education: Bank Policy and Operations.' World Bank, Population, Health and Nutrition Department, Washington (mimeo, limited circulation)

Cameron, J., and P. Hurst. 1983. *International Handbook of Education Systems II: Africa and Middle East*. New York: John Wiley and Sons

Cowen, R., and M. McLean. 1984. *International Handbook of Education Systems II: Asia, Australia and Latin America*. New York: John Wiley and Sons

De Ferranti, D. 1983. 'Health Sector Financing and Expenditure in Developing Countries: Current Issues' (draft for comment). Population, Health and Nutrition Department, World Bank, 8 February. Washington

– 1985. 'Paying for Health Services in Developing Countries: An Overview.' World Bank Staff Working Paper no. 721. Washington

De Tray, D. 1984. 'Schooling in Malaysia: Historical Trends and Recent Enrollments.' Rand Note no. N-2011-AID, Rand Corporation, Santa Monica, CA

De Wulf, L. 1975. 'Fiscal Incidence Studies in Developing Countries: Survey and Critique.' *International Monetary Fund Staff Papers* 22: 61–131

Dougherty, C., and G. Psacharopoulos. 1977. 'Measuring the Cost of Misallocation of Investment in Education.' *Journal of Human Resources* 12: 446–59

Eicher, J.C. 1984. 'L'Enseignement supérieur en Afrique de l'Ouest Francophone: Synthèse de cinq études de cas.' Education and Training Department, World Bank, Washington

Fields, G. 1980. 'Education and Income Distribution in Developing Countries.' In T. King (ed.), 'Education and Income,' World Bank Staff Working Paper no. 402. Washington

Foxley, A., E. Animat, and J.P. Arellano. 1979. *Redistributive Effects of Government Programs*. Oxford: Pergamon Press

Gersovitz, Mark. 1983. 'Savings and Nutrition at Low Incomes.' *Journal of Political Economy* 91: 841–67

Gillis, M., and C.E. McClure. 1978. 'Taxation and Income Distribution: The Colombian Tax Reform of 1974.' *Journal of Development Economics* 5: 233–58

Heller, P.S. 1979. 'The Underfinancing of Recurrent Development Costs.' *Finance and Development* 16: 38–41

– 1981. 'Testing the Impact of Value-Added and Global Income Tax Reforms on Korean Tax Incidence in 1976: An Input-Output and Sensitivity Analysis.' - *International Monetary Fund Staff Papers* 28: 375–410

Heller, P.S., and A. Cheasty. 1983. 'Sectoral Adjustment in Government Expenditure in the 1970s: The Educational Sector with Particular Emphasis on Latin America.' International Monetary Fund, DM/83/72. Washington (mimeo)

Heyneman, S., and W. Loxley. 1983. 'Import of Primary School Quality on School Achievement across 29 Higher and Lower Income Countries.' *American Sociological Review* 88: 1162–94

Hicks, N., and A. Kubisch. 1984. 'Cutting Government Expenditures in LDCs.' *Finance and Development* 21: 37–9

Hinchliffe, K. 1984. 'Higher Education in Sub-Saharan Africa.' Education and Training Department, World Bank, Washington

International Monetary Fund. 1982. *Government Financial Statistics*. Washington

Jimenez, E. 1987. *Pricing Policy in the Social Sectors: Cost Recovery for Education and Health in Developing Countries*. Baltimore: John Hopkins University Press

Mann, A.J. 1982. 'The Mexican Tax Burden by Family Income Class.' *Public Finance Quarterly* 10: 305–31

Meerman, J. 1979. *Public Expenditure in Malaysia: Who Benefits and Why*. New York: Oxford University Press

Meesook, O.A. 1984. 'Financing and Equity in the Social Sectors in Indonesia: Some Policy Options.' World Bank Staff Working Paper no. 703. Washington

Mingat, A., and G. Psacharopoulos. 1985. 'Education Financing Policies in Africa: Some Facts and Possible Lines of Action.' *Finance and Development* 22: 35–8

Mingat, A., and J.P. Tan. 1985a. 'On Equity in Education Again: An International Comparison.' *Journal of Human Resources* 20: 298–308

– 1985b. 'Subsidization of Higher Education versus Expansion of Primary-Enrollments: What Can a Shift of Resources Achieve in Sub-Saharan Africa?' *International Journal of Education Development* 5: 259–68

– 1986a. 'Expanding Education through User Charges in LDC's: What Can Be Achieved?' *Economics of Education Review* 5 (3): 273–86

– 1986b. 'Who Profits from the Public Funding of Education? A Comparison by World Regions.' *Comparative Education Review* 30: 260–70

Musgrove, P. 1983. 'Family Health Care: Spending in Latin America.' *Journal of Health Economics* 2: 245–58

Orivel, F. 1983. 'Costs and Financing of Education in Upper Volta: Current Situation and Prospects.' Country Policy Department, World Bank Discussion Paper no. 1984–2. Washington

Pinera, S., and M. Selowsky. 1981. 'The Optimal Ability – Education Mix and the Misallocation of Resources within Education.' *Journal of Development Economics* 8: 111–31

Prescott, N., and D.T. Jamison. 1983. 'Health Sector Finance and Expenditures in China.' Population, Health and Nutrition Department, World Bank, Washington
Psacharopoulos, G. 1985. 'Returns to Education: A Further International Update and Implications.' *Journal of Human Resources* 20 (4): 584–604
Ram, R. 1982. 'Public Subsidization of Schooling and Inequality of Educational Access: A New World Cross Section Study.' *Comparative Education Review* 26: 36–47
Richards, P.J. 1982. 'Meeting Basic Health Care Needs.' In Richards and Leonor, 1982, pp. 15–43
Richards, P.J., and M.D. Leonor (eds). 1982. *Target Setting for Basic Needs: The Operation of Selected Government Services.* Geneva: ILO
Schiefelbein, E. 1985. 'Education Costs and Financing Policies in Latin America.' Education and Training Department, World Bank, Washington (mimeo, limited circulation)
Selowsky, M. 1979. *Who Benefits from Government Expenditure?* New York: Oxford University Press
Tan, J.P. 1985a. 'Private Education: Some Macro Trends on Enrollment and Expenditures.' *International Review of Education* 3 (1): 103–17
– 1985b. 'Private Direct Cost of Secondary Schooling in Tanzania.' *International Journal of Educational Development* 5 (1): 1–10
Tan, J.P., K.H. Lee, and A. Mingat. 1984. 'User Charges for Education: The Ability and Willingness to Pay in Malawi.' World Bank Staff Working Paper no. 662. Washington
Thobani, M. 1984. 'Charging User Fees for Social Services: Education in Malawi.' *Comparative Education Review* 28: 402–23
UNESCO. *Statistical Yearbook.* Various years.
Wolff, L. 1984. 'Controlling the Costs of Higher Education in Eastern Africa: A Review of Data, Issues and Policies.' World Bank Staff Working Paper no. 702. Washington
Woodhall, M. 1983. 'Student Loan as a Means of Financing Higher Education: Lesson from International Experience.' World Bank Staff Working Paper no. 599. Washington
World Bank. 1980. *Education, Sector Paper.* Washington
– 1982. *World Development Report.* New York: Oxford University Press
World Health Organization (WHO). 1981. *Review of Health Expenditures, Financial Needs of the Strategy for Health for All by the Year 2000, and the International Flow of Resources for the Strategy.* Report by the Director General to the Executive Board, Document no. WHO/EB69/7. Geneva
Zschock, D. 1983. 'Medical Care under Social Insurance in Latin America: An Analysis.' USAID, Washington (mimeo)

5

Sites and Services – and Subsidies: The Economics of Low-Cost Housing

STEPHEN K. MAYO AND DAVID J. GROSS

This is a paper about a major innovation in delivering shelter and related services to the poor in developing countries: sites-and-services projects. These projects, which now have been sponsored by international aid agencies for a bit more than a decade,[1] are government-sponsored projects that deliver a package of shelter-related services, from a minimal level of 'surveyed plots' to an intermediate level of 'serviced sites' to an upper level of 'core housing' complete with utilities and access to community-based services, depending on the ability and willingness of beneficiary populations to afford a particular level of services. Typically, such projects represent a sharp break with pre-existing government shelter policies in that they attempt, in principle, to focus directly on lower-income groups and to deliver shelter and services with small or no subsidies.

In addition they constitute a package of policy alternatives on a small scale that, if extended more broadly, would address most land-use and shelter-policy areas in which governments have actively intervened. For example, sites-and-services project designers must confront issues of building codes, zoning and land-use regulations, tenure security, subsidy levels and mechanisms, housing and infrastructure standards and pricing policies, expropriation and compensation, cost-recovery mechanisms, financing instruments and terms, project siting and layout, land-acquisition mechanisms, the mix of public and private roles in project implementation, and a host of other administrative and institutional issues. Thus, to study the impacts of sites-and-services projects and to link those impacts to specific project design features and policies is in a real sense to study housing policy for the poor in a far more generic way than might at first appear to be required.

By now, large numbers of sites and services and slum-upgrading projects have been implemented. The World Bank alone, for example, had initiated some sixty-eight projects through 1984, each benefiting more than 25,000 households on average. After a decade of experience with such projects, it is instructive to look closely at how they have worked and to determine the lessons that can be learned from their successes and failures.

In order to understand better the workings of sites-and-services projects, it is useful to have an analytical framework. This paper uses such a framework, described in Mayo (1985), which looks at areas of impact such as housing consumption and investment, consumption of non-housing goods and services, incentives to sublet or to sell out to higher-income groups, and incentives to default on mortgages. The analytical framework provides a basis for estimating the economic benefits that accrue to project participants, the subsidies that are required to achieve certain project outcomes (such as housing that meets minimum project design standards), and the welfare losses to society associated with subsidy elements. In order to estimate these benefits, it is necessary to have information on housing-demand parameters in developing countries. Thus, the next section of this chapter reviews recent evidence on housing demand in developing countries based on an ongoing research project at the World Bank. Implications of that research for impacts of sites-and-services projects are then described. There follows a review of several major project outcomes of sixty-eight World Bank-sponsored sites-and-services projects in which it is suggested that failure to incorporate correct information on housing-demand behaviour in project designs has resulted in subsequent problems that seriously threaten the ability to achieve some of the most fundamental goals of sites-and-services projects. The most serious of these problems are creating conditions that lead either to large subsidies and hence poor prospects of replicability or to smaller subsidies but with benefits going to relatively higher-income groups. The chapter concludes with some comments and recommendations about improving both the design of sites-and-services projects and the choice of housing-policy instruments in developing countries.

1 Sites and Services: Background and Recent Evaluations

The growth of populations in developing countries and their increasing concentration in urban areas have put enormous pressure on governments to mobilize resources to meet the basic needs of their people. Shelter demands have been particularly acute. For example, between 1960 and 1980, the population of cities in developing countries is estimated to have increased by 135 per cent, from 234 million to 549 million; between 1980 and 2000, a further increase, to 1.2 billion people, is expected, thereby creating major demands on countries to provide both housing and related services (World Bank, 1975a).

The initial response of many developing-country governments to the press or urban population growth was to adopt the shelter 'solutions' of developed countries: heavily subsidized blocks of public-housing flats with high standards of construction and infrastructure, zoning and building-code regulations discouraging production of housing of lower standards, and, in many cases, destruction of slum areas and squatter settlements in the name of either 'law and order' or 'urban renewal.' These policies did not work.

Public housing did not reach most of the population; Grimes (1976), for example, reported that from one-third to two-thirds of urban populations could not afford the least expensive public housing unit in six developing-country cities he studied. Subsidy levels were high enough virtually to guarantee that public housing could not be made available to most of the population. Zoning and building regulations were widely flouted as 'informal housing' and squatter settlements proliferated. In Cairo, for example, where zoning laws forbid conversion of agricultural land to residential use and where building codes require approved architectural or engineering plans for legal housing construction, it was estimated that approximately 84 per cent of housing built since 1970 is 'informal' – built in violation of either zoning or building codes or both (Mayo et al., 1982). When squatter settlements were removed, hydra-like they returned, sometimes nearby but often in the same place.

By the 1970s, it was clear to many in positions to affect third-world housing policy that the failed (or failing) programs of the 1950s and 1960s had to be replaced by more constructive solutions. What was called for, and found expression in the works of Turner (1972), Mangin (1970), and others, was an approach more in harmony with the natural processes of shelter acquisition and with the development of the poor themselves. In place of previous policies, it was proposed that public programs capitalize on the untapped energies and resources of the poor through 'progressive-development' schemes that provided housing or simply serviced sites that were affordable by low-to-moderate-income households and that could be progressively upgraded over time. Complementing such sites-and-services schemes, there were to be 'slum-upgrading' or 'squatter-upgrading' schemes that focused on improving existing residential areas of the poor rather than on developing undeveloped land.

The key to making such projects work was to bring down the cost of shelter and infrastructure from the high and unaffordable levels prescribed by most governments. As noted in a World Bank policy paper (1975a, p. 5): 'This can be achieved, in the first instance and most rapidly, by reducing standards; permitting and encouraging the use of low-cost (frequently indigenous)) building materials and a lower quality of finish; providing communal rather than private plumbing and sanitary facilities; encouraging or providing higher density construction, with less land per dwelling unit; and providing less living space per dwelling unit.' Reducing standards was not enough, however. It was also seen to be important to deal with problems and constraints in urban land and housing markets, which were assumed to restrict the level of housing investment among low-income households – for example, shortages of urban infrastructure, uncertain and insecure land tenure, unavailability of formal housing finance, shortages of low-cost building materials, and difficulty in assembling land for development. Removal of such supply-side barriers to investment was seen as essential in establishing the context within which household resources could be mobilized to upgrade shelter and infrastructure beyond initial affordable but minimal levels.

It was also assumed that the progressive-housing development engendered by household resource mobilization and investment would be paralleled by a similar phenomenon at an institutional scale. That is, it was expected that public institutions responsible for implementing site-and-service schemes and upgrading projects would price sites and shelter at a level that would not only fully recover costs but generate a modest surplus that could be recycled in order to replicate projects at a larger scale. Although subsidies, particularly for the lowest-income participants, were not altogether ruled out of the sites-and-services paradigm, it was assumed that they would be modest, often generated internally by allocating profits earned on sales of higher-income and commercial sites to write down prices of sites for lower-income households. Thus, the important goal of 'replicability' of projects was seen to depend critically on both 'appropriate standards and sound pricing policies' (World Bank, 1983, p. 9). The latter implied prices that recovered costs and entailed small or no subsidies; the former implied that standards were not only affordable but represented a bundle of housing and infrastructure characteristics for which poor households were willing to pay. These principles were succinctly set out by the director of the World Bank Urban Projects, Department, who stated that 'affordability is the key to cost recovery, and cost recovery is the key to replicability. It's as simple as that' (Ayres, 1983, p. 162).

These principles were to be reflected in the 1970s and 1980s in a growing number of sites-and-services and upgrading projects sponsored by developing-country governments and funded in part by outside agencies such as the World Bank, U.S. Agency for International Development (USAID), regional development banks (e.g., Asian Development Bank, Inter-American Development Bank), and other bilateral aid agencies. The World Bank alone made loans for thirty-six sites-and-services or upgrading projects between 1972 and 1981, involving total Bank lending of more than $1 billion and estimated to have benefited nearly 2 million people (World Bank, 1983, p. 46). Under its Housing Guarantee Program, USAID sponsored preparation of a number of similar schemes, many of them in Latin America (World Bank, 1975a).

Evaluations of the workings of such projects, their impacts, and their potential problems are beginning to emerge in some numbers. For example, reviewing possible beneficial policy impacts of sites-and-services projects, Ayres (1983, pp. 176–7) concluded that 'The most obvious manifestation of these [policy] changes is held to be that publicly constructed housing, the model of the 1950s and 1960s, has given way to private investment through self-help, thereby reducing the role of the public sector,' citing as examples policy changes consistent with the sites-and-services approach in a number of countries. In addition to policy-level impacts, Ayres (p. 177) concluded that 'The Bank impact on project design, planning, and investment programming is more measurable. Changes in design standards have brought shelter costs way down.' In Zambia, for example, complete houses in sites-and-services projects were estimated to cost less than one-fifth as much as the least expensive government-subsidized housing; in El Salvador, the better-quality sites-and-services-project houses cost less than half as much as the cheapest conventional house (Keare and Parris, 1982, p. xiv).

In a recent evaluation study of four early World Bank projects jointly sponsored by the Bank and IDRC (International Development Research Centre), the authors stated that 'the experiment embodied in the first generation of Bank-supported urban shelter projects [has] been remarkably successful' (Keare and Parris, 1982, p. v), citing (1) increased production of housing and infrastructure, (2) stimulation of beneficiaries to produce housing of higher quality than had been expected, (3) continued investments by beneficiaries in both housing and community facilities, (4) allocation of plots as low as the twentieth income percentile, (5) residential turnover no greater among project residents than among control group households, (6) 'affordability' among target groups, and (7) generation of income and employment among project beneficiaries and producers of sites and services (Keare and Parris, pp. v–vi).

These relatively positive assessments indicate real accomplishments, achieved only at the expense of 'hard and sometimes bitter arguments ... to persuade borrowing nations to reduce their standards and costs, [and] to increase the amounts that were charged to project participants,' with the effect that available public resources were spread far more broadly among the population than they had been before the advent of sites-and-services and upgrading projects (Tym, 1984, p. 217). For these accomplishments, a generation of social innovators and implementors deserve considerable credit.

Despite the running accomplishments of sites-and-services and upgrading projects, a number of reservations and criticisms have been expressed concerning the way the sites-and-services paradigm is working. In many ways these critiques go to the heart of the paradigm, claiming variously that (1) shelter provided is not, in fact, affordable by the poor, (2) benefits accrue disproportionately to better-off households, (3) cost-recovery experience is poor, (4) subsidies persist at unsustainable levels, and, because of the above, (5) projects as they are now designed and implemented are not replicable on a large scale. Consider the arguments regarding each point.

Concerning affordability, Ayres (1983, p. 193) states that 'there is some evidence that the [World] Bank's project designs may have been overly optimistic about the ability of intended beneficiaires to afford improvements rendered by the projects,' citing the slow speed of housing consolidation beyond initial stages and biases in the distribution of sites-and-services plots toward higher-income groups in some projects. Payer (1982, pp. 336–7) goes further, claiming that 'the World Bank figures turn out to be highly unrealistic as a guide to "affordability" of the projects by the poorer slum residents,' and elsewhere elaborates by speculating that 'the "improvements", however desirable some of them may be, will eventuate in the collection of payments and taxes that are considerably higher than what the population is now paying, and that will be for many, if not most, more than they can afford' (p. 325). Jere (1984, p. 67), in reviewing the experience of a sites-and-services project in Lusaka, Zambia, notes that 'cost recovery in low-cost housing remains a major source of concern,' explaining that 'officials involved in the early planning stage had assumed that the residents would be willing to pay up to 20 to 25 percent of their monthly income towards housing costs. Now it appears that the question of affordability and willingness-to-pay were not studied with sufficient care.' The result of this oversight is 'the inability of some residents to pay even if they wanted to' (p. 67).

Over-optimism in design standards and the resultant inability of the poor to afford to be in the project has an inevitable corollary: that benefits will tend to accrue to higher-income households that can afford the higher standards. 'Leakage' of benefits to middle-income households in some sites-and-services projects is well known (Cohen, 1983, p. 95), and is in fact cited in the World Bank/IDRC evaluation: 'The principal finding ... with respect to accessibility [of different income groups to project benefits] is that, in both sites and services and upgrading projects, the participating populations span a wide range of incomes and tend to be more representative of median income groups than of the poorest urban households' (Keare and Parris, 1982, p. 12). The mechanism by which higher-income households become project beneficiaries varies. In some cases, they misstate incomes in order to meet initial project income-eligibility limits; in others, they may legally or surreptitiously purchase or lease project units from initial low-income occupants. For example, Keare and Parris (1982, p. 15) note that in the Philippines 'a number of cases of illegal selling of rights to tagged (censused) dwellings in the poorest area have been observed, and some other interim reports have suggested that a significant proportion of families may not be able to meet regular payments for reblocked housing.' Chana (1984, p. 52), in reviewing the experience of one of the most celebrated sites-and-services projects – the project at Dandora in Nairobi, Kenya – notes that about half of all occupied plots were rented out fully to non-allottees and some units had been illegally sold, presumably to members of higher-income groups. It should be noted that in many sites-and-services projects formal restrictions exist for a stipulated period on sales or rentals by initial allottees, with the effect that distributional consequences of initial design and pricing decisions may become apparent only over a number of years. This tendency for distributional consequences to be disguised initially is aggravated by the existence of subsidies. As Keare and Parris (1982, pp. 56–7) note, 'it is also likely that where subsidization of (a portion of) project costs coexists with barriers to transfer the subsidy in the event of resale, the participant may be, or at least feel, "locked in" for a time.' Subsidies can also disguise the existence of potential cost-recovery problems by creating situations whereby such 'locked-in' households undertake extraordinary financial sacrifices to reach a point at which they can either comfortably make payments on mortgage loans or, perhaps as likely, sell out to higher-income households.

Despite the incentive for low-income project beneficiaries to hold on in the face of economically precarious positions, cost-recovery problems have nevertheless arisen in World Bank and other sites-and-services projects. For example, Keare and Parris (1982, p. xii) note that cost recovery was a problem in three of the four projects they reviewed, although 'causes and severity of the problems varied significantly.' Reviews of cost-recovery experience at the World Bank have focused on the degree to which poor cost recovery depends on poor financial administration, lack of enforcement mechanisms or political will, unwillingness of populations to pay before services are connected and functioning adequately, and an endemic disdain for payment of charges for services (Keare and Parris, 1982, p. xii). Somewhat surprisingly, the possible inability or unwillingness of project beneficiaries to pay for project benefits has been discounted by Keare and Parris. Recalling the questions raised by Ayres, Payer, and others concerning the questionable appropriateness of affordability assumptions that underpin some project design standards, it may be appropriate to ask whether or not the explanations cited by Keare and Parris are 'derived variables' – the product of household unwillingness to pay for standards well beyond their needs and of governments' tacit recognition either of the validity of project beneficiaires' reluctance or of the risk to the government of admitting a mistake. That is, how much of an incentive exists for governments to increase subsidies quietly or to fail to pursue vigorously cost-recovery goals when it is clear to them that otherwise they would risk evicting or impoverishing a highly visible group in a highly visible project?

Regardless of the answer to such questions, it is clear that cost recovery is a significant problem in a number of World Bank (and undoubtedly other agencies') sites-and-services projects. And as Ayres (1983) notes, citing a Bank assessment, 'obviously more needs to be done to improve collections of monthly charges from sites and services occupants *and/or develop alternative financing sources.* Otherwise affordability cannot be equated with replicability' (p. 197, emphasis added). Unfortunately, even this prescription for improvement does not ring quite true, for, noting the italicized phrase, developing alternative financing sources almost inevitably means increasing subsidies, and it can almost never be true that affordability plus subsidies equals replicability.

Yet it appears that in many projects affordability has been purchased with subsidies that are considerably higher than the minimal levels envisioned by the original architects of the sites-and-services paradigm. For example, in one project in Ismailia, Egypt, undertaken by the Egyptian government (with some support from the British Overseas Development Council), selling prices for serviced land were set at Egyptian £2.25 per square metre when the market price was between Egyptian £10 and £15 per square metre (Davidson, 1984, p. 142); purchase was financed by the government at an interest rate of 5 per cent per annum at a time when the prevailing market rate was about 12 per cent. Such land-price write-downs and interest-rate subsidies are common in sites-and-services projects and can easily, as in the example just cited, constitute from half to as much as 90 per cent of the true resource cost of the shelter or land provided in a project. And despite the fact that many subsidy elements are implicit, off-budget transfers, they imperil the long-term replicability of projects just as surely as do direct government payments to project beneficiaries.

Reducing such subsidies has often proved to be extremely difficult for designers of sites-and-services projects, in that there is often a powerful inertia, of two major dimensions, at work in shelter policy. One dimension is that of standards, the other that of subsidies; each derives from earlier practice in shelter policy in developing countries – the often inappropriate policies of the 1950s and 1960s discussed above. The two are intimately related; as noted by Payne (1984, p. 8): 'The frequent exclusion of all land, financing, and administrative costs from project accounting may be considered to represent positive discrimination in favor of the poor and therefore a socially progressive approach. In practice, however, it is often an excuse to maintain unrealistically high standards irrespective of their appropriateness.' Another problem with subsidies is that little thought appears to be given in project planning to their form, magnitude, distribution among different sorts of households, or their impacts either on behaviour of beneficiaries (e.g., impacts on housing consumption, investment, or tenure choice) or on the viability of subsidy-generating institutions. In most developed countries with significant social-housing policies, such questions are at the heart of policy and technical debates concerning the choice of housing programs and policies; in most developing countries they are ignored – often at the peril of long-run replicability of low-income housing programs.

Yet it is on the basis of their replicability on a large scale that sites-and-services and upgrading projects will ultimately be judged. Achieving other project goals – physical implementation, affordability, cost recovery of 'scheduled costs' – at the expense of replicability simply cannot be viewed as the ultimate objective. Thus, as Cohen (1983) noted in reviewing the first decade's performance of World Bank shelter projects, 'by the end of the seventies, it was evident that the notion of replicability could no longer mean doing more of the same thing, but rather it had to involve seeking ways to increase the scale in the provision of housing whether through public or private sector efforts' (p. 91).

To meet this challenge means, among other things, having a clearer analytical understanding of how sites-and-services projects affect the behaviour of potential beneficiaries, as well as empirical information on expenditure on housing, in order to produce projects that are both affordable and replicable.

The next two sections, therefore, take up the issue of, first, the effective demand for housing in developing countries and, second, the actual planning practice of World Bank sites-and-services projects regarding affordability assumptions and the design and pricing decisions that follow from them.

2 Demand for Housing in Developing Countries

The previous section suggests the importance of getting good estimates of the effective demand for housing if sites-and-services projects are to be designed appropriately, that is, in ways that provide significant benefits to intended beneficiaries without adverse side-effects. Here we review recent research on household demand for housing in developing countries and present some of the major implications of that research for the design and likely outcomes of the sites-and-services projects.

A *Housing Demand*

Until recently few comparative studies of housing demand in developing countries existed. Most of the studies of household demand for housing services in developing countries were based on specialized data bases, not usually collected for the express purpose of estimating housing-demand relationships.[2] Different analyses used different variable definitions, different functional forms, and different stratification variables. This inconsistency made comparison of results regarding demand parameters across studies exceedingly tenuous.

In 1981, a major comparative study of housing demand in developing countries was initiated at the World Bank. In that analysis high-quality data were collected for sixteen cities in eight countries (Colombia, Egypt, El Salvador, Ghana, India, Jamaica, Korea, and the Philippines) and were used to estimate housing-demand relationships using relatively comparable variable definitions and identical functional forms and stratifying variables. For comparative purposes, identical models were estimated for two U.S. cities - Pittsburgh and Phoenix. A description of much of that research is contained in Malpezzi and Mayo (1985). The following represents a highly abbreviated description of the study and of its major empirical findings.

Malpezzi and Mayo first estimate a simple log-linear model of housing expenditures in each of the sixteen cities:

(1) $\ln R = a + \epsilon_y(\ln y) + bH + cH^2 + u,$

where R is rent; y is income; H is household size; ϵ_y is the estimated income elasticity of demand; a, b, and c are regression coefficients; and u is an estimated disturbance. The model is stratified for renters and owners. For renters, rent is defined as net rent, exclusive of utility payments. For owners, rent is defined variously as owner imputations of net rent, hedonic estimates of net rent based on applying renter-based hedonic price equations to owners' housing characteristics, or imputed rents based on applying a fixed amortization ratio (from 1 per cent to 1.5 per cent per month depending on the country) to owners' estimates of housing value. Although other functional forms were tried, and many other demographic variables were included in alternative estimated equations, results from the simple log-linear model were found to provide adequate fits and robust findings regarding major demand parameters.

Table 5.1 presents the estimated parameters of housing expenditures functions for renters and owners.[3] In general the results are remarkably consistent with results from developed countries (see Mayo, 1981). The regression fits are typical for this type of equation: typical R-squared statistics are in the 0.1–0.3 range (minimum 0.06, maximum 0.57). Fits are similar for owners and renters.

The median of all renter income elasticities is 0.49; developing-country elasticities range from 0.31 (Busan, Korea) to 0.88 (Davao, the Philippines). Most cluster between 0.4 and 0.6, with estimated U.S. elasticities, however, lower than developing-country estimates. The median of all point estimates of owner income elasticities is 0.46, with extremes of 0.17 in Cairo and 1.11 in Santa Ana, El Salvador. Most point estimates lie between 0.4 and 0.6. In nine of fourteen cases where comparison is possible, estimated developing-country owner income elasticities are greater than those for renters; this finding parallels findings in the literature for developed countries (Mayo, 1981). Comparing expenditure equations across countries reveals practically no systematic variation of income elasticities with country or city income level or population size, but considerable variation in dollar-adjusted intercepts, which are positively related to average city income. Rent-to-income ratios, therefore, decline systematically with income *within* cities, but increase with income *across* cities.[4]

These relationships are shown graphically in figure 5.1 for renters in four representative cities. Relationships for owners are similar, although average rent-to-income ratios are invariably higher at every income level for owners within given housing markets.[5]

The relationships portrayed in figure 5.1 are very similar to the consumption patterns within and across countries documented by Kuznets (see Kuznets, 1961, and other works cited therein). Qualitatively, housing con-

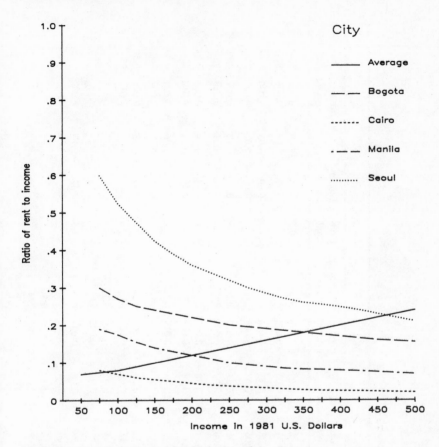

Figure 5.1 Rent-to-income ratios by income for renters

sumption is remarkably similar to total consumption; that is, within-country differences are markedly smaller at various income levels than are between-country differences at different average income levels. Malpezzi and Mayo explore alternative theoretical explanations for these results and then test a series of cross-country housing expenditure models, which are designed to explore presumably long-run cross-country housing-demand relationships. The simplest cross-country model they test parallels the log-linear within-country model, but with the addition of a price term, the relative price of housing, which is constructed using data from Kravis, Heston, and Summers (1982). Defining p_H as the relative price of housing, they estimate the following models[6] for renters and owners in developing countries:

TABLE 5.1
Estimated parameters of housing expenditure functions

Country	City		Renters					Owners				
			Constant	Log income	HH size	HH size squared	R squared and N	Constant	Log income	HH size	HH size squared	R squared and N
Colombia	Bogota (1978)	(coef)	1.11	0.66	0.09	-0.006	0.40	0.77	0.75	-0.00	-0.003	0.49
		(std err)		0.03	0.03	0.003	1016		0.03	0.04	0.003	821
	Cali (1978)	(coef)	2.81	0.44	0.13	-0.006	0.27	1.25	0.69	-0.05	-0.000	0.38
		(std err)		0.06	0.07	0.007	257		0.06	0.07	0.005	256
Egypt	Cairo (1981)	(coef)	0.25	0.46	-0.17	0.010	0.16	0.89	0.17	0.12	-0.009	0.06
		(std err)		0.06	0.09	0.008	303		0.12	0.21	0.019	76
	Beni Suef (1981)	(coef)	-1.2	0.51	0.38	-0.047	0.25	-.09	0.42	0.14	-0.003	0.23
		(std err)		0.14	0.28	0.029	63		0.13	0.14	0.010	63
El Salvador	Santa Ana (1980)	(coef)	0.37	0.48	0.13	-0.014	0.16	-2.5	1.11	-0.06	-0.004	0.37
		(std err)		0.11	0.08	0.007	131		0.11	0.12	0.009	169
	Sonsonate (1980)	(coef)	0.79	0.50	-0.10	0.007	0.16	0.39	0.79	-0.13	0.001	0.57
		(std err)		0.12	0.09	0.007	83		0.15	0.17	0.012	27
Ghana	Kumasi (1980)	(coef)	0.82	0.33	0.02	0.000	0.11					
		(std err)		0.04	0.03	0.002	814					
India	Bangalore (1975)	(coef)	0.66	0.58	-0.08	0.003	0.18	2.84	0.43	-0.17	0.007	0.15
		(std err)		0.04	0.04	0.002	1041		0.08	0.06	0.004	205
Jamaica	Kingston (1975)	(coef)	-0.12	0.70	0.16	-0.012	0.30					
		(std err)		0.08	0.07	0.007	223					

Region	City	stat	(1)	(2)	(3)	(4)	(5)	(6)	(7)	(8)	(9)	(10)
Korea	Seoul (1979)	(coef)	5.04	0.45	0.07	-0.004	0.15	6.06	0.44	-0.04	0.002	0.12
		(std err)		0.03	0.04	0.005	952		0.04	0.04	0.003	952
	Busan (1979)	(coef)	6.26	0.31	0.05	-0.001	0.08	5.93	0.45	-0.05	0.002	0.10
		(std err)		0.07	0.06	0.006	508		0.08	0.10	0.011	296
	Taegu (1979)	(coef)	4.95	0.44	0.03	-0.003	0.23	6.32	0.47	-0.19	0.011	0.18
		(std err)		0.07	0.07	0.008	292		0.08	0.08	0.006	152
	Kwangju (1979)	(coef)	2.70	0.62	0.09	-0.002	0.32	7.53	0.41	-0.27	0.018	0.14
		(std err)		0.09	0.13	0.014	134		0.11	0.18	0.016	84
	Other Korean cities (1979)	(coef)	3.33	0.54	0.04	0.002	0.17	2.16	0.79	-0.12	0.003	0.26
		(std err)		0.05	0.05	0.007	1000		0.05	0.05	0.005	779
Philippines	Davao (1979)	(coef)	-1.6	0.88	0.00	-0.002	0.42	-3.2	0.99	0.04	-0.004	0.28
		(std err)		0.03	0.05	0.002	1376		0.04	0.04	0.003	1968
	Manila (1983)	(coef)	1.27	0.56	0.01	-0.002	0.22	2.46	0.57	-0.02	-0.000	0.31
		(std err)		0.04	0.04	0.003	605		0.04	0.05	0.003	390
United States	Pittsburgh (1975)	(coef)	3.07	0.26	-0.02	-0.002	0.15	3.50	0.18	0.08	-0.005	0.21
		(std err)		0.02	0.04	0.005	946		0.01	0.02	0.002	2378
	Phoenix (1975)	(coef)	3.68	0.18	0.12	-0.015	0.13	3.62	0.18	0.13	-0.011	0.24
		(std err)		0.02	0.03	0.005	918		0.01	0.01	0.002	2284

Renters

(2) $\ln R = -5.39 + 1.60 \ln y + 0.15 \ln p_H$
                    (0.18) (0.29)

        $R^2 = 0.90,$ d.f. $= 13$

Owners

(3) $\ln R = 3.57 + 1.38 \ln y + 0.65 \ln p_H$
                    (0.35) (0.50)

        $R^2 = 0.76,$ d.f. $= 11$

where the dependent variable, rent (R), and income (y) are city means and are converted to 1981 U.S. dollars.[7]

The implications of these models, which are confirmed with alternative specifications, are straightforward: in the very long run, housing consumption is income elastic. Price elasticities are smaller in absolute value than income elasticities, although confidence intervals are quite wide for the former. Long-run income elasticities are estimated to be higher for renters than owners. This means that as cities' economies develop over the very long run, owner and renter consumption patterns increase at a similar pace, *ceteris paribus*. However, because relative housing prices arise with income (at least in our sample) and because renter price elasticities are estimated to be higher than owner elasticities, the net effect of both incomes and prices rising with economic development is that owners' consumption increases faster than renters' consumption over most of the range of the data.

These findings have important implications for the design of housing programs and, in particular, of sites-and-services projects. An obvious general rule is that the fraction of income allocated by households for housing is highly variable, depending on income, the level of economic development, the relative price of housing, and tenure (own or rent). Thus, it is inappropriate to use any single rule-of-thumb 'affordability ratio' as the basis for establishing design standards in sites-and-services projects. If a single value is used, particularly if it is higher than normal spending patterns would indicate, then subsidies might be required to induce target groups to participate and higher-income groups might find their way into projects, either initially or by purchasing from initial allottees.

In order to get a sense of how serious these problems might be, it is useful to examine (1) the minimum subsidy (or benefit) necessary to induce typical target groups to participate and (2) the likely income levels of participants in the absence of subsidies based on the empirical findings on housing demand presented above and assuming alternative affordability rules of thumb.

B Minimum Subsidies Necessary to Induce Participation

Theoretical work by Mayo (1985) has developed a general procedure for estimating minimum subsidies (benefits) necessary to induce participation by households whose normal housing equilibria are below those implied by project standards. Here we operationalize that procedure by assuming a particular utility function, the parameters of which can be approximated using our empirical results, and examine the impact on required subsidies as they vary with alternative affordability planning assumptions.

Specifically, assume that household preferences can be approximated by a Stone-Geary utility function:[8]

$$(4) \qquad U = (H - \theta_h)^{b_h} (X - \theta_x)^{b_x}$$

where H is the housing consumption, X is the consumption of other goods, and θ_h, θ_x, b_h, and $b_x = (1 - b_h)$ are parameters. Applying the procedures described in Mayo (1985), the following expressions can be derived for the minimum housing necessary to induce participation, H_{min}, and the minimum subsidy (benefit) necessary to induce participation, S_{min}:

$$(5) \qquad H_{min} = \left(\frac{y - R_0 - \theta_x}{y - R_s - \theta_x} \right)^{b_x / b_h} (H_0 - \theta_h) + \theta_h$$

and

$$(6) \qquad S_{min} = p_h H_s - R_s,$$

where R_0 is the initial pre-project rent, R_s is the within-project rent, and $p_h H_{min}$ is the market value of shelter and services provided in the project. If the project is designed according to the typical site-and-service paradigm, within-project rent reflects the 'design affordability ratio,' a, and hence $R_s = ay$. Thus equations (5) and (6) become:

$$(7) \qquad H_{min} = \left(\frac{y - R_0 - \theta_x}{y(1 - a) - \theta_x} \right)^{b_x / b_h} (H_0 - \theta_h) + \theta_h$$

and

$$(8) \qquad S_{min} = p_h H_{min} - ay,$$

where R_0 is determined by the housing expenditure function.

The parameters of a Stone-Geary utility function may be locally approximated using knowledge of the parameters of a log-linear housing expenditure function; the resulting parameters can then be used to evaluate equations (7) and (8) for various values of a.[9] Figure 5.2 presents results of such a procedure based on the actual housing expenditure equations estimated in Malpezzi and Mayo where, for simplicity, it was assumed that a within-city income elasticity of 0.5 and a corresponding price elasticity of -0.4 typified developing-country cities, and where a typical target income group for sites-and-services project is in the thirty-fifth percentile of the income distribution.[10] The horizontal axis is monthly household income in 1981 U.S. dollars and the vertical axis is the minimum subsidy necessary to induce participation as a percentage of the market value of the housing provided in a project for various values of a, the design affordability ratio. For reference, estimated monthly household incomes in 1981 dollars in most African countries and countries on the Indian subcontinent were below $100; some of the countries with incomes between $100 and $200 were Botswana, Cameroon, Egypt, El Salvador, Indonesia, the Philippines, and Thailand; countries between $200 and $400 included a number of Latin American and North American countries, Nigeria, and Zambia; and countries above $400 included Caribbean, Latin American, and East Asian countries, such as Jamaica, Bahamas, Brazil, Mexico, Panama, and Korea.

The figure indicates clearly the effect that project standards (as derived from 'design affordability levels') have on target-group households' incentives to participate, and on the need to provide subsidies to induce participation when standards are set too high. for example, suppose that it were assumed that households in a typical African country, say Kenya, with a 1981 household income of roughly $100 per month would be willing to pay for a unit designed to cost 20 per cent of income. According to figure 5.2, a subsidy of roughly 60 per cent of the market value of such a unit would have to be provided in order to induce households in the thirty-fifth percentile of the income distribution to participate. In Burundi, with a monthly household income of only about $70 in 1981, a subsidy of over 90 per cent would be required to induce thirty-fifth-percentile households to participate if the design standard is based on an affordability assumption of 20 per cent of income. Subsidies of these levels are, of course, a reflection of the low average propensities to consume housing indicated by the cross-country expenditure functions presented above.

In higher-income developing countries by contrast, a 20 per cent affordability standard may be entirely appropriate. For example, for countries (cities) with average household monthly income above about $175, subsidies of less than 20 per cent would appear to be adequate to induce target groups to participate. Required subsidies are, however, extremely sensitive to the

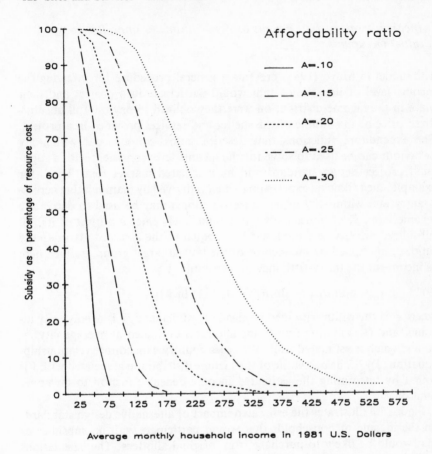

Figure 5.2 Minimum subsidies necessary to induce participation of thirty-fifth percentile households at alternative design affordability ratios

choice of design standards. Although the difference between 20 per cent and 25 per cent of income may not sound like much to a project planner, such a difference represents a 25 percentage-point difference in monthly shelter costs and can easily mean the difference between required subsidies in the range of 60–70 per cent rather than the range of 20–35 per cent. Depending on whether subsidies of the required magnitude are forthcoming or not, target income groups may not even participate or, if they do, they may have strong incentives to sell out to higher-income groups. It is useful to examine now the influence of planning subsidies on the income levels of participants if subsidies are not provided or, alternatively, if initial allottees sell out to higher-income households at the full market price.

C *Income Levels of Participants at Zero-Subsidy or upon Resale by Initial Occupants*

The model in Mayo (1985) presents a general procedure for inferring the income level of households that would participate in a project and their place in the income distribution were they obliged to pay the full unsubsidized price of the bundle of the shelter and services provided in a project. The expenditure functions that describe across-country and within-city behaviour can be used to solve for the income level consistent with a stipulated project design standard and its associated market rent. Thus, for example, the following expression (which is derived by manipulating across-country and within-city expenditure functions) may be used to derive the income level, $\hat{y}$, of households that would freely enter a project of its full subsidized price, where the latter is set equal to the assumed affordability ratio, a, multiplied by the income of the typical target group, defined here as income at the thirty-fifth income percentile, y_{35}:

(9) $\quad \hat{y} = \exp[\ln ay_{35} - \{\ln(\bar{R}/y) - (\epsilon_y - 1) \ln \bar{y}\}]/\epsilon_y$

where ϵ_y is the within-city income elasticity of demand, $\bar{y}$ is average city income, and $(\bar{R}/\bar{y})$ is the rent-to-income ratio evaluated at average city income (which is estimated using the cross-country expenditure relationship, equation (2)).[11] The percentile of the income distribution associated with $\hat{y}$ is found by integrating the estimated income density function to an upper limit of $\hat{y}$.

Figure 5.3 illustrates the estimated impact of alternative design standards on the income of households that would participate with no subsidies or that would be likely to purchase from original allottees. The calculations underlying the figures are based on a generalized or average income distribution in developing countries that was estimated by fitting a fourth-degree polynominal to Lorenz curve data presented in Kakwani (1980) for a sample of thirty-three developing countries.[12] A within-city income elasticity of 0.5 was assumed, and it was assumed that the design standard was based on the product of income of the thirty-fifth-percentile households and various assumed affordability levels, ranging from 10 to 30 per cent of income.

The figure clearly illustrates the effect of alternative design standards of unsubsidized projects on the income of probable participants. Not only does increasing the design affordability ratio increase the income level of likely participants, but it does so with particularly dramatic effect at various thresholds. For example, for households in low-income countries (e.g., $y = \$100$ per month), setting the design standards on the basis of an assumption that households are willing to spend 20 per cent of income on

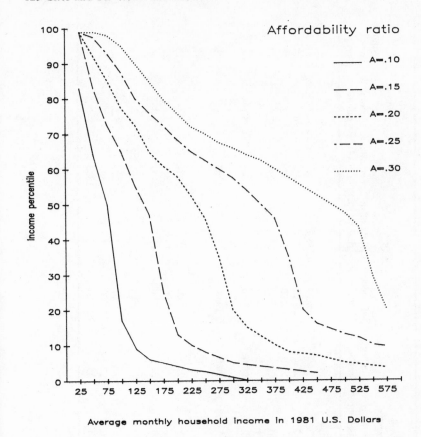

Figure 5.3 Income percentile of participating households with no subsidy at alternative design affordability ratios

housing implies that households in approximately the eightieth percentile of the income distribution could afford to participate without subsidies. Dropping the standard to one based on 15 per cent of income has only a modest effect, inducing participation down to the sixty-fifth percentile in the absence of subsidies. Dropping the standard still further to one based on just 10 per cent of income permits reaching even below the original target group, all the way down to the fifteenth percentile. Similar thresholds exist at each level of income, suggesting that dramatic improvements can be realized in the ability to reach the poor through sites-and-services projects by finding the 'correct' design standard – the one that reflects true willingness to pay by low-income groups.[13]

TABLE 5.2
Median values of project planning and economic variables of World Bank-financed shelter projects 1972–84

	Minimum income sites-and-services projects ($)	Per cent down payment	Afford-ability ratios	Project rates (%)	Rate of inflation[a] (%)	Per capita GDP[b] ($)	% of income held by lowest income quintile	Number of projects
By region								
E. Africa	49	0	20.0	9.00	15.7	339	4.5	15
W. Africa	131	10	20.0	9.25	9.0	765	6.1	7
E. Asia & Pacific	60	10	25.0	12.00	15.7	779	5.7	13
S. Asia	27	10	20.5	12.00	12.0	249	7.0	7
Europe, Middle East, and North Africa	141	10	20.0	7.00	9.6	944	5.1	8
Latin America and Caribbean	78	5	20.0	10.00	15.1	1763	2.9	18
By period[a]								
1972–6	74	5	22.5	8.00	16.0	730	3.4	13
1977–80	62	10	20.0	10.00	13.5	835	4.8	29
1981–4	60	10	21.3	11.00	11.1	741	5.3	26
By per capita GDP[b]								
Below 600	32	5	20	9.00	14.2	296	5.2	25
601–1200	75	10	20	10.00	9.4	835	5.2	23
Over 1200	109	10	25	11.00	18.0	1833	3.2	20

[a] Defined as year of appraisal report
[b] Expressed in 1983 US$ per annum

Having examined the behavioural evidence on developing-country housing demand and having explored some of the implications of that evidence
for sites-and-services project planning, it is useful now to consider the actual planning practice and some of the project outcomes of typical sites-
and-services schemes. Planning practice can be evaluated in terms of its
consistency with external evidence on household behaviour, and project
outcomes can be interpreted in part in light of discrepancies between planning assumptions and actual behaviour.

3 Project Design Practice and Project Outcomes

The previous section has emphasized the important role played by planning
parameters in influencing outcomes in sites-and-services projects. In this
section we review briefly important aspects of planning practice in sixty-
eight World Bank–financed sites-and-services projects, particularly affordability assumptions, and examine the consistency of planning parameters
with external evidence on willingness to pay for housing. In addition, we
look at the magnitude of subsidies that have been provided in a subset of
Bank-financed sites-and-services projects – those that have been completely
implemented with all loan amounts disbursed. Implications of these findings for the ability to achieve the nominal goals of sites and services are then
evaluated.

Among the most important planning criteria in sites-and-services projects
are the income levels of the principal target groups, the affordability ratio,
the percentage down payment, and the interest rate to be charged on project
financing. Table 5.2 presents median values of each for sixty-eight World
Bank–financed sites-and-services projects initiated between 1972 and 1984,
along with median values of three variables that indicate market conditions.
Results are disaggregated by region, by the time period of project initiation,
and by 1983 per capita GDP (gross domestic product).

Consider each project design variable in turn. First, the minimum income
level intended to be reached by sites-and-services projects varies considerably among regions, ranging from a low of $27 per month in South
Asian projects to a high of $141 in European, Middle East, and North
African projects. Much of this variation is a result of differences among
regions in GDP per capita; the minimum income level of target groups
ranges from $40 per month in countries with per capita GDP less than $600
per year to $112 per month in countries with GDP per capital greater than
$1200 per year. Planned minimum target-group incomes have fallen slightly
over time, indicating a concern with reaching relatively farther down the in-

come distribution. Median target groups (not shown here) tend to be at about the thirty-fifth percentile of the income distribution.

Down payments in sites-and-services projects have generally been minimal. No region has had a median down payment greater than 10 per cent of the sales price. There are only weak positive associations between down-payment percentages and time and GDP per capita. Further investigation reveal that 79 per cent of World Bank projects required down payments of 10 per cent or less. Such low down-payment requirements reflect an implicit assumption that the ability to accumulate pre-project assets through savings is negligible. In contrast, as discussed below, project designs appears to assume that within-project savings propensities, in the form of mortgage-loan repayments, are quite high. The two assumptions do not appear to be consistent.

Affordability ratios reflect assumptions concerning the fraction of income that households are willing to pay for shelter and related services. As table 5.2 indicates, there is strikingly little variation by region, time, or GDP per capita in the affordability ratios embodied in sites-and-services project designs. Medians for all substrata are from 20 to 25 per cent. Further investigation reveals that 74 per cent of all projects initiated by the World Bank have assumed affordability ratios of 20–25 per cent, with 17 per cent below those levels and 9 per cent above. This percentage comes close to the very definition of a rule of thumb.

Median interest rates charged for project-related loans have ranged from a low of 7 per cent in the Europe, Middle East, and North Africa region to a high of 12 per cent in the South Asia, East Asia, and Pacific regions. Interest rates have increased systematically over time and are highest among countries with the highest GDP per capita. The spread between interest rates charged in projects and inflation rates has narrowed appreciably over time, indicating a rise in real interest rates on project loans.

Let us now examine in more detail how the planning assumptions inherent in sites-and-services projects, particularly affordability ratios, correspond to empirical evidence on actual willingness to pay for shelter and services. Figure 5.4 superimposes two pieces of information concerning World Bank–financed sites-and-services projects. First, a scatter of points is presented that indicated for each project its design affordability ratio in relation to estimated average household monthly income expressed in 1981 dollars.[14] Second, figure 5.4 also presents three curves that relate estimated rent-to-income ratio to income, based on the cross-country and within-city econometric results presented in section 2.[15] Curves are shown for city average income and for households at the twentieth and thirty-fifth percentiles of the income distribution. The figures may be interpreted as follows: if

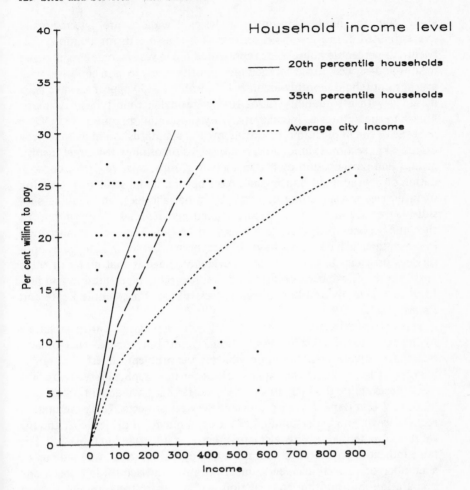

Figure 5.4 Assumed willingness to pay in World Bank sites-and-services projects in relation to empirically estimated willingness to pay

the target income group is assumed to have been households at city average income, then the lowest curve indicates our estimate of their actual willingness to pay for housing as a fraction of income; if the target group is assumed to have been the thirty-fifth or the twentieth income percentile, then the two higher curves represent estimates of their willingness to pay as a fraction of income. Recall that because the income elasticity is less than one, lower income emplies higher rent-to-income ratios. The figure clearly suggests that regardless of the relative income of the target group, affordability and, by implication, project design standards are systematically overestimated in low-income countries. If it is assumed, for example, that twentieth-percentile households represented the lowest-income target group in sites-and-services projects, then the majority of projects in countries with average household monthly incomes below about $150 appear to have been designed with affordability ratios that were higher than typical ratios of housing expenditures to income, many by substantial margins.

Some of the implications of setting project standards too high have been discussed in section 1; among these are exclusion of intended target income groups and participation by higher-income groups, relatively slow consolidation or upgrading of housing and plots beyond initial standards, creation of incentives for subletting or resale by initial allottees, and making subsidies necessary in order to reach intended beneficiaries. The critiques of sites-and-services projects summarized in section 1 presented anecdotal evidence that such outcomes have, in fact, been observed in many sites-and-services projects. In contrast, other evidence suggests that many of these problems may have been isolated and that project implementation and performance have, by and large, been successful (see for example Keare and Parris, 1982).

This apparent paradox in the range of outcomes can be partly explained by the existence of subsidies. As section 2 points out, the existence of subsidies can mitigate a number of possible project problems, in effect purchasing project feasibility at the expense of longer-term replicability. Thus, it is useful to examine the magnitude of subsidies that have actually been provided in World Bank–financed sites-and-services projects. This examination requires having an understanding of the components of project cost and the sources of potential subsidy elements; these are illustrated in table 5.3. The table indicates that 'total development and operating costs' are made up of a number of discrete elements, most notably land-acquisition costs, site preparation and housing construction, off-site infrastructure and project administration, and recurring costs such as utilities and maintenance. A proper account of resource costs means costing them at their full opportunity cost; for example, even though government land may be provided at small or no cost, its market value is the proper resource-cost measure. The total resource cost of a project, however, should account for the market value of the 'finished product.' Thus, the market value of the project, which is equal to the capitalized value of resource costs, is equal to the total development and operation costs multiplied by a factor equal to one plus the project's economic rate of return. The annualized resource cost is then equal to the total resource cost multiplied by the market rate of interest.

TABLE 5.3
Cost and subsidy elements in sites-and-services projects

Cost elements	Subsidy elements
Site preparation and housing construction	Cross-subsidies from higher- to lower-income households within project or government-provided cost write-downs
+ Land acquisition	Government or expropriated private land at below cost
+ Off-site infrastructure and project administration	Ignored or charged at less than marginal cost
+ Recurring costs (utilities, maintenance)	Ignored or charged at less than marginal cost
= Total development and operation costs × (1 + economic rate of return)	Prices set to recover scheduled costs, not resource costs
= Total resource costs × Market rate of interest	Subsidized interest rates
= Annualized resource costs	

Associated with each cost element is a possible subsidy element. These elements are indicated in the table and take the form of cross-subsidies from higher-to-lower-income project participants; government capital cost write-downs; low-cost or free government or expropriated land; exclusion of all or part of off-site infrastructure, project administration, or recurring costs; pricing to recover only 'scheduled' costs rather than full resource costs; and subsidized interest rates. These sorts of subsidies are prevalent in many World Bank–financed sites-and-services projects and are present as well in similar projects not under World Bank auspices – both sites-and-services projects sponsored by other aid organizations and government housing schemes that pre-dated the sites-and-services paradigm.

Consider, for example, only one subsidy element, but an extremely widespread and significant one: interest-rate subsidies. As Table 5.2 indicates, median interest rates charged on sites-and-services project loans ranged from about 7 to 12 per cent across regions. At the same time, inflation rates among those regions ranged from 9 to about 16 per cent at the time of project appraisal. Assuming that the market rate of interest is, conservatively, from two to three percentage points above inflation, median interest-rate subsidies appear to have ranged from roughly 20 to 55 per cent of annual market interest charges in the six World Bank administration regions. Were one to calculate real interest rates in World Bank sites-and-services projects as nominal interest rates less the rate of inflation in the year of project appraisal, 61 per cent of Bank projects are estimated to have had negative real rates of interest at the time of project appraisal. Such subsidies are often part of a general pattern of subsidized interest rates that pervade public-sector interventions in developing countries; they are, thus, difficult to eliminate or control at the level of planning an individual sites-and-services project.

Other subsidy elements, which are more amenable to project-level control, can also be significant, however. Pricing policies for land, off-site infrastructure, administrative costs, utilities, and maintenance are all more subject to project-level negotiation than are interest-rate policies. Also, decisions about whether or not to price sites and services at a level that recovers full resource costs or simply scheduled costs can be made within the project planning context.

In order to estimate the rough order of magnitude of subsidies in Bank projects, a simplified version of the cost-accounting framework presented in table 5.3 was applied to six of the earliest Bank projects, for which it was possible to examine actual pricing policies rather than the hypothetical projections contained in initial project appraisals. Subsidies were calculated as the difference between a measure of the annualized resource cost and actual charges to project beneficiaries. Annualized resource costs were estimated based on reported project development costs not including community facilities and not including recurring costs. These generally include, but are not limited to, stated development costs, land-acquisition costs, pro-rata shares of off-site infrastructure, and project administration. These development costs are then increased by a percentage equal to the project's projected economic rate of return to get an estimate of the market value of the project. This market value is then multiplied by a rate of interest equal to 12 per cent per year to get an annualized resource cost; as is discussed below, this cost represents in general a conservative estimate of the opportunity cost of money in each of the six countries.

Table 5.4 presents the estimated subsidy level as a percentage of annualized resource costs (assuming an opportunity interest rate of 12 per cent). Also shown in the table are the interest rate charged within the project, the actual inflation rate in each country in the year of project appraisal, and the annual compound rate of inflation for the years 1973–8 (approximately the first five years of operation of each project). With the exception of the Indonesia project, which features market-level pricing for all components (but has a subsidized interest rate), the subsidies range from roughly one-

TABLE 5.4

Estimated subsidies in sites-and-services projects (per cent of annualized resource costs)

Country	Subsidy as a per cent of resource costs[a]	Interest rate charged in the project (per cent)	Inflation rate in year of project appraisal	Compound inflation rate (1973–8)
Botswana	72	8.0	19.3	12.7
Indonesia	18	5.0	33.0	14.4
Ivory Coast	68	13.0	5.5	10.5
Jamaica	62	8.0	16.0	17.1
Senegal	55	7.0	2.9	10.7
Tanzania	67	6.0	18.8	25.0

[a] Assuming market rate of interest – 12 per cent

half to three-quarters of project resource cost. The subsidies have several sources: all six projects have subsidized interest rates and beneficiaries are in general charged less than the market price for their land, building materials, or completed dwellings. Cross-subsidies, which can raise the price charged to low-income households without affecting total project revenue, were implemented only in Indonesia.

It should be emphasized that although these subsidy estimates form a large part of project costs, they are probably underestimates of the true subsidy. This is particularly true in regard to interest subsidies. As table 5.4 indicates, for example, interest rates charged to project beneficiaries are generally considerably less than inflation rates and, of course, less than market interest rates. The only exception among the six early projects is the Ivory Coast, where the project interest rate is in fact close to a market rate.

What should be made of subsidies of the magnitudes in evidence here? The analytical model of section 2 suggests a number of implications. First, it is clear that the subsidies provided in early World Bank projects were large enough to have overcome many of the potential problems that might have resulted from upward-biased affordability assumptions and project standards. Comparing the actual subsidies provided with the estimated 'minimum subsidies necessary to induce participation' by typical (say thirty-fifth-percentile) target groups suggests that subsidies were probably instrumental in inducing many low-income households to participate that might not otherwise have done so. Even so, subsidies were sufficiently large for many project beneficiaries (those induced to distort their shelter consumption by consuming at overly ambitious project standards) that large relative welfare losses must certainly have occurred. That is, for many households whose participation in sites-and-services projects required them to spend more out of pocket than before entering the project (even after accounting for subsidies), the net benefit of participation must certainly have been worth considerably less than the resource cost of the subsidy. Also, for such households, incentives to sell out to higher-income households and propensities to default in the face of income shocks would have been substantial. Housing upgrading would have been limited in early years of the project for such households, unless subsidies were generous enough (as for example in the case of heavily subsidized building loans) to permit continued housing investment at low cost. The one possible beneficial side-effect for such households and for the housing market in general would have been the encouragement of providing additional space for low-income renters through subletting.

At the same time, many households participated in the projects that would probably have done so without subsidy, either higher-income households or households with stronger-than-average housing preferences. Each such group would have had incentives to invest in upgrading their units beyond initial standards. For the former group, receipt of large subsidies is inequitable; for the latter group, it is inefficient.

By and large, however, sites-and-services projects appear to have worked as intended: target groups have been reached; affordability by target groups has generally been evident – indeed some groups have been observed to be spending even more than initial affordability targets; reported defaults on account of 'affordability problems' have not been overwhelming. The comparatively small scale of many projects has also worked in favour of project success because households with relatively stronger preferences for the bundle of shelter and services offered by projects tend to enter projects through a process of self-selection. Much of the evidence concerning project impacts cited in section 1 appears to paint just such a picture.

Even while project-by-project assessments indicate the appearance of success, much of it purchased at the expense of significant subsidies, a broader view of the sites-and-services experience is consistent with Cohen's (1983) view cited above that replicability does not mean doing more of the same thing. The most obvious concern is that large subsidies will frustrate the ability to replicate projects on a large scale, thereby failing to meet the immense needs for shelter and services for the poor. Another concern is that the subsidies that are provided are not particularly rational. The types of subsidies provided, their magnitude, their distribution among potential beneficiaries, and their impacts on either beneficiaries or subsidy-granting organizations are rarely addressed in a thorough way when projects are designed. As a result, the subsidies provided are likely to be inefficient, sometimes inequitable, and harmful to the long-term viability of the subsidy-granting institutions.

4 Suggestions for Future Policy

This paper has reviewed evidence on the performance of sites-and-services projects, observing that although projects have been successful in many ways as implemented, there are limits to their effectiveness as a strategy to meet the needs of the poor in developing countries. The single most-serious problem in extending the breadth of application of the sites-and-services paradigm is the existence of subsidies that are simply too high to permit large-scale replication of projects.

Reasons for the existence of such subsidies are complex, in part because of the inertia of previous government shelter and services policies that established even larger subsidy amounts. To a considerable degree, however, subsidies are a reflection of ambitious planning standards, which require that large subsidies be maintained to make projects affordable by intended beneficiaries. In many cases, these standards are the result of the inappropriate application of a rule of thumb that households can spend from 20 to 25 per cent of their incomes for shelter and related services. As a general rule, this one is wrong.

The empirical analysis of housing demand in developing countries presented in section 2 indicates that the actual fraction of income that households are willing to pay for shelter varies with household income, a country's level of economic development, the relative price of housing, tenure status, and a number of other variables. The fraction actually spent on housing generally falls with income within cities but increases with average income across cities - relationships that parallel those observed by Kuznets (1961) regarding the way that consumption varies with and across countries.

When one compares actual spending patterns with the 'affordability assumptions' used in World Bank sites-and-services projects as the basis for project design standards, it is apparent that there has been a systematic upward bias in affordability and hence in design standards. This upgrading is acute for low-income countries, but largely disappears for better-off developing countries. Although the incentives created by such projects are complex and affect households differently, two implications of 'too-high' standards stand out. Either subsidies have to be provided to induce target groups to participate or groups with higher income than the target group will find their way into the project (either initially or as initial allottees sell out).

Section 3 explored empirically the magnitude of the subsidies required to reach typical target groups of World Bank projects (roughly the thirty-fifth percentile of the income distribution), and also the likely incomes of project participants if subsidies are not provided. Each outcome was examined in relation to alternative affordability assumptions and hence planning standards. There it was shown that subsidies as high as 80 or 90 per cent of project costs might be required to induce typical target groups to participate in low-income countries with planning standards that are derived from the rule of thumb that households can spend 20–25 per cent of income for housing. Alternatively, if no subsidies are provided, households with incomes in the eightieth percentile or above might be the most likely project participants. It was indicated, however, that required subsidies and income levels of likely participants are highly sensitive to the level of standards (and hence pricing) of project units. Thus, by choosing standards judiciously, at levels consistent with empirical evidence on housing demand, it should be possible to reach the intended beneficiary groups with small or no subsidies – a clear prerequisite for large-scale replicability in most countries.

A review of actual planning practice in World Bank sites-and-services projects (section 3) focused on planning parameters such as affordability ratios, down-payment requirements, and interest rates charged to project beneficiaries. Actual subsidies in six early projects were also analysed. It was found that all the projects had significant subsidy elements, with a median subsidy equal to about 65 per cent of total resource cost. Sources of subsidies included (1) failure to account for all project costs at their true resource cost (e.g., use of written-down government land), (2) pricing units at or below cost rather than at market value, and (3) charging below-market interest rates. The last is widespread, with 61 per cent of projects analysed estimated to have been charging interest rates below the inflation rate during the year of project appraisal. It appears, however, that the real rate of interest being charged in World Bank projects has risen over time, perhaps in response to an explicit goal to rationalize project design policies.

Subsidies of the magnitude of those found in early Bank-financed projects (which are not atypical of similar projects sponsored by other aid organizations) appear to be sufficiently high to have induced target-group households to participate, despite requiring them to spend more for shelter and services than they would normally be expected to do. Thus, subsidies have mitigated potential problems from overly ambitious planning standards, namely, high levels of defaults, slow rates of housing consolidation, or upgrading, turnover among project beneficiaries with higher-income households replacing initial allottees, and lack of participation by the intended target group. Although some authors have noted the existence of these problems in sites-and-services projects, it seems certain that they have been less severe than they might have been because high subsidies in effect purchase the participation and co-operation of project beneficiaries.

There are costs to such subsidies, however, the most severe of which is that they defeat the goal of cost recovery within the projects and hence imperil the ability to replicate projects on a large scale. In effect they perpetuate some of the problems inherent in public-housing policies of many developing countries prior to sites and services. In addition, the subsidies that are provided are not particularly rational; there is little explicit consideration given in much project planning to the magnitude, type, or distribution of subsidies; also little consideration is given to their impacts on beneficiaries or subsidy-generating institutions. As a result, while subsidies do buy a measure of small-scale success in sites-and-services projects, they do so at the expense of replicability, equity, and efficiency.

Despite what may seem a somewhat hair-shirted view of sites-and-services projects, it is clear that straightforward means exist, at least in principle, to fix many of the problems noted above. For example, the discussion has noted the inimical role played by large subsidies in reducing prospects for large-scale replication of sites-and-services projects. There are several ways to reduce subsidies: one is to reduce project standards and hence project costs; another is to change pricing policies to better reflect true resource costs; another is to provide a bundle of sites and services that increases household willingness to pay, while leaving project costs unchanged. Consider each in turn.

The analysis above indicates clearly that project standards are too high in most low-income developing countries, the result in part of having assumed that households would pay 20–25 per cent of incomes for housing when, in fact, formal expenditures are far less. In better-off developing countries, however, this assumption is entirely appropriate. The solution to this problem is simple: start planning on the basis of actual housing-demand patterns rather than on the basis of inappropriate rules of thumb. Actual patterns can be established on the basis of either the sorts of research findings presented in section 2 or local housing surveys. In the case of the former, a forecasting model has been developed by the authors that uses easily available macro-economic data (or, if it is available, household-survey data) to establish rough willingness to pay estimates in developing countries (details are available on request). In the case of the latter, materials have been developed by Malpezzi, Bamberger, and Mayo (1984) and by Malpezzi (1984) that discuss how to design and analyse urban-housing surveys. Simply getting the 'affordability assumption' straight can go a long way to bringing standards down to an appropriate level in many countries. This necessarily implies affordability standards that vary considerably among countries depending on their level of development and that vary among population groups depending on household income and other variables.

Reducing standards to an appropriate level is not sufficient to reduce subsidies, however. Pricing policies for sites-and-services projects must be revised to reflect true resource costs. This means costing project elements (land, building materials, infrastructure, administration, and recurring costs) at their full resource costs and then charging accordingly. Loans to beneficiaries should also be made at market rates of interest in order to allow loan-granting organizations to generate a sufficient surplus to ensure their institutional viability and growth.

If there are to be departures from resource-cost-based pricing in order to subsidize some households, these should be explicitly recognized, analysed and discussed by project planners. Subsidies, rather than being treated in the ad hoc or accidental ways that now characterize their use, should be explicitly justified and should, to the extent possible, be rationalized to serve equity, efficiency, and project-impact criteria. Procedures should be established for identifying subsidy elements, for quantifying them, and for estimating their incidence and impacts on project beneficiaries and their consequences for institutions responsible for them.

Another way of reducing subsidies is to provide households with a bundle of shelter and services that maximizes the perceived benefit for a given level of cost of provision. For example, if information is available on the trade-offs made by households among different elements of the housing and infrastructure bundle (e.g. relative preferences for size and location of plot, size and quality of structure, proximity to community facilities, quality and type of infrastructure), it may be possible to design packages of shelter and infrastructure characteristics for which households are willing to spend a good deal more than they normally do, and which cost no more to provide than the households' existing shelter. In some cases, dealing with capital-market and land-market imperfections by making available long-term finance or secure tenure may induce significant changes in household willingness to pay for shelter. Research on such trade-offs in developing countries has been conducted recently by Quigley (1982), Follain and Jimenez (1985a), and with particular reference to the demand for secure tenure, by Jimenez (1984) and by Friedman, Jimenez, and Mayo (1985). Related work by Gross (1984) looks not only at the trade-offs made by households among shelter and infrastructure attributes, but also at the influence of providing different bundles of characteristics on groups most likely to participate in a project. More empirical research into the nature of such trade-offs and their implications for project design could be of great benefit.

The analysis presented here has implications at the level of housing-sector policy, as well as at the level of project planning and design. The emphasis here on reducing and rationalizing subsidies in order to improve the equity, efficiency, and replicability of sites-and-services projects is useful advice at the sectoral level as well. Government shelter and services policies for other than sites and services can benefit from more vigorous attempts to reduce standards to truly affordable levels, to modify pricing policies to improve cost recovery, and to attempt to package shelter and services in ways that maximize their attractiveness to potential beneficiaries. It is particularly important to rationalize subsidy policies at the sectoral level, for although subsidy policies can in part by addressed at the project level, there are often severe limits to the extent of low-level reform that can be accomplished. Limitations exist particularly in the case of interest-rate policies, for which the legacy of subsidized rates for higher-income households makes it politically difficult to charge unsubsidized rates in sites-and-services projects; similarly, pricing policies for urban services must often be addressed at a sectoral level before project-level reform can occur successfully.

Two directions in shelter policy that follow from the observation that standards have been upward-biased in low-income countries are (1) to do relatively more upgrading projects than sites and services and (2) to focus policies relatively more on improving the supply of rented housing than predominantly on owner-occupied housing. Although upgrading and sites and services are and will remain useful complements in shelter policy, it seems clear that the task of reducing standards to affordable levels is often more easily accomplished within the context of slum-upgrading projects than in sites-and-services projects. Particularly in low-income countries, a product mix more heavily oriented toward upgrading would appear warranted on grounds of both equity and efficiency. Evidence that just such a shift has already begun is presented by Ayres (1983, p. 158), who indicates that the World Bank has increased emphasis on slum upgrading 'partly because some of the earlier sites and services projects proved too costly for the urban poor, partly because the number of beneficiaries in sites and services projects tended to be small, [and] partly because it fit better with the Bank's emphasis on realism and lower standards.' This tendency to undertake such changes based on the lessons of experience deserves further encouragement on the basis of the analysis presented here.

Reduction in standards can also be attained by emphasizing production of private rental housing rather than focusing largely on production of housing for owner occupancy. A reasonable strategy would be to encourage existing property owners to intensify development of their properties, creating additional dwelling units for rental occupancy by their horizontal or vertical expansion. Incentives for such development can be created by many of the same instruments used in upgrading schemes; particularly in cities with large and growing fractions of renters, it is logical to explore housing strategies that are consistent with general market trends. Such strategies have the potential in many cities to accommodate larger portions of the low-income population in adequately serviced housing than do those that emphasize higher standards, lower densities, and owner occupancy.

In conclusion, it must be noted that the innovative approach of sites and services as a way of improving the lives of poor households in developed countries remains a valid one. The approach has, in fact, delivered a great deal of shelter and related services to households that might not otherwise have attained them, has by and large reached more lower-income households than were than were typically served by other government-sponsored housing projects, and, despite still-significant subsidy levels, has probably reduced average subsidy levels per household below levels of previous programs. As important, the process of undertaking sites-and-services projects has served as a catalyst and focal point for discussions of housing and land policies, institutional roles and capacities, and training needs, the outcome of which have stimulated reform that goes well beyond the boundaries of the projects themselves.

These real accomplishments, however, cannot yet be seen as having achieved the goal of large-scale replicability that is so much the object of the sites-and-services paradigm. For upgrading and for sites and services to move beyond the level of demonstration projects, reforms must be undertaken at the level of both the project design process and sectoral policy. In most cases, simultaneous reform is necessary in order for standards to be set appropriately, for pricing and subsidy policies to be rationalized, and for resource mobilization and cost-recovery goals to be met. This will not be easy. But, as experience has shown, a great deal can be accomplished by applying technical skills and political will in support of a well-founded sites-and-services strategy to serve the shelter needs of the poor in developing countries.

Notes

Opinions expressed herein are solely those of the authors and should not be interpreted as those of any organization. The authors gratefully acknowledge the comments and suggestions of many of their colleagues while research for this paper was in progress, especially Alain Bertaud, Anthony Churchill, Michael Cohen, Emmanuel Jimenez, Richard Westin, and James Wright. Major substantive contributions to analyses of housing demand and analysis of sites-and-services projects was made by Stephen Malpezzi; Waleed El-

Ansary provided competent and responsive research assistance; and Sylvanus Best typed this draft with impeccable efficiency.

1 The earliest sites-and-services schemes (in South Africa, Chile, and Kenya) were undertaken largely without external assistance in the 1940s and 1950s. It was not until the late 1960s and early 1970s, however, that international agency assistance began in earnest.

2 For a review of the pre-1984 literature see Malpezzi and Mayo (1985).

3 Malpezzi and Mayo (1985) discuss findings concerning household size; here we focus only on income elasticity and intercept estimates.

4 It should also be noted that the relative variation in rent-to-income ratios is greater at low-income levels than at high-income levels, a result that has implications for the degree to which self-selection problems occur within sites-and-services projects with high standards. See Malpezzi (1984) for evidence.

5 On average, owners' housing consumption is roughly 80 per cent greater than that of renters at given incomes within particular markets.

6 Models were also estimated for a pooled sample of U.S. and developing-country cities; these are reported in Malpezzi and Mayo (1985).

7 Note that in a log-linear expenditure equation the coefficient of price is equal to one plus the price elasticity; thus the price elasticity is the estimated coefficient minus one, or -0.85 and -0.35 for owners.

8 See Phlips (1974) for an extended discussion of the properties of this function.

9 This approximation requires knowing the price elasticity of demand, ϵ_p, the income elasticity of demand, ϵ_y, and the rent-to-income ratio at the point where the function is to be approximated. These parameters are successively substituted into the expenditure equation consistent with the Stone-Geary utility function ($R = \theta_h (1 - b_h)p_h + b_h y - b_h \theta_x$), and the expressions for ϵ_y and ϵ_p ($\epsilon_y = b_h y/R$ and $\epsilon_p = \epsilon_y (y - \theta_x)/y$) to solve for θ_h, θ_x, b_n, and b_x.

10 Our research indicated that, on average, income at the thirty-fifth percentile was about 43 per cent of city average income. The quantity R_0 was estimated in two steps, first, estimating average rent at average city income using equation (2), for renters, and then moving up the within-city expenditure equation (assuming $\epsilon_y = 0.5$) to $y = 0.43\hat{y}$ and the corresponding value of R_0. Renters' rather than owners' expenditure functions are used here. The main reasons are (1) that often it is 'homeless' or renter households that represent the designated sites-and-services-project target group; (2) owners' current consumption relative to current income reflects on average greater longevity and thus more chance to have upgraded housing services than would renters'; and (3) in some markets, owners' current housing consumption reflects both windfall price appreciation and possible overconsumption due to high transactions costs of moving.

11 Details of the derivation will be provided by the authors on request.

12 Details will be provided on request.

13 This assertion is obviously a simplification because the goals of projects are numerous and choice of a design standard must reflect a number of compromises among the abilities to satisfy various program objectives. A highly simplified way of improving project design might be to view the minimum required subsidy to reach the intended target group and the income-group percentile likely to be attracted at unsubsidized prices as arguments in a limited social-welfare function, with the design standard being chosen to maximize such a function.

142 Stephen K. Mayo and David J. Gross

14 The scatter diagram is constructed on the basis of information in project appraisal reports. The affordability ratio is that given for the minimum-income taget group. Income is estimated by adjusting GDP per capita figures to get household disposable income expressed in 1981 dollars. Details will be furnished on request.
15 Equation (2), for renters, is used as the basis of the average city income relationship. Other curves are based on the assumption that the within-city income elasticity of housing demand is 0.5, and that income levels at the twentieth and thirty-fifth percentiles are related to average income levels based on the generalized developing-country income distribution discussed in section 2.

References

Ayres, R.L. 1983. *Banking on the Poor*. Cambridge: MIT Press
Chana, T.S. 1984. 'Nairobi: Dandora and Other Projects.' In G. Payne (ed.), pp. 17–36
Cohen, M. 1983. 'The Real Challenge of Replicability.' *Regional Development Dialogue* 4: 90–9
Davidson, F. 1984. 'Ismailia: Combined Upgrading and Sites and Service Projects in Egypt.' In G. Payne (ed.), pp. 125–48
Follain, J., and E. Jimenez. 1985a. 'Estimating the Demand for Housing Characteristics: A Survey and Critique.' *Regional Science and Urban Economics* 15: 77–107
– 1985b. 'The Demand for Housing Characteristics in Developing Countries.' *Urban Studies* 22: 421–32
Friedman, J., E. Jimenez, and S. Mayo. 1985. 'The Demand for Secure Tenure in Developing Countries.' Water Supply and Urban Development Department, World Bank, Washington (mimeo)
Grimes, O.F., Jr. 1976. *Housing for Low-Income Urban Families: Economics and Policy in the Developing World*. Washington: World Bank
Gross, D.J. 1984. 'Designing a Suitable Housing Project: Integration of a Demand Module into a Supply Side Planning Model.' Water Supply and Urban Development Department, World Bank, Washington
Jere, H. 1984. 'Lusaka: Local Participation in Planning and Decision-Making.' In G. Payne (ed.), 1984, pp. 55–68
Jimenez, E. 1984. 'Tenure Security and Urban Squatting.' *Review of Economics and Statistics* 66: 556–67
Kakwani, N.C. 1980. *Income Inequality and Poverty*. New York: Oxford University Press
Keare, D., and S. Parris. 1982. 'Evaluation of Shelter Programs for the Urban Poor.' World Bank Staff Working Paper no. 547. Washington
Kravis, I.B., A. Heston, and R. Summers. 1982. *World Product and Income: International Comparisons of Real Gross Product*. Baltimore: Johns Hopkins University Press
Kuznets, S. 1961. 'Quantitative Aspects of the Economic Growth of Nations. VI. Long-Term Trends in Capital Formation Proportions.' *Economic Development and Cultural Change* 9: 3–56

Malpezzi, S. 1984. 'Analyzing an Urban Housing Survey: Economic Models and Statistical Techniques.' Urban Development Department Discussion Paper no. 52, World Bank. Washington

Malpezzi, S., M. Bamberger, and S. Mayo. 1982. 'Planning an Urban Housing Survey: Key Issues for Researchers and Program Managers in Developing Countries.' World Bank Water Supply and Urban Development Discussion Paper no. 44. Washington

Malpezzi, S., and S. Mayo. (with D.J. Gross). 1985. 'Housing Demand in Developing Countries.' World Bank Staff Working Paper. Washington

Mangin, William. 1970. Peasants in Cities. Boston: Houghton-Mifflin

Mayo, S.K. 1981. 'Theory and Estimation in the Economics of Housing Demand.' Journal of Urban Economics 10: 95–116

Mayo, S.K. (with D. Gross). 1985. 'Sites and Services – and Subsidies: The Economics of Low-Cost Housing in Developing Countries.' World Bank Water Supply and Urban Development Department Discussion Paper UDD–83. Washington

Mayo, S.K., et al. 1982. Informal Housing in Egypt. Cambridge, MA: Abt Associates

Payer, C. 1982. The World Bank: A Critical Analysis. New York: Monthly Review Press

Payne, G.K. (ed.) 1984. Low-Income Housing in the Developing World. New York: John Wiley and Sons

Phlips, Louis. 1974. Applied Consumption Analysis. Amsterdam: North Holland

Quigley, J. 1982. 'Nonlinear Budget Constraints and Consumer Demand: An Application to the Public Programs for Residential Housing.' Journal of Urban Economics 12: 177–201

Turner, J. 1972. Freedom to Build. New York: Macmillan

Tym, R. 1984. 'Finance and Affordability.' In G. Payne (ed.), 1984, pp. 209–20

World Bank. 1975a. Housing. Sector Policy Paper. Washington: World Bank

– 1975b. Sites and Services Projects. Washington

– 1983. Learning by Doing: World Bank Lending for Urban Developing, 1972–82. Washington

6

Food Subsidies and the Poor: A Case Study of Tanzania

SUSAN HORTON

Food-subsidy programs have large and visible costs that affect government macro-economic policy and the agricultural sector. Hence such programs are often vulnerable in times of economic difficulty because of pressures that are internal as well as external to the country. However, food-subsidy programs have potentially important benefits for income distribution and nutrition. These benefits are not always gained in practice because political considerations frequently affect program design. This chapter examines the costs and benefits of food-subsidy programs in a number of selected countries. The findings and some hypotheses are then compared with a case study of the subsidy on maize meal in Tanzania, 1980–4. I suggest that abolition of the subsidy in Tanzania did not have the adverse effects on poverty and nutrition that might develop in some other countries if subsidies were removed. The potential operation of food subsidies is rather different in sub-Saharan Africa than elsewhere. Tanzania presents an extreme example of the difficulties of using food subsidies in sub-Saharan Africa.

The survey of selected countries in the following section examines two of the costs (macro-economic and agricultural) and two potential benefits (improved income distribution and nutrition) of food subsidies. The survey is based on country studies in Horton and Taylor (1986), and draws also on Horton (1984). Section 2 gives a brief history and description of the food subsidy in Tanzania and section 3 analyses the subsidy based on the survey findings in section 1. The final section contains some conclusions.

1 A Survey of Selected Countries

One definition of food subsidies is that they exist where the consumer price of food in a region is held below some free market price that would otherwise prevail. Explicit subsidies exist where there is some budgetary outlay by the government, while implicit subsidies are where the supply price is also held down. Using this definition means that food subsidies are endemic throughout the developing world, exist in several centrally planned economies, and exist at certain times in developed countries. A study of thirty-seven developing countries indicated that at least thirty-one of them used explicit food subsidies at some point between 1968 and 1980 (Horton, 1985). Several development models, such as the Fei-Ranis one, argue that implicit subsidization of food (at the expense of agricultural producers) is necessary for development. The same idea has affected government policies during industrialization in the USSR (the 'scissors crisis'), India, and Latin America (import substitution). However, more recent development literature has emphasized the disadvantages of such a policy.

This section focuses on countries that make explicit subsidies, i.e., where government outlays exist. As will be seen, there is a great temptation for governments to try to cut costs by using additional implicit taxes on the agriculture sector, and hence the implicit/explicit distinction is not always clear. This survey examines macro-economic and agricultural costs and potential income-distribution and nutritional benefits of food subsidies.

There are three possible methods for financing a consumer subsidy on food. These are government expenditure, a producer tax, and food aid. Government expenditure can in turn be financed by increasing taxation, reducing other expenditures, borrowing, or printing money. The exact macro-economic consequences depend on how a subsidy is financed. The effects are, however, quite large, given the scale of subsidy programs in some countries. Various macro-models have been used to simulate the effects, which tend to vary according to model specification (Cavallo and Mundlak, 1982; Quinzon and Binswanger, 1984; de Janvry and Subbarao, 1984; Gibson, Lustig, and Taylor, 1982; and others).

Table 6.1 presents some figures on the size of budget outlays. The total subsidy has been even larger, given that cheap imported food flows (mainly U.S. PL-480 wheat and rice) have been quite large, as has implicit taxation of the domestic agricultural sector. The data from table 6.1 are taken from very different sources, and are for different years, and hence should be interpreted with caution. Nevertheless, the magnitude of the expenditures is quite striking.

Food subsidies also have an obvious effect on worsening the balance of trade in food. The size of the effect depends on the size of the consumer subsidy and the elasticity of demand for food, and the size of (any) producer tax and the elasticity of supply of food domestically. These price distortions combine to decrease food exports, or more frequently to increase food imports. The effect is somewhat ameliorated by food aid. One

TABLE 6.1
Cost of food subsidy program, selected countries

Country	Year	Direct cost	(%)[a]	Domestic procurement price (%)	Source
Egypt	1979	8.1	27[b]	82% of world price (wheat)	Alderman, von Braun, and Sakr
				61% of world price (rice)	(1982); Scobie (1981)
Brazil	1973–82	0.4	3[b]	125% of world price (wheat)	Calegar and Schuh (1984)
Colombia	1980	n/a	0.2[b]	n/a	Horton and Taylor (1986)
Mexico	1972–81	0.5	3[b]	131% of world price (maize)	Lustig (1984)
China	1974–8	6.4	23–26[c]	70% of domestic price (wheat)[d]	Lardy (1983)
				55% of domestic price (rice)[d]	
India	1978–9	0.6	4[b]	70–90% of domestic price (wheat)[d]	Swamy (1979); Krishna and
				60–90% of domestic price (rice)[d]	Raychaudhuri (1980)
Pakistan	1976	1.4	10[c]	99% of domestic price (wheat)[d]	Brown (1978)
				66% of world price	
Bangladesh	1972/3–	0.6–	21–36[c]	58–103% of domestic (rice)[d]	Ahmed (1979)
	1975/6	1.3		50–107% of world	
Sri Lanka	1964/5–	3.0	10–18[b]	95% of domestic price (rice)[d]	Gavan and Chandrasekera
	1975				(1979)
Korea, Rep.	1980	1.2	6[c]	n/a	Horton and Taylor (1986)

[a] As per cent of GDP in first column
[b] Per cent of government current expenditure
[c] Per cent of government revenue
[d] Domestic wholesale price
SOURCE: Horton (1984)

study for Egypt (Scobie, 1983) suggested that a 10 per cent increase in food subsidies would increase inflation by 5 per cent and cause an effective devaluation of the free-market exchange rate of more than 3 per cent.

Food-subsidy schemes may cause foreign-exchange difficulties not only by their size but also by their stabilizing effect on domestic demand. If food-subsidy schemes increase the government commitment to insulating consumers from price fluctuations, then other importing sectors are forced to bear the burden of adjustment to fluctuations in domestic food production or world food prices. Scobie (1983) shows that, for Egypt, the volume elasticity of food imports to total import expenditures is only 0.05, i.e., that maintaining food imports has had very severe effects on other sectors in the economy.

Food subsidies do have one potential macro-economic benefit: they can be a useful domestic response to adverse external shocks. They provide a reasonably convenient way for governments to bolster domestic consumption in the face of (temporary) external shocks.

Food subsidies often impose costs on the agricultural sector. Implicit agricultural taxation is very common among countries with food subsidies (not that it is absent elsewhere). In particular the poor developing countries frequently have implicit agricultural taxation at the same time as they subsidize consumers. Only the more affluent Latin American countries with larger non-agricultural sectors seem to be able to subsidize both consumers and producers. Countries that hold down output prices frequently have offsetting input subsidies, which do not usually fully offset the output taxes. For example, Brown (1978) estimates that, for Pakistan, input subsidies were only about 10–20 per cent of the value of the output tax.

Output price distortions cause several problems. First, there are overall disincentives to agriculture and food production. Second, the output mix is distorted. And third, design and implementation of procurement schemes can harm producer incentives, adding to the adverse effects of low prices. Because agricultural incentives are a major topic in their own right, the discussion below is rather brief.

Table 6.1 provides some information on the relative level of consumer and producer prices. Without further information on marketing costs, it is not possible to ascertain whether producers are being taxed and, if so, to what degree. However, the operation of many government procurement schemes suggests that producers are taxed. Governments frequently impose levies, quotas, or some other means of compulsory procurement. For example, in Egypt there are levies on rice, beans, lentils, and sugar-cane, as well as on some export crops. In India there has been a rice levy (at the milling stage), although wheat is procured on the open market. India also operates zoning restrictions that restrict trade between surplus and deficit states. An ostensible reason for these restrictions is to reduce price variation, but in fact they reduce the government's procurement costs, and if anything increase price disparities (Krishna and Raychaudhuri, 1980). China also has a procurement system with several tiers of producer prices, ranging from a quota price, a second tier of quotas (euphemistically called 'above quota' amounts), a third tier of prices negotiated between state and producers once both quotas have been filled, and finally a rural market price (Lardy, 1983). Several African countries have legal state monopolies over important food crops.

Some countries also have state export monopolies,[1] which have to be supplemented by border controls. For example, in times of crisis Bangladesh has enforced laws restricting the amount of grain that can be held or traded within a certain distance of the border.

A final procurement technique is the one employed, for example, by Bangladesh, where small farmers may be forced to sell very quickly after harvest, either because of lack of storage capacity on the farm or because of liquidity requirements. Such farmers thus sell at the time when free-market prices are at a seasonal low, and hence may find it more profitable to sell to the government although, taking an all-year average, free-market prices may exceed government ones. Hence the government can reduce its procurement costs, at the expense of the poorest farmers.

The size and importance of the adverse effect of low producer prices on aggregate output are highly debated topics. Recent World Bank documents, such as those on Africa, have emphasized the harmful effects. However, other researchers have argued that factors such as infrastructural investment and agricultural research have stronger effects. It has also been argued that the use of world prices as a benchmark is misleading, given that only a small fraction of output is traded, and that internal terms of trade between sectors are more important.

Empirical evidence surveyed by Scandizzo (1984) suggests that the long-run price elasticity of aggregate output is in the range of 0.3 to 0.5. Scandizzo also concludes that prices can be an effective component of policy packages to increase aggregate output. Thus, food subsidies, which increase the pressure hold down producer prices, may have some adverse effects on total output. However, the distortions between crops are probably more marked.

Government procurement policies often distort the output mix because governments frequently discriminate against the crops that enter the subsidy scheme. In Egypt, this type of pricing policy led to a decrease in rice production, an increase in wheat production, and an increase by small farmers in labour-intensive livestock production (Alderman and von Braun, 1984). In

Sri Lanka, procurement policies were run adroitly in the 1960s, with a high rice procurement price, partly because of the availability of cheap imported wheat, which did not compete with a domestic crop. However, coconuts and starchy staples such as cassava, both significant sources of calories in the diet, were neglected. In China, the existence of a 10:1 poultry-to-grain price differential in contrast to a grain conversion rate to poultry of only 3:1 apparently had an incentive effect on poultry production that may not have been socially desirable (Lardy, 1983).

If they are badly designed, procurement schemes can have disincentive effects beyond those resulting from low prices alone. For Bangladesh a series of problems have been cited relating to inadequate infrastructure (Ahmed et al., 1980). Farmers disliked having to make two separate trips to procurement centres – one to sell grain and one to exchange their sale vouchers for cash. It was also argued that insufficient numbers of purchasing centres and personnel caused small farmers to sell at a discount to an intermediary dealer, rather than waiting to sell directly at the government price. A lack of bags for grain created inconvenience because farmers had to guard their grain at the purchase centre before selling. Finally, there were complaints related to the lack of an objective measure of moisture content and quality of rice that affected the government price offered. Some similar problems were also reported in Sri Lanka (Yoshimura et al., 1975), although the magnitude of problems seems much greater in Bangladesh.

Food subsidies have important potential benefits. Given that the poor spend a large proportion of their income on food (as much as 70–80 per cent in South Asia, for example), changing the price of food can affect income distribution and nutrition of the poor. Food subsidies are also potentially more egalitarian than subsidies on other expenditure items because the income elasticity of demand for food is low. It is also possible to select the particular subsidized food so as to target the subsidy somewhat towards poorer households, i.e., some foods have self-targeting properties. One condition for such properties is that the income elasticity of the food should decline (or even become negative) as income increases. It is also desirable that the price elasticity of demand should decrease with income. Both criteria ensure that richer households are less sensitive to the subsidy, and there is thus less spillover of the subsidy to non-target households.

Table 6.2 provides some figures on the expenditure elasticities for some subsidized foods in different countries. These show that wheat is a better subsidy vehicle than rice in the three countries chosen, and that oil, sugar, and bean subsidies in Egypt favour the poor less than a wheat subsidy.

The income-distribution effects also depend on eligibility for subsidized food. Several countries have restricted eligibility to certain more-affluent groups, in which case political rather than nutritional or income-distri-

TABLE 6.2
Expenditure elasticities for various subsidized foods

Food item	Bangladesh percentile		Sri Lanka percentile			Egypt (urban) quartile	
	10	75	20	50	90	Lowest	Other
Rice	0.94	1.19	0.45	0.36	0.13	0.36	0.13
Wheat	−0.24	−0.10	−0.15	−0.15	−0.15	0.09[a]	−0.06[a]
Sugar						0.14	0.20
Oil						0.08	0.10
Beans						0.09	0.14

[a] Coarse (balady) flour
SOURCE: Pitt (1983) for Bangladesh; Alderman and Timmer (1980) for Sri Lanka; Alderman and von Braun (1984) for Egypt

bution considerations are paramount. These include China, where state employees are the main recipients, and Bangladesh, where certain urban groups, including government employees, are favoured. Several countries restrict the eligibility of rural households. In Pakistan, wheat-producing rural areas are not eligible for the wheat ration (although they receive sugar), despite the fact that such households on average purchase 61 per cent of their wheat intake (Horton and Taylor, 1986). Colombia did target its food-subsidy scheme for more-disadvantaged areas of the country, but doing so may only have been politically feasible for such a small scheme.

Even in countries where rural households are in theory eligible for subsidies, there is, in practice, an urban bias. In India the population served per ration shop is higher in rural areas, despite the lower population density, indicating that much of the rural population is inadequately served (Swamy, 1979). In Egypt, bread is available more frequently in urban areas, and workplace co-operatives selling subsidized frozen meat, etc., are mainly an urban phenomenon (Alderman and von Braun, 1984). However, rural Egypt benefits relatively more from the flour subsidy. In Mexico only 43 of the 1467 national distribution agency's (DICONSA) outlets were in rural areas in 1970 (Grindle, 1975). Food subsidies in Zimbabwe, Ivory Coast, Mali, and elsewhere in Africa have been almost wholly urban oriented. The two exceptions are Kerala and Sri Lanka's discontinued ration scheme. In the latter, the aim was to have ration shops within three miles of any member of the population. In both cases, high population density may have contributed to the success of the shop network.

In order to minimize the cost of transferring nutrients, there are some additional requirements. First, the income and own-price elasticities of demand for food should be high, to minimize leakage to non-food items. Second, increased income should lead predominantly to consumption of a larger quantity of food, rather than a higher quality. McCarthy (1978) found that in Pakistan, for example, over half the increase in expenditure on wheat went to increased quality wheat, with little change in nutrient content. Third, cross-price elasticity with respect to non-food items should be high, and with respect to other foods should be low, so that the increase in consumption of the subsidized food is not at the expense of other food items. Fourth, the subsidy vehicle should preferably be a good source of nutrients.

We can compare the criteria above with empirical evidence to examine how well actual subsidy schemes minimize the costs of transferring nutrients and reach target households. One finding is that food-subsidy income may have a greater effect on nutrient intake than cash income, because it has been observed empirically that the marginal propensity to consume food (MPCF) obtained by food rations or food stamps is higher than if the food is purchased from cash income. Gavan and Chandrasekera (1979) found, for Sri Lanka, that the MPCF out of money income ranged from 0.22 to 0.58, but was on average 0.85 of the value of the food ration. Kumar (1979) found, for Kerala, that ration transfers had an effect on nutrition (as measured by child nutritional status and household dietary quality) that was 6–10 times as large as that of an equivalent increase in money income. West and Price (1976) found, for the United States, that the MPCF out of money income was 0.05, as compared to 0.30 out of food stamps, and even more out of income transfers in kind, such as school lunches. However, other studies in the United States (Madden and Yoder, 1972; West, 1978) did not find that in-kind transfers acted differently from cash ones. This issue deserves careful empirical testing because it could provide a justification for food subsidies rather than equivalent income transfers.

Figures obtained from the analysis of conventional household-expenditure surveys can be very helpful in evaluating how appropriate the subsidy vehicle is. Estimates of the price and income elasticities of demand for nutrients can help to evaluate how effective a subsidy will be in transferring nutrients. Table 6.3, from Pitt (1983), provides some useful evidence for Bangladesh on the characteristics of different foods as potential subsidy vehicles. The figures show that rice is a poor subsidy vehicle in this particular country because rice has less nutrient content per unit of expenditure, and also because the pattern of substitution among foods is much better whens the wheat price changes, than when the rice price does. A good sub-

TABLE 6.3
Nutrient price elasticities, tenth percentile

	Protein	Fat	Carbo-hydrate	Calories	Calcium	Iron	Thiamine	Ribo-flavin	Niacin
Uncompensated nutrient price elasticities									
Rice	−0.191	−0.441	−0.553	−0.484	−0.087	0.129	0.055	0.009	−0.394
Wheat	−0.261	−0.112	−0.203	−0.210	−0.177	−0.391	−0.373	−0.329	−0.254
Compensated nutrient price elasticities									
Rice	0.201	0.041	−0.061	−0.011	0.308	0.403	0.362	0.365	0.065
Wheat	−0.186	−0.020	−0.109	−0.119	−0.102	−0.339	−0.314	−0.261	−0.170

SOURCE: Pitt (1983)

sidy vehicle should have large, negative, uncompensated nutrient-price elasticities, in order for the subsidy to increase nutrient intake. Wheat is better than rice under this criterion.

Thus, food subsidies in practice have been rather costly as a way to improve income distribution and nutrition, and arguably could have been more cost effective by being restructured. Their design has, of course, been influenced by political considerations. It is no accident that politically vocal groups such as urban consumers, civil servants, and government employees have been beneficiaries of many food-subsidy schemes. The political difficulty of reforming or reducing subsidies is exemplified by unrest in Egypt, the Dominican Republic, Poland, Tunisia, and Morocco, following rises in the price of subsidized foods.

Recently interest has shifted to the possibility of targeting subsidies in order to reduce costs and to minimize leakage of benefits to non-needy groups. However, targeting is neither costless nor perfectly accurate in practice. Means-testing, as practised in developed countries – for instance, in the U.S. food-stamp scheme – is much more difficult in developing countries. In the latter no good data on income flows are accessible to the government. It is particularly difficult to monitor incomes where a large proportion of the population is rural or self-employed. The Sri Lanka food-stamp scheme introduced in 1979 provides an example. Although households with incomes above the mean were not officially eligible to receive stamps, one study found that 30 per cent of them did (Edirisinghe, 1987).

Alternative targeting methods have been used in various countries. These include the use of household characteristics such as age, family size, and geographic location as indicators of need, the imposition of work requirements (food for work programs), and the use of rationing and queuing.

These all have administrative costs and entail leakage (see Horton, 1985), but can potentially improve allocation of benefits. The trade-off between additional administrative costs and better targeting is likely to be of future interest to researchers and policy-makers.

2 History and Description of the Tanzanian Maize Subsidy

The explicit consumer subsidy on *sembe* (maize-meal) was begun in Tanzania in 1980, as a way of protecting urban consumers while the government introduced various measures designed to deal with the country's economic difficulties. It ended in 1984, partly because the economic difficulties proved so severe that the fiscal costs of a subsidy could not easily be met. It was administered by the National Milling Corporation (NMC), the marketing body for most food grains and some other food crops.

To understand the effects of the subsidy, and of its removal, it is useful to know some background details about the agricultural marketing system in Tanzania, about food and agricultural policy, and about how the subsidy was operated. It is particularly important to examine the background to the subsidy in Tanzania because economic difficulties were so pervasive as to constrain seriously the operation of government policies.

The history and role of the agricultural marketing boards in Tanzania have been described in some detail by Kaberuka (1984), Temu (1984), Wagao (1982), Clark (1978), and others. State intervention has been of long standing. There were marketing boards during the Second World War, and following the war until 1956 the Grain Storage Department operated in the food-crop market. There was a brief period of free-market operation until the 1962 Agricultural Products (Control and Marketing) Act led to the establishment of several crop marketing boards, including the National Agricultural Products Board (NAPB) for food crops as well as boards for various export crops. The government continued to extend it influence in the food sector and in 1967 nationalized seven private milling companies, which formed the National Milling Corporation (NMC).

Throughout the 1970s, the government continued to extend its influence. One move was to limit the role of the co-operatives, at first by encouraging *ujamaa* (communal) villages to deal directly with the crop boards, and in 1976 by abolishing co-operatives and transferring their functions to the marketing boards. Another move was to allow the food-crop boards to participate directly in production. In 1973 the NAPB was broken up, and NMC assumed responsibility for trade in cereals. It was granted monopsony powers over the main food crops (maize, paddy/rice, wheat, cassava, sorghum, millet, and beans) in 1976 when co-operatives were abolished.

The pan-territorial pricing policy (whereby a single price was paid to farmers and by consumers, irrespective of geographic location) was instituted in 1973 and continued until 1981. The institutional structure of food marketing has remained unchanged from 1976 to the present, although in 1984 the government announced that co-operatives would be allowed to return. The National Milling Corporation has functions ranging from production, distribution, milling, processing, storage, imports, and exports to managing the strategic Grain Reserve. It also has interests in a winery, a paper-bag factory, and other enterprises.

The agricultural parastatals have been widely criticized. They have been often accused of inefficiency: Lamade (1970) documents this for the 1960s, and figures for 1978/9 (see table 6.4) show that agricultural producers were paid between 26 and 62 per cent of the realized value of their output (the range for food crops was 39–62 per cent). A Marketing Development Board (MDB) Study (MDB, 1980) found that marketing costs also increased rapidly. In the five years from 1972/3 to 1977/8, sales of the NMC increased by 49 per cent, but operating costs rose by 672 per cent. The NMC has also been criticized for high storage losses (7.5 per cent on imported grain as against 4 per cent on domestic) and losses in milling. For instance, in maize, the extraction ratio achieved was only 50 per cent instead of the intended one of 90 per cent (MDB, 1982). The deficiencies of the boards are described in more detail in World Bank (1983), Stewart (1984), and Kaberuka (1984).

Increased marketing costs and inefficiency had consequences for the agricultural and food sectors, which have been analysed by Ellis (1982) and others. Real producer prices declined over time, more particularly for export crops than food crops. Table 6.5 from Lipumba (1983) presents figures for 1972/3 to 1982/3, although the decline had begun even earlier. Production statistics are not very reliable: however, available evidence suggests that a result of the fall in producer prices was a stagnation in the volume of agricultural exports, a switch into non-controlled crops such as fruits and vegetables, and the development of a parallel market in controlled food crops. One consequence of the last development was a rather large fluctuation in official cereal procurement, depending on conditions in the parallel market.

The development of a parallel market in foods was quite important. For one thing, it exaggerated the substitution out of export crops (because opportunities to sell export crops on the parallel market are more limited). The difference between parallel market and official prices are quite substantial. Lipumba and Mbogoro (1984) give figures for the ratio of parallel market to official consumer prices in thirteen lake-region villages. The figures are 4.98:1 (maize), 2.42:1 (paddy), 4.58:1 (cassava), 4.68:1 (sorghum), and 4.63:1 (millet). MDB (1985) gives similar figures for

TABLE 6.4
Producer price as a per cent of market realization, various crops, 1978/9

Crop	Percentage
Export	
Coffee	51
Tea	58
Tobacco	39
Pyrethrum	26
Sisal	64
Food	
White sorghum	50
Finger millet	62
Bulrush millet	50
Cassava	39
Maize	58
Rice	53
Wheat	39

SOURCE: Export crops: Msambichaka, Ndulu, and Amani (1983), ch. 3; food crops: MDB (1982) using official consumer prices and assuming milling ratios of 85 per cent (wheat and maize) and 65 per cent (rice)

September 1983 to August 1984, based on the average for all regions of the country: 3.32:1 (maize), 2.19:1 (wheat), and 2.79:1 (rice). Because the parallel market is illegal, prices tend to fluctuate greatly in it. It thus makes management of the food sector much more difficult for the government, and complicates the lives of producers and consumers as well. It also makes it more difficult to conduct economic analysis because published price indexes only imperfectly include parallel market prices, and because figures are not available on quantities transacted.

The inefficiencies of the NMC were related directly to the need for a consumer subsidy. Throughout the 1970s, the efficiency costs were passed on to the producers in the form of lower real product prices. In fact, assuming a shadow exchange rate, it is likely that producers were implicitly subsidizing consumers for grain going through the NMC. However, there were limitations on the extent to which producer prices for food crops could be held down because of shifts between crops and the development of the parallel market, which limited NMC's ability to procure grain. Thus, by 1980, the government was forced to either raise consumer prices or operate an explicit subsidy. It chose the latter course. Since the abolition of the explicit subsidy in 1984, there has been a reversion to an implicit subsidy on grain passing through official channels. NMC grain remains cheaper than parallel market

TABLE 6.5
Real producer prices for agricultural products (Index, 1982/3 = 100)

	1972/3	73/4	74/5	75/6	76/7	77/8	78/9	79/80	80/1	81/2	82/3	83/4
Preferred staples	99	100	116	153	146	139	125	121	98	114	100	100
Drought staples	109	165	151	163	182	186	173	145	110	92	100	103
Oilseeds	149	131	131	144	136	137	130	134	110	103	100	96
All export crops	144	128	125	133	236	178	152	156	129	120	100	n/a
All agricultural products	136	124	123	137	220	178	154	153	119	119	100	n/a

SOURCE: Lipumba (1983)

grain, and is sold below the world price if that is measured at a reasonable shadow exchange rate.

The consumer subsidy on maize was introduced along with other measures to aid economic recovery. Tanzania was experiencing severe economic difficulties in the late 1970s, following two oil price shocks, the war with Uganda, the dissolution of the East African Economic Community, and terms-of-trade problems. Domestic policy may have weakened the country's ability to respond to external shocks, particularly the relative neglect of agriculture and agricultural exports. A series of economic survival measures were introduced in the 1980s: e.g., the 1981 National Economic Survival Plan, the 1982/3 to 1984/5 Structural Adjustment Plan, and the 1983 National Agricultural Plan. As part of these measures, the minimum wage was raised in 1980 and 1981 and wheat and rice prices were raised, but at the same time maize flour was given an explicit subsidy.

The maize subsidy did not prevent the continued erosion of the real value of the minimum wage, but it was intended to protect food consumption somewhat (see table 6.6). In terms of the ratio of the minimum wage to the maize price, consumers were better off in 1980/1 than in any year since 1973/4. In 1984 when the maize subsidy was reduced, the minimum wage was raised to compensate. However, the real value of the minimum wage continued to fall, and the ratio of the minimum wage to the maize price declined markedly.

The maize subsidy was paid for 75 per cent by explicit government expenditure and 25 per cent by a tax on sugar. The subsidy was put on maize flour but not on unmilled grain, and the latter, in fact, cost 33 per cent more than flour, after the subsidy. Maize flour in 1980 was absolutely cheaper (at 1.25 sh/kg) than the less-preferred staples such as sorghum flour (3.00 sh/kg), millet flour (3.05–3.25 sh/kg), and even cassava flour (1.50–1.65 sh/kg). The subsidy was also unfortunately commenced at a time when NMC had relatively low stocks of *sembe*.

NMC is not supposed to deal directly with the public. Subsidized grain was distributed mainly to institutions (the armed forced, hospitals, parastatals, universities), who distributed it to their employees in a manner of their choice. For instance, the University of Dar es Salaam made allotments on a departmental basis and sold grain through the co-operative shop. The rest of the grain was distributed to ration shops (*maduka ya kaya*). Each urban household since 1983 has had a ration card, which entitles it to purchase subsidized grain and scarce items (e.g., sugar, soap, cooking oil). The system is apparently not as formalized as in South Asia, however, and there is little written information available on it. Supplies of scarce commodities are not assured and may be unavailable for several weeks at a time.

TABLE 6.6
Official retail prices of cereals, urban minimum wage, and ratio of minimum wage to maize price

Category	1973/4	74/5	75/6	76/7	77/8	78/9	79/80	80/1	81/2	82/3	83/4	84/5
Food prices, in sh/kg												
Current prices												
Sembe	0.80	1.25	1.25	1.75	1.75	1.75	1.75	1.25	2.50	2.50	2.50	8.00
Rice	1.65	2.00	4.00	4.00	3.50	3.50	3.50	5.35	5.35	5.35	7.20	13.40
Wheat flour	1.65	2.40	3.75	3.75	3.75	3.75	3.75	5.65	5.65	5.65	8.00	14.50
Constant 1982 prices												
Sembe	3.70	4.90	3.90	3.10	4.50	4.10	3.60	2.00	3.10	2.50		
Rice	7.70	7.80	12.40	11.60	9.10	8.10	7.20	8.40	6.70	5.30		
Wheat flour	7.70	9.40	11.60	10.90	9.70	8.70	7.70	8.90	7.10	5.70		
Urban minimum wage, in sh/month												
Current prices	240	340	380	380	380	380	380	480	600	600	600	810
Constant prices	1120	1330	1180	1100	990	880	780	760	760	600		
Kg staple/day's wage												
Sembe	10.0	9.1	10.1	7.2	7.2	7.2	7.2	12.8	8.0	8.0	8.0	4.1
Rice	4.8	5.7	3.2	3.2	3.6	3.6	3.6	3.0	3.7	3.7	2.8	2.1
Wheat flour	4.8	5.7	3.4	3.4	3.4	3.4	3.4	2.8	3.5	3.5	2.5	1.9

NOTE: For comparison purposes, the exchange rate in December 1984 was 17.90 Tanzanian shillings to the U.S. dollar.
SOURCE: MDB (1982); MDB (1984)

There is little information available on allotments of NMC grain to different institutions, and any figures that are available are in any case thought to be unreliable. The reason is that certain individuals do have access to NMC grain, through connections. This type of transaction is not officially sanctioned, but apparently amounts recorded as going to the ration shops may, in fact, be diverted.

The main problem is that NMC is only able to satisfy a portion of urban demand, which is not easy to quantify. If one uses the 1976/7 Household Budget Survey, one can estimate that urban consumers purchased 114 thousand tonnes of *sembe* in a year in which NMC distribution was 120 thousand tonnes, i.e., NMC apparently supplied most of urban requirements. However, the implied per capita annual consumption (50 kg) is suspiciously low, perhaps by a factor of two or more. The MDB has made an alternative estimate for 1984/5 (MDB, 1984) based on estimates of the share of maize in calorie intake. The board estimates that 5 per cent of production, or 24 per cent of marketed production, of maize will be through the NMC. The urban population was in 1976/7 about 14 per cent of the total mainland population. Hence, even if all NMC maize goes to urban areas, and assuming urban consumption is no more than 15 per cent of the total, NMC would supply no more than a third of urban demand in 1984/5, and probably less. Dar es Salaam has also taken the lion's share of subsidized grain. In 1976/7 it received about 40 per cent of NMC's maize, slightly less than its percentage of the urban population (about 50 per cent). By 1983 or 1984, its share of NMC maize had risen to about 70 per cent.

By 1984, Tanzania's economic difficulties were very serious. Over three and one-half years, the subsidy had cost 1233 million shillings; in addition, NMC had accumulated a deficit of 750 million shillings from the late 1970s. The cost of the maize subsidy was expected to raise to 800 million shillings in 1984-4. The government, therefore, abolished the subsidy in the 1984 budget and introduced a package of reform measures. These included ending the fertilizer subsidy, increasing fees such as those for passports and examinations, introducing secondary-school fees, raising certain taxes, reducing the number of parastatals, reducing the number of items controlled by the Prices Commission (from about 2000 to 75), and partially liberalizing the use of private foreign exchange.

The maize subsidy has not entirely ended. There remains a 1 shilling subsidy on maize grain, financed by a tax on rice and wheat. Also maize remains implicitly subsidized because consumer and producer prices remain below world prices measured at the shadow exchange rate, and below parallel market prices. Competition to obtain cheaper NMC foodstuffs remains intense.

The NMC also continues to cross-subsidize certain regions at the expense of others. The much-criticized policy of pan-territorial pricing was discontinued in 1981. This policy gave a uniform producer price for a particular cereal, irrespective of geographic location. It tended to discourage efficient spatial location of production and increased transportation costs. However, political considerations rather than economic efficiency seem to have governed the setting of consumer prices spatially since 1981. In a free market, the areas of greatest deficit would tend to have the highest price, to induce food to move over longer distances from surplus areas. However, Dar and Dodoma (the intended site of the new capital), both heavy deficit areas, face lower maize-flour prices than the national average (6.60 and 7.40 sh/kg respectively, compared to the average of 8.00 sh/kg), whereas areas that are almost self-sufficient are penalized (the price in Rukwa is 9.80 and in Ruvuma 9.20 sh/kg). Thus the NMC is operating a cross-subsidy favouring Dar es Salaam and Dodoma.

3 Analysis of the Tanzanian Maize Subsidy

In analysing the Tanzanian food subsidy, using the framework derived from the cross-country survey in section 1, this section examines the costs of the subsidy (macro-economic, agricultural) and the benefits (income distribution and nutritional).

The fiscal costs of the maize subsidy were relatively small compared to those in China and Sri Lanka. The cost was 1233 million shillings over three and one-half years (United Republic of Tanzania, 1984), or about 0.9 per cent of GDP, 2.2 per cent of government expenditure, and 5.1 per cent of government recurrent revenue annually. These costs were, however, perceived as high in a situation in which the government's ability to raise additional revenue was limited, and where control over the domestic credit expansion was perceived as important.[2]

However, abolition of the consumer food subsidy has not solved the problem of deficits of the agricultural parastatals. Since the early 1980s, the real producer prices of export crops have been raised, in recognition of the problems caused by stagnant export volumes and receipts. However, the government was for several years (until 1986) unwilling to devalue further (which would raise the shilling value of export-crop sales), and the result was large deficits by the export crop parastatals. These were 907 million shillings in 1982/3 and 500 million in 1983/4 (MDB, 1983), and were similar in magnitude to the annual costs of the *sembe* subsidy.

The balance-of-payments effects of the subsidy were probably not a serious constraint, since a large proportion of food imports are given as aid.

Of more serious concern was the high foreign-exchange intensity of urban food supply (see figures in section 2) resulting from inefficiencies in transport and in regional pricing. Also the choice of technology and crop mix in agriculture has large balance-of-payments implications. The wheat sector in particular uses tractor technologies that are very foreign-exchange intensive. Thus the negative balance-of-payments effect of the subsidy was probably unimportant relative to balance-of-payments effects of other distortions in the agricultural sector.

Similarly, it might be argued that the *sembe* subsidy had a relatively minor distortionary effect on agriculture, given the existence of other distortions. The real producer price for preferred staples had declined continuously since 1975/6 (refer back to table 6.5) and continued to decline while the subsidy was operative.

In any case, the existence of the parallel market limited somewhat the adverse effects of low official producer prices. Instead, it probably distorted incentives between producers with different volumes of output. Those farmers with large surpluses were more likely to come under pressure to sell at least partly through official channels. It probably also distorted incentives across regions. Regions closer to Dar es Salaam and other urban areas were more likely to be able to transport grain and sell it on the parallel market, whereas in more distant areas illegal grain movements were easier to detect. For instance, according to MDB (1984) a large proportion of NMC's procurement in 1983/4 was due to a crack-down on procurement in a single region, Arusha.

One question that might be asked is whether the consumer subsidy led to an expansion of the parallel market and, if so, whether that expansion was a bad thing. It seems likely that the subsidy did encourage the parallel market. Theory suggests that if the income elasticity of demand for maize is fairly high, then income transfers via a subsidy will increase demand for maize. If demand is not satisfied through official channels, it must be met through the parallel market. Theories of rent-seeking would also suggest that the wider the gap between the subsidized and the parallel market price for maize, the more resources will be diverted to (and wasted, from the social point of view) obtaining subsidized maize. However, there is very little empirical evidence that can be used to examine the effects of the subsidy on the parallel market.

Hence, the main conclusion regarding costs of the subsidy is that although they were not trivial, they were small relative to the costs of other existing distortions. Partial analysis is less helpful in Tanzania's case than for other countries. The reason is that the severe economic difficulties in Tanzania put serious constraints on the operation of government policy.

The shortage of one key input (foreign exchange) has made individual sectors of the economy much more dependent on what happens elsewhere.

The income-distribution effects of the subsidy were potentially substantial. As table 6.6 shows, removal of the subsidy halved the purchasing power of the minimum wage in terms of NMC maize. However, there are several reasons why removal of the subsidy is unlikely to have substantially worsened inequality in income distribution. First, the subsidy was urban biased and favoured the most wealthy city, Dar es Salaam. Second, within urban areas it seems likely that higher income earners had greater access. Third, the consumption characteristics of maize suggest that it was not the best subsidy vehicle, if income distribution were thought to be important. The following paragraphs examine the evidence for each of these assertions.

First, with regard to the urban/rural distribution of benefits, the Tanzanian subsidy (like most of those surveyed in section 1) is urban biased. In most countries it is obvious that urban incomes are on average higher than rural, and hence an urban subsidy is inegalitarian. For Tanzania however, the ILO (1982) has made calculations suggesting that urban minimum wage earners, in fact, had lower real incomes by the 1980s than smallholders, in which case an urban food subsidy might not have worsened overall income distribution. The ILO's methods have been disputed (see, for example, ILO, 1983). It is immediately obvious that purchasing power of the minimum wage has been severely eroded. However, it is less obvious that calorie intake in rural areas has remained constant over time, a crucial assumption underlying the ILO's calculations.

I would use two pieces of evidence to argue that the ILO has overstated the case, and that urban real incomes probably remain above rural ones, although the differential almost certainly has narrowed. However, resolution of the debate requires better data. Possibly ongoing work by Collier (at Oxford University, Institute for Economics and Statistics) will help resolve the issue. Collier has traced a sample of urban and rural households from the 1976/7 Household Budget Survey and resurveyed them in 1983.

I would advance the following evidence: first, there is evidence on birth weight from Bantje (in progress). He has information from particular hospitals in four rural and one urban area (Dar). His data suggest that birth weight may have fallen somewhat since the late 1970s, in both urban and rural areas, but that urban birth weights are consistently higher than rural. Of course, birth weights depend on many different factors. However, these factors do include maternal nutrition in the third trimester of pregnancy and health services. Bantje's explanation is that crop yields have been declining slowly since the late 1970s because of the shift to sedentary agriculture without a simultaneous intensification of inputs – an occurrence barely remarked upon by agricultural economists (Bantje, personal communication). Bantje's data do not include those rural areas that were affected by the drought.

Second, there is anecdotal evidence suggesting that published statistics may underestimate real incomes in Dar es Salaam. Urban residents apparently increasingly supplement their incomes by other activities. These include cultivating *shambas* (small farms) in the region around the city, producing food in small plots within the city, working in a second job. These activities frequently divert resources: for example, the cultivation of *shambas* may use official transport and gasoline on weekends, having a second job may reduce time and effort on the main one. Income supplementation of this type is more feasible in Dar es Salaam – the political centre, main port, and headquarters of aid agencies and of most government agencies – than it is elsewhere. Income supplementation is probably more feasible for higher-income earners, but even for minimum-wage earners such opportunities are likely to be most favourable in Dar. Thus, although urban incomes have undoubtedly fallen sharply, it is by no means clear that they are on average below rural incomes.

Within urban areas, it has been argued that operation of the maize subsidy favoured higher-income groups. Rugumisa and Semboja (1984) argue that richer households obtained more NMC grain, either through direct contacts with NMC or because they were associated with large institutions. Poorer households relying on the ration shops received a lower priority. There is little evidence available to quantify this statement, however, Bryceson (1985) uses 1976/7 household-budget data to show that low-income households (those with less than 6000 shillings annually) derived 61 per cent of their *sembe* from non-market sources in 1976/7, as opposed to only 16 per cent for other (higher-income) urban households. Comparable figures for the 1980s are not available, but the figures suggest that poorer households were less able to rely on marketed grain (both NMC and non-NMC marketed grain). It is also possible that the subsidy was initially operated in a more egalitarian way than at the end (Helleiner, personal communication).

Analysis of the consumption characteristics of maize suggests that although maize was not the worst item to subsidize as far as income distribution was concerned, it was also not the best. Figures on the income elasticity of demand for specific foods are not available, but table 6.7 gives information on budget shares by expenditure group. These show that maize is not a luxury, unlike rice and wheat (maize's share of food expenditure declines as expenditure rises). However, the budget shares of millet, sorghum, and starches, particularly cassava, also decline. Table 6.8 gives in-

TABLE 6.7
Share of certain items in total food expenditure, for urban households in Tanzania, 1976/77

| | Annual expenditure group (in shillings) | | | |
| | 0–3999 | 4000–5999 | 6000–9999 | 10,000 + |
Category	Low I	Low II	Medium	High
Cereals	0.348	0.268	0.230	0.177
Rice and paddy	0.070	0.109	0.120	0.095
Maize	0.146	0.121	0.090	0.037
Millet and sorghum	0.062	0.004	0.002	0.001
Wheat	0.002	0.008	0.008	0.024
Others	0.006	0.002	0.001	0.013
Cost of grinding	0.003	0.002	0.001	0.002
Starches	0.130	0.068	0.055	0.046
Cassava	0.046	0.015	0.010	0.000
Maize				
Grain	0.004	0.002	0.001	0.001
Flour	0.142	0.119	0.089	0.037
Share of food/total expenditure	0.760	0.598	0.499	0.275
Per cent of all households	32.6	19.5	25.1	22.8

NOTE: The low/medium/high categorization is one used by the Household Budget Survey. The low-income group has been subdivided.
SOURCE: Calculated from Bureau of Statistics, *Household Budget Survey* (1985)

formation on the share of the lowest third of urban households, in total urban consumption of particular foods. The lowest third consume less than one-third of total maize, and hence a maize subsidy benefits the rich relatively more. However, the poorest third consume more than one-third of total cassava, starch, millet, and sorghum available; hence these items are potentially better subsidy vehicles.

The least-preferred staples may have some disadvantages as subsidy vehicles. Cassava is bulky; it stores and transports badly; and NMC has suffered losses on this crop in the past. Markets in the drought staples may be rather thin, and there has been relatively little research on technical change. The NMC also had losses on sorghum and millet in the late 1970s, when it accumulated quantities it could not easily sell. However, greater attention to tastes (people strongly prefer traditional varieties whereas improved varieties are sometimes cheaper to produce) and attention to the millet/maize price differential facing consumers could help. For these reasons NMC might

TABLE 6.8
Share of lowest-expenditure group of households (below 4000 sh) in total consumption of particular foods, Tanzania 1976/77, urban areas

Category	Share
Number of households	0.326
Urban rice consumption	0.224
Urban maize consumption	0.285
Maize grain	0.409
Maize flour	0.261
Urban millet + sorghum consumption	0.705
Urban wheat consumption	0.041
Urban starch consumption	0.338
Urban cassava consumption	0.485

SOURCE: Calculated from Bureau of Statistics, *Household Budget Survey* (1985)

not have wanted to subsidize the least-preferred staples instead of maize. However, it should at least have subsidized them to the same extent, rather than making maize absolutely cheaper.

Thus, several considerations suggest that the maize subsidy had few, if any, benefits in relation to income distribution, and that its removal was not a highly regressive measure. Compared to food subsidies in other developing countries (see, for example, Horton and Taylor, 1986), the Tanzanian subsidy was not well designed to benefit income distribution. Nor was state administrative capacity such that the subsidy could be administered in an egalitarian manner.

However, it is undoubtedly true that those among the urban poor who had had access to subsidized grain had negative effects on their real incomes because of the removal of the subsidy. At the time the subsidy was removed, other measures could have been implemented aimed at buffering the effect on the urban poor. Ultimately, long-run improvements in agricultural and food policy were required to ensure an adequate supply to urban areas. However, short-run solutions such as school feeding, food distribution via health centres, or a redirection of NMC grain towards shops in the poorer urban areas might have been considered (although the economic crisis seriously constrained the government's ability to implement many of these options).

It is difficult to obtain direct evidence on the nutritional benefits of the maize subsidy. If the subsidy favoured higher-income groups, then we would infer that its effect on maintaining nutrient intake of poorer households may have been limited. This conclusion is hard to substantiate because there is very little information on nutritional status over time for Tanzania. The ILO (1983) uses a number of small surveys of different regions and concludes that the percentage of the population exhibiting severe protein-energy malnutrition (PEM) declined from 4.8 to 2.3 per cent between 1970 and 1981, but the percentage with moderate PEM rose from 22 per cent to 40–60 per cent. This finding has an appealing interpretation (Tanzania's policies reduced income inequality but per capita incomes and food intake fell on average), but the survey evidence is very shaky.

Bantje's (1985, and in progress) evidence on birth weights is likely to be more reliable. Birth weights are sensitive to nutrition in the last trimester of pregnancy, and hence the impact of food shortages shows up quite quickly. However, other factors are involved. Bantje finds that birth weights have declined slightly over time in Dar es Salaam since the late 1970s. The declines are more pronounced in certain groups (females, and first and second births). Seasonal dips are also becoming more apparent over time, and were especially low in March 1980 and even lower in March 1981. It should be noted that by March 1981, the food subsidy had been in operation for almost a year. Things might have been worse in the absence of the subsidy, but apparently the subsidy was not entirely successful in protecting the nutritional status of vulnerable groups.

Finally, concerning possible nutritional benefits resulting from greater food security, the Tanzanian food subsidy was apparently not particularly successful. The NMC's ability to intervene in food markets is rather circumscribed because it sells mainly to urban areas and deals with only a small proportion of total production and of marketed output. (The figures are 5 and 24 per cent, respectively, for maize; 11 and 21 per cent for rice; and 43 and 58 per cent for wheat [MDB, 1984, estimates for 1984–5]). Its purchases of maize have varied greatly over time (ranging from 23.9 million tons in 1974/5, to 220.4 in 1978/9 and 71.0 in 1983/4), since the existence of the parallel market tends to make NMC the buyer of last resort (i.e., NMC provides a floor price for sellers). The NMC, therefore, tends to accumulate grain in years with good harvests, when consumer purchases from NMC are also low. Thus, there is potentially a role for stabilizing prices intertemporally. In practice, NMC does not have the necessary finance, storage capacity, and probably management capability (to turn over stocks). Nor is holding physical stocks necessarily the best way to provide food security. However, one alternative, the use of trade in food to improve food security, is not viable. Export possibilities are limited because at the present exchange rate, Tanzania is a relatively high-cost producer and food imports are constrained by lack of foreign exchange.

NMC also has had problems in balancing the supply and demand for individual crops. The price of drought staples was raised after the 1973/4 food crises and led to an accumulation of stocks that could not easily be sold in the late 1970s. The NMC is currently accumulating stocks of cassava, which may lead to a similar problem (NMC, various years).

4 Some Policy Findings

The cross-country survey suggested that food-subsidy programs can have considerable macro-economic and agriculture-sector costs. They also have important potential benefits. Because food represents such a large share of the expenditure of the poor, food-price interventions have important effects on the real incomes of those poor households who participate in food markets. Moreover, there are potential 'self-targeting' properties if the food-subsidy vehicle is selected carefully. Thus, food subsidies can potentially improve income distribution, as well as improve the nutrition of poor households. However, political considerations (which are not discussed here) often affect program design, and many existing schemes are urban biased and probably regressive.

If the Tanzanian subsidy is examined in the above framework, it would seem that its costs were not particularly high, especially when compared to costs of existing distortions in the agricultural sector. However, the subsidy did not succeed very well in maintaining consumption of lower-income urban households. There are several reasons for this result. The NMC purchases only a small fraction of maize production and even of maize marketed, and satisfies only a fraction of urban demand. Thus, it does not have the market power to maintain a low consumer price without administrative fiat. Moreover, bureaucratic resources are already strained, without the extra responsibilities of a food subsidy financed partly by a procurement that effectively taxes producers. The subsidy was even more difficult to run because the subsidized consumer price was set very low in real terms, relative to prices over the previous decade, and absolutely below the price of less-preferred staples. Thus, the result was that the parallel market flourished, there was strong competition for the subsidized grain, and the beneficiaries were likely not the urban poor.

In Tanzania, any food subsidy would have been difficult to run. Tinkering with one small policy area did not produce the expected results in an economic system subject to serious constraints, and with large existing distortions. Perhaps aiming for a substantial explicit subsidy was too ambitious, whereas a more modest effort such as the existing (small) cross-subsidy between maize, and rice and wheat, is more feasible. The analysis of the preceding section suggests that millet, sorghum, and cassava should also be involved in any such cross-subsidy because they are predominantly consumed by the poor.

Ultimately, securing the consumption of the urban poor in Tanzania might require an examination of overall food and agriculture policy. Particular aspects might be the role of drought staples, and a reconsideration of the role of wheat, a crop which is foreign-exchange intensive to produce and with luxury-consumption characteristics. Other analysts have stressed broader requirements, such as provision of more resources to the agricultural sector and a rationalization of the use of bureaucratic resources (which might include delegating some of their existing functions).

More generally, African policy-makers have argued that running food subsidies in sub-Saharan African is different from (and perhaps more difficult than) elsewhere. Food subsidies are inevitably more urban biased because there is less of the problem of rural landlessness than in Asia, and because rural populations probably participate less in markets. African countries are also rather smaller and more likely to experience domestic production variability. The usual recommended response to the latter (to trade in food) may be limited by current foreign-exchange shortages, as well as over-valued exchange rates, which restrict the ability to export agricultural products. In addition, managerial capacity is less well developed, and private marketing and distribution mechanisms are less likely to exist. The tax base may also not be adequate to finance explicit subsidies. Studies of food subsidies in a variety of countries (e.g., Horton and Taylor, 1986) seem to bear out in practice the arguments that food subsidies work least well in sub-Saharan Africa.

However, food subsidies may be a less-appropriate policy intervention in Africa. Urbanization is a relatively recent problem and the urban poor tend to maintain stronger ties to the rural areas than are maintained in Asia or Latin America. Thus, in times of food scarcity, urban residents have more potential capability to obtain food from family members who remain behind in the rural areas, or to migrate temporarily back to their village. Urban food subsidies run the risk of accelerating rural-to-urban migration. Long-run improvements in the food-marketing system in Africa may be a better method of ensuring food security for urban residents than (possibly ineffective) food subsidies.

There is a need for more studies of African food policy. Analysis of the Tanzanian case was hampered by the lack of data, in particular lack of data on real incomes after 1976/7, on the parallel market, on nutritional status over time, etc. There are also fewer studies of food subsidies in other

African countries and such studies face similar data problems to those for Tanzania. Tanzania's food-marketing system is similar to that of other countries in East Africa, but Tanzania's experience is not necessarily representative.

Notes

I would like to thank the faculty of the Department of Economics, and the research staff of the Economics Research Bureau, of the University of Dar es Salaam, as well as Gerry Helleiner of the University of Toronto, for their help while I was researching the Tanzanian case study. Research travel was funded by the International Development Research Centre of Canada, and enabled by a postdoctoral fellowship from the Social Sciences and Humanities Research Council of Canada. The survey of other countries is based on a longer paper written in conjunction with Lance Taylor. The author alone remains responsible for any errors or omissions remaining.

1 Scandizzo and Swamy (1982) calculate that for India this has a substantial effect on decreasing consumer prices.
2 Hanak (1982) cites that the 1980 agreement with the IMF failed when Tanzania exceeded the money-supply guidelines.

References

Ahmed, J.U., M.L. Rahman, and A.F.M.F. Huq. 1980. *Paddy/Rice Procurement System in Bangladesh*. Dacca: Government of Bangladesh, Ministry of Agriculture and Forests
Ahmed, R. 1979. 'Foodgrain Supply, Distribution, and Consumption Policies within a Dual Pricing Mechanism: A Case Study of Bangladesh.' International Food Policy Research Institute (IFPRI) Research Report no. 8. Washington
Alderman, H., and Timmer, C.P. 1980. 'Consumption Parameters for Sri Lanka Food Policy Analysis.' Sri Lanka, *Journal of Agrarian Studies* 1: 1–12
Alderman, H., and J. von Braun. 1984. 'The Effects of the Egyptian Food Ration and Subsidy System on Income Distribution and Consumption.' IFPRI Research Report no. 45. Washington
Alderman, H., J. von Braun, and S.A. Sakr. 1982. 'Egypt's Food Subsidy and Rationing System: A Description.' IFPRI Research Report no. 34. Washington
Bantje, H. 1985. 'Long-Term and Seasonal Variations in Birth Weight in Dar es Salaam.' University of Dar es Salaam, Institute of Resource Assessment, draft (mimeo)
– In progress 'Long-Term Changes in Birth Weight Distribution in Tanzania.' University of Dar es Salaam, Institute of Resource Assessment, draft
Brown, G.T. 1978. 'Agricultural Pricing Policies in Developing Countries.' In T. Schultz (ed.), *Distortions of Agricultural Incentives*, pp. 84–113. Bloomington: Indiana University Press
Bryceson, D.F. 1985. 'Food and Urban Purchasing Power: The Case of Dar es Salaam, Tanzania.' *Africa Affairs* 84, no. 337: 499–522

Bureau of Statistics. 1985. *Household Budget Survey 1975/6*. 2 vols. Dar es Salaam: Government of Tanzania Printing Office

Calegar, G.M., and G.E. Schuh. 1984. 'Brazilian Wheat Policy and Its Income Distribution and Trade Effects: A Case Study.' Paper presented at IFPRI workshop on consumer-oriented food subsidies, May, Washington

Cavallo, D., and Y. Mundlak. 1982. 'Agriculture and Economic Growth in an Open Economy: The Case of Argentina.' IFPRI Research Report no. 36. Washington

Clark, W.E. 1978. *Socialist Development and Public Investment in Tanzania, 1964-73*. Toronto: University of Toronto Press

De Janvry, A., and K. Subbarao. 1984. 'Agricultural Price Policy and Income Distribution in India.' Division of Agricultural Sciences Working Paper no. 274. Berkeley: University of California

Edirisinghe, N. 1987. 'The Food Stamp Scheme in Sri Lanka: Costs, Benefits, and Options for Modification.' IFPRI Research Report no. 58. Washington

Ellis, F. 1982. 'Agricultural Price Policy in Tanzania.' *World Development* 10: 263-83

Gavan, J.D., and I.S. Chandrasekera. 1979. 'The Impact of Public Foodgrain Distribution on Food Consumption and Welfare in Sri Lanka.' IFPRI Research Report no. 13. Washington

Gibson, B., N. Lustig, and L. Taylor. 1982. 'Terms of Trade and Class Conflict in a Computable General Equilibrium Model for Mexico.' University of Massachusetts (mimeo)

Grindle, M.S. 1975. 'Bureaucracy and Public Policy in Mexico.' PhD dissertation, Department of Political Science, Massachusetts Institute of Technology

Hanak, E.E. 1982. 'The Tanzanian Balance of Payments Crisis: Causes, Consequences and Lessons for a Survival Strategy.' University of Dar es Salaam, Economic Research Bureau Paper no. 82-91

Horton, S. 1984. 'A Survey of Food Subsidy Programs in Selected Countries.' Paper presented at a conference on consumer-oriented food subsidies, International Food Policy Research Institute, Washington

- 1985. 'Food Prices: Reconciling Consumer and Producer Interests.' Draft to FAO for Committee on Agriculture Price Policy Study, Rome (mimeo)

Horton, S., and L. Taylor. 1986. 'Food Subsidy Programs: Theory, Practice and Policy Lessons.' University of Toronto, in preparation (mimeo)

International Labor Organization (ILO). 1982. *Basic Needs in Danger*. Addis Ababa: ILO JASPA

- 1983. *Basic Needs and Development in Tanzania*. Report of a seminar sponsored by JASPA. Addis Ababa

Kaberuka, D. 1984. 'Evaluating the Performance of Food Marketing Parastatals.' *Development Policy Review* 2: 190-216

Krishna, R., and G.S. Raychaudhuri. 1980. 'Some Aspects of Wheat and Rice Price Policy in India.' World Bank Staff Working Paper no. 381. Washington

Kumar, S.K. 1979. 'Impact of Subsidized Rice on Food Consumption and Nutrition in Kerala.' IFPRI Research Report no. 5. Washington

Lamade, W. 1970. 'Policies of Marketing Boards in East Africa.' In P. Zajadacz (ed.), *Studies in Production and Trade in East Africa*. Munich: Weltforum Verlag

Lardy, N.R. 1983. 'Agricultural Prices in China.' World Bank Staff Working Papers no. 606

Lipumba, N. 1983. 'Basic Needs and Agricultural Development Policy: A Critical Review.' In International Labor Organization, *Basic Needs and Development in Tanzania,* report of a seminar sponsored by JASPA. Addis Ababa: ILO

Lipumba, N., and D. Mbogoro. 1984. 'Agriculture in Economic Stabilization Policies.' Workshops on Economic Stabilization Policies in Tanzania, University of Dar es Salaam, Feb. 20–23

Lustig, N. 1984. 'Fiscal Costs and Welfare Effects of the Corn Subsidy Program in Mexico.' Paper presented at IFPRI workshop on consumer-oriented food subsidies, May, Washington

McCarthy, F.D. 1978. 'Food and Nutrition Planning in Pakistan.' International Nutrition Planning Program, Massachusetts Institute of Technology, Discussion Paper no. 12

Madden, P.J., and M.D. Yoder. 1972. *Program Evaluation: Food Stamps and Commodity Distribution in Rural Areas of Central Pennsylvania.* Pennsylvania State University, Agricultural Experiment Station Bulletin no. 80

Marketing Development Board (MDB), Ministry of Agriculture, Tanzania. 1980. *Financial Aspects of NMC Cereal and Pulses Trading*

– 1982. *Price Policy Recommendations for the July 1982 Agricultural Price Review.* Summary volume, Annex 1 (Maize, Rice and Wheat) and Annex 2 (Sorghum, Millets and Cassava)

– 1983. *Price Policy Recommendations for the 1983 Agricultural Price Review.* Summary volume

– 1984. *Price Policy Recommendations for the 1984 Agricultural Price Review.* Summary volume, vol. 1 (Maize, Rice and Wheat) and vol. 2 (Sorghum, Millet, Cassava and Beans)

– 1985. *Price Policy Recommendations for the July 1985 Agricultural Price Review.* Summary volume

Msambichaka, L.A., B.J. Ndulu, and H.K.R. Amani. 1983. *Agricultural Development in Tanzania: Policy Evaluation, Performance and Evaluation.* Bonn: Friedrich-Ebert-Stiftung

Pitt, M.M. 1983. 'Food Preferences and Nutrition in Rural Bangladesh.' *Review of Economics and Statistics* 65: 105–14

Quizon, J.B., and H.P. Binswanger. 1984. 'Income Distribution in India: The Impact of Policies and Growth in the Agricultural Sector.' World Bank Agriculture and Rural Development Department, Discussion Paper no. ARU 21. Washington

Rugumisa, S.M.H., and J.J. Semboja. 1984. 'Possible Income Redistribution Effects of Recent Policy Changes in Tanzania: Some Thoughts on the 1984/5 Government Budget.' University of Dar es Salaam, Economics Research Bureau, draft (mimeo)

Scandizzo, P.L. 1984 'Aggregate Supply Response: Empirical Evidence on Key Issues.' FAO draft. Rome (mimeo)

Scandizzo, P.L., and G. Swamy. 1982. 'Benefits and Costs of Food Distribution Policies: The India Case.' World Bank Staff Working Papers no. 509. Washington

Scobie, G.M. 1981. 'Government Policy and Food Imports: The Case of Wheat in Egypt.' IFPRI Research Report no. 29. Washington

- 1983. 'Food Subsidies in Egypt: Their Impact on Foreign Exchange and Trade.' IFPRI Research Report no. 40. Washington

Stewart, F. (in co-operation with J. Sharpley). 1984. 'Tanzania: Macro-economic Policies and Agricultural Performance.' OECD Development Centre, Paris (draft, mimeo)

Swamy, G. 1979. 'Public Food Distribution in India.' World Bank, AGREP Division Working Paper no. 25. Washington

Temu, P.E. 1984. *Marketing, Board Pricing, and Storage Policy with Particular Reference to Maize in Tanzania*. New York: Vantage Press, Inc.

United Republic of Tanzania. 1984. *Speech by the Minister of Finance Introducing the Estimates of the Public Revenue and Expenditure for the Financial Year 1984/5 to the National Assembly on 14th June 1984*. Dar es Salaam: Government Printer

Wagao, J. 1982. 'State Control of Agricultural Marketing in Tanzania, 1961-76.' University of Dar es Salaam Economic Research Bureau Paper no. 82-7

West, D.A. 1978. 'Food Program Evaluation: The Washington State Experience.' U.S. Department of Agriculture, Economics, Statistics and Co-operatives Service, AFPR-2

West, D.A., and D.W. Price. 1976. 'The Effects of Income, Assets, Food Programs and Household Size on Food Consumption.' *American Journal of Agricultural Economics* 58: 725-30

World Bank. 1983. *Tanzania: Agriculture Sector Report*. Report no. 4052-TA. Washington

Yoshimura, H., M.P. Perera, and P.J. Cunawardene. 1975. 'Some Aspects of Paddy and Rice Marketing in Sri Lanka.' Agrarian Research and Training Institute, Occasional Publication Series no. 10. Colombo

7

Agricultural and Rural Policies for the Poor

R. ALBERT BERRY

Most poor people in developing countries live in rural areas; the poorer the country the more marked is this pattern. Hence, it seems plausible to expect that in any economic strategy that puts weight on poverty alleviation, agricultural policy and, more generally, any policies particularly affecting rural populations will be quite important if not dominant components of the overall policy package.

We accept that in most of the poorer LDCs (less developed countries) growth of output and productivity in agriculture is the pivotal first step for successful development, and that the process of agricultural growth is certain to have impacts of one sort or another on a large group of the country's poor. In most countries there is no significant agricultural frontier to permit output increases at constant costs through 'horizontal' expansion of the sector, so capital formation and technological improvement must be central to the growth process. Population growth, meanwhile, has reached extreme levels in many of the poorer countries, especially those in Africa, and is usually higher in rural than in urban areas. In many countries rural poverty is associated with the state of being landless (or not having good access to water, in countries where it is the key input). In most countries there is some degree of urban or industrial bias in policy (Lipton, 1977), either in the sense that industry is protected at the expense of agriculture or in the sense that a disproportionate share of government expenditures or of imports benefits an urban elite or the urban population as a whole.

Rural poverty could be alleviated in most LDCs by improved income distribution in rural areas (as after the Chinese or other revolutions) or between rural and urban areas, or by growth whose fruits are reasonably widely distributed. In many poorer LDCs, redistribution, while it would help, could not be the key element of a long-term strategy to eradicate poverty (and such a strategy usually has to be long term) because the size of the existing pie is too small and the population growing too fast. So the growth process is central to poverty alleviation in general. In other countries, especially those of Latin America, redistribution could eradicate poverty.

From a technical point of view, it now appears that substantial output increases of agricultural products and of other rural activities are quite feasible in most, perhaps all, developing countries. At the same time, it is evident that if population growth continues unchecked at 2.4 per cent per year, most of the outputs gains will be eaten up just to feed the expanding population and will not lead to permanently raised standards of living. Population growth impinges especially negatively on the poor because it depresses the equilibrium wage rate on which the poor, especially, depend for their living. So no policy package can provide any guarantee of a resolution of the problems of rural poverty, or of poverty in general, if it does not include a mechanism whereby population growth will be curtailed. Thus, a successful set of policies would (1) raise output fairly quickly, (2) assure a widespread distribution of the resulting benefits, and (3) lead to a slowing of population growth.

In most developing countries, adequate allocation of resources to research, infrastructure, and other investments, together with effective administration of those resources, would probably assure a growth of agricultural output that would exceed population growth, at least for a decade or two, while the opportunities that are now visible are run through. Such success would probably be more difficult in many of the countries of sub-Saharan Africa than elsehwere in the third world because of the greater reliance on uncertain rainfall and the smaller benefits thus far obtainable from the major genetic breakthroughs (especially in wheat and rice) coming from international research centres. In terms of taking advantage of the growth potential of agriculture, however, many LDCs seem to have remained far below their potential, and this fact required an explanation involving primarily non-technical considerations.

Achievement of widespread distribution of the fruits of growth, and more generally of an acceptable distribution of rural income, is also technically simple: all it seems to require is a fairly equitable distribution of resources, and especially land (or sometimes water). But it is not surprising that this distribution does not often happen, for economic and political power are highly correlated.

Reduced population growth in most of the countries that have achieved it has been mainly the result of rising standards of living and more education and urbanization; public policy has played a role in a good number of countries but seldom, with the probable exception of China, has it been the major factor at work. Of particular interest in the present context is how agricultural policy, and in particular the adoption of a small-farm strategy, bears on population growth. If such a policy were to delay the reduction of birth rates, then its advantages on other counts would be seriously reduced.

The next section of this chapter describes what appears to be the best rural development strategy for rapid alleviation of poverty. It goes without saying that the appropriate components would vary across countries according to their natural resources, level of development, and so on, and that various of the components may be politically or administratively unfeasible in many countries. Available evidence gives us many highly relevant ideas about what policies produce better results than others, but when one gets to the practical level of asking which among the policies feasible in a given setting are likeliest to produce good results, our 'knowledge' shrinks and modesty becomes the order of the day. Much of the problem lies in our innocence of the 'how to' of development. The institutions, attitudes, administrative skills, and other determinants of how a given objective will be pursued in a given country are often more important than the precise policy followed (see Johnston and Clark, 1982). There is much still to be learned in this area as well as in the area of *how much* the results of alternative rural development strategies differ. Though it appears that the strategy outlined in the next section is a clear front-runner, it is less clear how great an advantage it may have over other approaches, and how this advantage varies across economic and political settings. It seems logical to expect that the implementation of some less-attractive agricultural and rural strategy would have lower costs in a middle-level country where agriculture's relative role has already been greatly diminished than in a really agrarian society.

The last quarter-century of thinking about development problems has seen a shift from the nearly exclusive emphasis on growth to a broader concern that also encompasses equity. The new conventional wisdom – that because the trickle down is not a guaranteed solution to poverty,[1] conscious attention must be given to income distribution and employment – is conceptually obvious enough, though it might be argued that for want of evidence that attention has not yet paid off in much new insight. This problem plagues the analysis of rural poverty, as that of poverty in general, making it hard to assess 'growth-first' types of strategies.

Neither economic nor administrative/institutional theory is anywhere nearly adequate to the task of accurate prediction of the outcome of various strategies and structures, so careful analysis of the historical record is the main and ultimately the only reasonably safe guide to policy. The shared view of most students of rural development on the best-bet strategy is rooted in the experience of a few countries that have followed or approximated it, especially Taiwan. Less-careful attention has been given to the record in countries following different routes; in this essay I take a partial look at the particular experiences of Brazil and India, along with that of Taiwan, in an attempt to get a better feel for how sensitive outcomes may be to policies or patterns of rural development.

A further methodological point should be noted here. Whether the attack on rural poverty is mainly a matter of rural and agricultural policy depends partly on the way rural/urban migration occurs and on other rural/urban linkages, such as the intersectoral terms of trade and remittances. If migration is sufficiently sensitive to urban/rural income gaps, any policy whose direct effect is to raise incomes in a given sector will lead to migration into that sector with a different distribution of benefits than what would have occurred in the absence of such migration. In many LDCs, rural/urban migration does appear to respond rather sensitively to relative employment opportunities, so it may make little sense to treat rural poverty separately from overall poverty. In the context of many of the poorer LDCs, however, the major group of poor people is, in any case, found in rural areas. Hence, even if impacts of policies are effectively spread throughout the economy, their main effect would still be on rural people, so it would make sense to assess the relationship between agricultural/rural policy and rural poverty.

1 A Policy Package for Rural Growth with Equity, and the Obstacles to Its Implementation

The professional's model for successful agricultural development is that corresponding to Japan, Korea, and Taiwan, involving an equitable distribution of land, good public-sector support in terms of development and dissemination of improved seed varieties, infrastructural improvements, supportive rather than damaging price and marketing interventions, and good coverage of rural education. The contribution of a good rural educational system to the package's success may be less obvious than that of the other components and, in current application to the poorer countries, one would add a population policy as an important ingredient. One would accept as given that administrative competence, together with farmer interest and involvement, is very important to success. In each of the cited countries, after their land reforms in the early post–Second World War years, agricultural output rose quickly, as did rural incomes and wage rates.[2] The agricultural labour force began to fall in Taiwan in the 1970s and in Korea probably around 1980. In each case, labour productivity in the agricultural sector rose rapidly. Land distribution was equalized in the original reforms, and reconcentration was discouraged by land ceilings; mean farm size was just a few hectares. In terms of agricultural price policy these have been cases more of support than of below-equilibrium prices.[3] The recognition of agriculture's importance and the structure of domestic politics has been reflected in a relatively high level of public expenditure on the sector and, as important, in effective use of that expenditure.

An additional feature of the experience in Taiwan and Japan, though less so for Korea, has been the prevalence of non-agricultural employment opportunities in the rural areas. The share of farm families' income coming from off-farm employment surpassed 50 per cent fairly early in both Japan and Taiwan. Research has not focused enough on this issue to clarify why such opportunities have been greater in these countries than in most LDCs. Probably the fairly high level of rural incomes and their relatively equitable distribution have been factors, as has the fact that inputs for small-scale agriculture are easier to manufacture locally than those of larger farms. The relative density of rural populations in these countries is another likely factor. Perhaps a more positive attitude toward small industry (rural non-agricultural enterprises are nearly all small) has contributed. There appears, in any case, to be a relationship between the existence of a small peasantry and public support for it with the existence and potential of rural non-agricultural activities. These latter may be doubly important in a successful small-farm strategy because they can provide a satisfactory outlet for energies, savings, and pressures in the system. The basic need for land redistribution, farm-size ceilings, and the like lies in the absolute limit to available land, in contrast with the cases of capital, labour, etc. The individual who wishes to expand to better exercise his capacities can be frustrated if no oulet is available. Rural non-agricultural activities provide local and known investment opportunities.

These cases of what Johnston and Cownie (1969) referred to as a unimodal agricultural strategy are the exception rather than the rule in LDCs. In some countries the total public-sector support for agriculture has clearly been less than optimal; further, it has typically been biased, often strongly, in favour of large farms or of farms favoured by the existing regime (see, for example, Bates, 1981). It is often the mirror image of the Japan/Korea/Taiwan model. Research is limited and focused on export crops or on the products of large farms. Prices are often held below their equilibrium levels, either because export crops are heavily taxed or because there are price controls on food products. Credit and modern inputs are frequently subsidized for favoured (usually large) farmers but unavailable for smaller ones. Public-sector marketing agencies often introduce inefficiencies into the process of intermediation. Even in cases where public policy is very discriminatory in its treatment of different groups of farmers, output growth may be satisfactory (e.g., Brazil), but the fruits of that growth are very unlikely to be well distributed. In the poorer countries, where agricultural population is certain to continue rising for the foreseeable future, such a scenario has the seeds of social crisis implicit in it.

What changes of scenario, of decision-making skills, or of other factors could lead to better decisions as far as poverty-related agricultural/rural policies are concerned? At first glance the problem appears intractable, inasmuch as the bimodal sort of strategy just described reflected the perceived interests of the power groups; one cannot, therefore, expect it to be changed just because technocrats might argue that GDP would rise faster or be better distributed under some other approach. A closer look does suggest that some of what we may here label 'defects' in rural policy-making may be more easily attacked than others because they are or appear to be less in conflict with the major vested interests. Even with respect to the probably least-tractable problem – that of unequal distribution of land – some enlightened oligarchs can be persuaded that there must be some give if social unrest is not to reach the boiling point. So it is not irrelevant to consider even land-distribution policy, though it is clearly the least likely of those discussed here to come in for major non-revolutionary change in developing countries.

Strategies exist that will achieve both growth and equity, so there is no essential or unavoidable conflict between the two. And it is clear also that some policy combinations will tend to produce neither. An important general question is how much the achievement of one of the two goals will deter achievement of the other, if at all, for in-between cases. Of particular importance, perhaps, is the issue of whether, when growth occurs under the more-or-less typical policy package that favours the larger and powerful farmers, the fruits will usually be limited to these groups or will be spread more widely in the rural population. Is there, in other words, a significant amount of trickle down to poorer people when the growth process is 'dualistic'?

At a more detailed level are questions of how success would be affected, in various types of LDCs, by the absence of specific components of the locally desirable package. How successful can a credit program for small farms be in a country where land is mainly concentrated in large farms? How will the fruit of agricultural research be distributed in a country where land is concentrated and labour-saving innovations are favoured by the tax- and import-incentive systems. Common sense suggests that the dilemmas created by not having an ideal setting for growth with equity in the rural area are more serious in a still mainly agricultural country where the agricultural population continues to rise quickly than in a middle-level developing country where agricultural employment is a reduced share of total employment and is perhaps falling in absolute terms.

Assessing the impact of alternative policy combinations in various settings involves drawing on any evidence or understanding of how specific component policies would be likely to affect income distribution and poverty, but also on the historical record of how poverty trends have behaved under various policy combinations. The more the countries for which such a record is available the better, but it would be important at a minimum to be able to compare cases involving 'good' and 'bad' policy packages for pairs of countries where the rural population has fallen to a moderate share of the total and others in the earlier stages of development where that share is still quite high. India falls in the latter category and its growth experience has not been very successful, despite the adoption of new high-yielding varieties of seeds in parts of the country. The Brazilian case has become the major locus for debate on whether the introduction of those varieties helps or hinders the poor. The Asian trio of Japan, Korea, and Taiwan can be compared to a country like Brazil to get some feel for how much difference agricultural and rural policy as a whole makes in the middle and later stages of LDC growth. In the first three, the record of successful broad-based growth is well known; where debate lies, naturally enough, is on the question of which policies and characteristics of these economies led to a growth whose fruits have been relatively widely shared. Focusing mainly on Taiwan and Korea, one finds arguments in support of land reform, of the agricultural policy package as a whole, of a broad-based educational system, and of an outward-oriented trade strategy as key contributors to the outcome. Disentangling the casual mechanisms at work will doubtless be a slow process for economic historians of this period. But in contrast to a case like Brazil, it is of interest to note that Brazil also moved to an outward-oriented strategy, albeit more recently than the other two countries. If one then hypothesized that the difference in the scope of rural education (much less in Brazil) was mainly a result of the generally greater income inequality in that country (especially vis-à-vis Korea, where much [secondary] education is privately financed), it could be argued that the leading candidate to explain the different outcomes would be agricultural policy. First, however, it is worth contrasting the outcomes in more detail, and in particular assessing the distribution of the fruits of growth in rural Brazil. To provide a benchmark of success, we turn briefly to the Taiwanese success story.

2 Evidence from Selected Country Experiences

A *Taiwan*

In Taiwan, per capita income had by 1980 reached a level 5.1 times that of
1953 (Kuo, 1983, pp. 96–7), for an average increase of 6.2 per cent per year.
Population growth was rapid, about 3.5 per cent over 1953–63 and 2.7 per
cent over 1963–73 (Kuo, 1983, p. 336). Over the decade 1973–83 it was
down to 1.9 per cent and by 1983–4 had fallen to 1.5 per cent (Republic of
China, 1984, p. 2). The labour force grew at nearly 3 per cent per year over
1953–83; the share located in agriculture fell from 60.5 per cent in 1952 to
30 per cent in 1973 and to 18.6 per cent in 1983 (Republic of China, 1984,
pp. 50–1). The agricultural labour force peaked in the late 1960s at about
1.75 million persons and had by 1983 fallen to about 1.3 million (Galenson,
1979, p. 387; Republic of China, 1983, p. 50). Industry's share (i.e., the
secondary sector, including mining) rose from 18.4 per cent of the labour
force in 1952 to 41.1 per cent in 1983.

Taiwan's income distribution history is dramatic; the Gini coefficient
among families as of 1953 may well have been around 0.50 or higher, and
by 1980 it had fallen to 0.30; in other words, in 1953 it was probably in or
near the Latin American range, and by 1980 it was perhaps the lowest
among all LDCs and one of the lowest in the world.[4] If the figures are even
close to accurate, the 1950s, when land reform was implemented,[5] witnessed
a marked drop in inequality; so did the short period 1968–70, a time of
rapid growth of demand for labour resulting from the successful growth of
exports.[6] Those two phenomena were doubtless very important aspects of
Taiwan's success story. A closer look at the evolution of the income-distribution pattern suggests some of the details of the process of change and
some hypotheses about other factors at work.

In Kuznets's (1963) original description of why distribution so often
deteriorates in the early stages of modern economic growth with industrialization and urbanization, he focused on the widening gap between urban or
non-farm incomes and farm incomes. Eventually, this gap narrows or the
farm sector is small enough that its low average income has little effect
on overall inequality.[7] In Taiwan, farm-family[8] incomes rose quickly
throughout the post-1953 period. Over 1952–65 as a whole, average income
per worker in agriculture grew at the same rate as that for non-agricultural
workers, being around 43 per cent of the latter in both years (Kuo, 1983).
Over 1964–79, Kuo reports some widening of the gap between farm and
non-farm family incomes, though not enough to prevent a decline in overall
inequity; there was a decline in inequality within both the farm and the non-

farm groups. And between 1966 and 1980, there was a marked decline in the Gini for the least-urbanized quarter of the population and a greater gain in life expectancy for this group than for other groups (Kuo, 1983). An important factor in preventing a greater widening of the farm/non-farm income gap was the increase in non-farm income of farm families from 34.1 per cent of their total income in 1966 to 72.7 per cent in 1979. The agricultural income of these families did not grow in real terms, so the nearly 5 per cent annual increase in their total income was more than completely accounted for by the 11 per cent annual increase in non-agricultural income.

Kuo identifies the increased degree of multiple cropping and the fast agricultural diversification as key facets of agricultural change during Taiwan's transition period of the 1950s and 1960s. With Taiwan still characterized by labour surplus, the multiple-cropping index rose from 171.9 in 1952 to its peak of 190.0 in 1966, subsequently falling to 179.3 in 1971 as the economy moved toward full employment. The number of working days per hectare of land rose from about 170 in 1948–50 to about 260 in 1963–5 (Kuo, 1983). A shift towards more labour-intensive crops such as vegetables and fruits raised output per hectare and also paved the way for the rapid expansion of food processing. Such marked and rapid shifts in the composition of output are easier to achieve in a small trading economy than in a larger one like Brazil or (especially) India. Some of Taiwan's success was thus probably a result of its smallness.

Taiwan's land reform focused substantially on replacing tenancy with ownership; unlike the current evidence from many countries, which tends not to show significantly higher (and sometimes lower) land productivity on owner-operated than on tenanted farms, ownership in Taiwanese agriculture has been associated with above-average land productivity. Replacement of tenancy probably not only contributed to output increases[9] but also tended to diminish the share of land devoted to rice production, as rice was a medium of rental payment (Kuo, 1983). A very considerable 'hidden' tax on rice – which took several forms – existed up to 1971 and also contributed to the shift away from this crop; it did help to stabilize the rice price but the government was also stabilizing prices of other more remunerative products. By the 1970s, the farm-gate rice price was relatively high.

The Taiwanese experience suggests that it may be very difficult, perhaps impossible, for technology to transform agriculture without a concomitant restructuring of the institutions of traditional agriculture. Certainly a major restructuring occurred in Taiwan. It placed a great demand on administrative, organizational, and technical skills, which Taiwan did not possess, and which therefore had to be brought from Japan. To promote scientific agriculture, the Japanese government invested heavily in institutional development, especially the farmers' associations (FAs). According to Ho (1978, pp. 63, 64):

> FAs eventually took charge of such important functions as the improvement and extension of seeds, the maintenance of a seed multiplicatior system, the prevention and control of animal and plant diseases, the training of agricultural technicians, the execution of agricultural surveys, the purchase of fertilizers, seeds, and equipment needed by members, and the management of warehouses ...
>
> Supporting the FAs were other newly formed organizations such as the Small Agricultural United (SAU) and the credit cooperatives.

Although these rural institutions were separately administered, their efforts to develop agriculture were coordinated through the influence and supervision of the colonial government. Between the FAs and the agricultural cooperatives, the Japanese had created an institution that was second only to the government in size. In the late 1920s and the early 1930s, when they were at their heights, the FAs and the agricultural cooperatives employed approximately 40,000 people. Of these 13,000 were extension workers, 9,000 of who were agricultural advisers working with the small agricultural units at the village level. On a per farm household basis, this would amount to approximately one extension worker for every 32 farm households. The size of the operation is perhaps indicative of the magnitude of effort needed to transform traditional agriculture.

Rural primary education expanded very rapidly in Taiwan under Japanese reoccupation.[10] Many observers have felt that widespread primary education contributed to the raising of factor productivity in Taiwanese agriculture (Ho, 1966). It is a serious hypothesis that for technological improvements to be at the heart of the agricultural growth process in small-farmer agriculture, widespread education is an important complement to successful research, as is an extension system that can reach the many farmers involved.

There seems no reason to doubt that the land reform had a significant impact on rural and overall income distribution.[11] In 1951-3, agriculture and related industries accounted for 33.2 per cent of gross domestic product (GDP) (Kuznets, 1979). Nearly half of farm households benefited from the redistribution of land (public land sale and land allotted to the tiller program) (Ho, 1978) and 43 per cent from the rent-reduction program; for poorer farm households these shares would be greater.

Rural poverty alleviation can be aided by emigration to urban areas or by the expansion of non-agricultural activity in rural areas. With respect to the latter, we saw above that Taiwan's experience is dramatic: the share of farm-family income coming from non-farm sources rose from 13 per cent in 1952 to 25 per cent in 1962, 43 per cent in 1975 (Ho, 1979) and – if the figures presented by Kuo can be believed – 72.7 per cent in 1979. He mentions that in Korea, whose evolution has in many important respects paralleled that of Taiwan but whose industries are concentrated in or near the principal cities of Seoul and Pusan, this share has remained roughly constant at around 23 per cent since 1962.[12] In contrast

Taiwan's industrialization has followed a more decentralized pattern, which has enabled its economy to grow as an organic unit by promoting interaction among its components. In other words, by allowing rural industry and agriculture to grow in a mutually reinforcing manner, decentralized industrialization has created rural employment opportunities and enabled greater numbers of Taiwan's rural population to participate in industry without having to leave the countryside. This has not only reduced the total need for urban housing and infrastructure but also made the transition from agricultural to non-agricultural activity less abrupt, with fewer disruptions of family life and the rural social fabric. The evidence from Taiwan also shows that decentralized and rural industrialization brings to the countryside important income distribution benefits. (Ho, 1979, pp. 77, 78)

Because off-farm income is more important for families with small farms (or appears to have been in the 1960s), off-farm activities probably helped to lessen inequalities.[13]

Although other factors (including the density of the agricultural population) no doubt played a role, Ho (1979) argues that decentralized industrialization in Taiwan was facilitated by the presence of a highly commercialized and productive agricultural sector, the development of a diversified agro-industry, and the early development of infrastructure and human capital in rural areas. Agricultural development transformed rural Taiwan into a well-developed and important market for non-farm goods and services. Although it is difficult to say to what extent this increased demand is responsible to the growth of rural non-farm activities, it is clear, according to Ho, that practically all the services as well as many of the non-food consumer goods demanded by farm households can be and probably have been produced in rural areas. As noted earlier, rural Taiwan early possessed a highly literate population, a result of the Japanese colonial government's initiating in the 1930s an intensive program to educate the Taiwanese. Rural electrification also began early in Taiwan and, by the 1960s, electricity had reached 70 per cent of its farm households. Transportation was also quite adequate.

TABLE 7.1
Fertility rates by degree of urbanization: 1971, 1977, and 1983

	General fertility rate[a]			Total fertility rate[b]		
	Cities	Urban townships	Rural townships	Cities	Urban townships	Rural townships
1971	105	110	119	3.355	3.670	4.085
1977	86	96	105	2.360	2.800	3.090
1983	70	84	89	1.920	2.325	2.415

[a] Average number of births per thousand women in the age range 15–49

[b] Average number of births per woman passing through the child-bearing years 15–49 and being characterized in each age category by the age-specific fertility rates of the year in question

SOURCE: Republic of China (1984), p. 30

In the spectrum of developing countries, Taiwan seems to be an extreme case in its moderate rural/urban differentials[14] – in income levels, in employment structure, and in other dimensions. Of particular interest is the relatively small gap in female fertility rates by place of residence (see table 7.1).

B *Brazil*

Brazil's recent rural and agricultural history is of interest as a test of the existence of trickle down to the rural poor in a setting where policy is mainly designed to assist the better-off layers of society, rural and urban. Land distribution is highly unequal, rural education is amazingly limited, and income-distribution considerations appear to be nearly absent from the decision-making process. But Brazil has grown fast, and its agricultural labour force appears to have peaked and begun falling around 1970 or soon thereafter. Can rapid overall economic growth, and perhaps the ending of a surplus labour condition, partially substitute for the sort of successful unimodal small-farm strategy pursued par excellence in Taiwan?

Brazil's well-known combination of fast growth and extreme income in-equality was especially notable during the 1960s and 1970s. Over that twenty-year period, GDP grew by an average of about 7 per cent per year, per capita output by about 4.5 per cent, and per capita income by about 5 per cent (World Bank, 1982). Most Gini coefficient estimates are in the range 0.55 to 0.60.

The extreme income inequality in Brazil results from a highly unequal distribution of income-earning assets, including land and human capital. Parts of the economy toward the modern end of the technological spectrum are quite capital intensive, whereas at the other extreme many people work with virtually no capital. This general feature is manifest in agriculture where the labour/land ratio varies greatly between small and large farms. And, as in most countries, incomes are lower in agriculture and in the rural economy generally than in urban areas.[15] The country also suffers wide regional income gaps associated with major differences of economic structure; the southeast region is far more developed than, at the other extreme, the northeast.

Another strand of thinking reflected in part of the literature is a concern that recent decades have witnessed a trend towards proletarization – a shift from self-employment to wage labour – and an associated increase in the concentration of land in the larger farms. Certainly it would be consistent with Brazil's pro-large bias if such patterns were occurring, and they would create a context in which one might predict a widening gap between the rich and the poor in the sector where most of Brazil's poor are found. It is important to trace, in the degree possible, the fate of the rural and agricultural poor over the last few decades, and to study how this group has benefited from or coped with the dramatic growth that has occurred.

The few available studies that have made use of the 1980 population census results have concluded that, after the widening inequality generally accepted to have characterized the 1960s, little overall change occurred during the 1970s; probably there was a slight decline in inequality. Denslow and Tyler (1984) note that the near constancy of distribution in the 1980s was the result of two offsetting factors: narrowing of the gap between rural and urban income, and greater inequality in the rural sector. Their figures indicate an increase in the average income of deciles of rural income earners in the range of 30–40 per cent for most deciles, but highest by far for the tenth decile. A look at the figures pertaining to agriculture indicates, as one would expect, that the patterns of rural income trends reflect those of agriculture – gains for all groups but greatest for those at the top. Assuming these positive patterns are an accurate reflection of the true course of events, it is of interest to look at the underlying events in Brazilian agriculture that could be responsible for those events.

The sector's labour force appears to have peaked (though if the present economic crisis endures, its earlier upward trend might be restored). According to population census figures, it grew at 1.8 per cent per year over 1950–60, 1.0 per cent over 1960–70, and then fell a little over 1970–80. Meanwhile, total farm land reported in the agricultural census rose by a total of 7.6 per cent over 1950–60, by 17.7 per cent over 1960–70, and by 25.6 per cent over 1970–80. Land cultivated, which is a small share of total land in farms (12.0 per cent in 1975), rose more rapidly, at an annual rate of 2.9 per cent over 1950–80, and the reported stock of cattle rose at over 3 per cent per year. Value added in agriculture rose by a little under 5 per cent (4.8 per cent) per year over 1950–75, a high rate by international standards and one which implied a rapid increase in average labour productivity of over 3.5 per cent per year. Accepting the agricultural census figures on area in farms and the population census data on the agricultural labour force, we would conclude that the land/labour ratio fell by a total of 10 per cent over 1950–60 and rose by 10 per cent over 1960–70 and 30 per cent over 1970–80. Thus, for 1950–80 as a whole, the ratio of land in farms to labour rose by about 30 per cent. Because intensity of use rose over the period, however, the ratio of cropped land to total labour force (the large majority of whom were engaged in crop production) rose by 70 per cent or so over 1950–80, i.e., by 1.75 per cent or a little more per year.

Data on wages, income, and housing conditions suggest that, for poorer rural people, the 1970s witnessed quite different trends from the 1960s. Landless families tend to be the poorest of Brazil's rural groups,[16] and data on rural wages are scanty. The longest wage series refers to daily wages of rural casual labourers in the state of Sao Paulo, where from the late 1940s to the early 1970s there was no trend, though fluctuations were marked (Pfefferman and Webb, 1979). But between 1970 and 1977 a doubling occurred, suggesting a qualitative change in labour-market conditions, perhaps an end of a 'surplus-labour' condition. In the rest of Brazil the casual rural wage grew less but still sharply in the 1970s; the smallest increase registered in any state over 1968–77 was 38 per cent in Rio Grande do Norte (Pfefferman and Webb, 1979). Income data from population censuses and samples (see table 7.2), while they cannot be relied upon to give a fully accurate picture of income trends, support the evidence of the wage statistics and imply an equally marked improvement for the self-employed in the 1970s.[17]

The 1970s was a decade of rapid income increase for paid employees from top to bottom, probably in the neighbourhood of 50 per cent for most deciles except the top one, where the increase was considerably faster. For the self-employed, the bottom few deciles gained by less than 50 per cent but the top six probably by considerably more, with the top decile or so probably by over 100 per cent.[18]

With respect to trends in the structure of the agricultural labour force, it seems likely, on the basis of the available data, that (a) there has been no

TABLE 7.2
Income levels (1970 cruzeiros per month) of selected percentiles of male agricultural
workers in Brazil by occupational category and by year: 1960–80

Occupational category and percentile in the income ranking	August 1960	September 1970	November 1976 (males & females)	August 1980
Paid workers				
10th	n/a	30–40	55.8–66.7	49.9–61.5
25	46.0–51.0	58.4	87.7–104.8	81.6–100.5
50	87.5	88.1	128.6–153.7	122.0–150.3
75	133.7	132.1	198.5–237.3	178.0–219.4
90	< 189.1	176.4	281.6–236.7	244.1–300.4
95	215.4	196.3	394.0–470.9	399.0–417.1
Independent farmers				
10	n/a	30–40	57.2–68.4	41.3–50.9
25	> 61.9	59.5	95.3–114.0	80.1–98.7
50	110.4	90.3	153.5–183.5	137.3–169.2
75	172.1	145.4	283.3–338.3	225.5–277.8
90	266.1	212.7	611.9–731.5	469.6–577.9
95	341.6	293.7	722.2–923.0	715.3–880.1
All income earners				
10	0	0		0
25	Very low	30–40		56.5–69.6
50	77.1	78.0		116.8–144.0
75	141.6	130.9		195.2–240.5
90	212.0	191.4		374.1–461.0
95	312.5	277.4		626.4–771.8
99	< 682.3	< 756.6		2256.4–2780.2

SOURCES AND METHODOLOGY: The current price figures for 1980 are deflated to 1970
cruzeiros using the conservative index of the price of consumption expenditures in GDP
developed by Denslow and Tyler (1984, p. 1027n17); deflation by that index provides the
lower of our two figures in 1980. For the upper figure we assumed prices rose 23-fold
(rather than the 28.34-fold of the previous index), a little less than the 24.7-fold increase of
the wholesale price index and above the approximately 21-fold increases of the various cost-
of-living indexes I have seen – mostly adjusted for the alleged irregularities of the early
1970s.

Between 1960 and 1970 we assumed a price index of 36.26 (above that of the GDP
deflator, 35.7, or the wholesale price index, 33.3, but below that of the Sao Paulo cost-of-
living index of 38–40).

Between 1970 and 1976 we assumed a high price index of 4.90, based on the GDP deflator
plus 4 per cent, in an attempt to approximate the Denslow-Tyler consumption index, and
allowing two months for the difference in date between the 1970 and 1976 data. For the
lower price increase, we assumed an index of 4.10.

measurable longer-run (i.e., 1950–80) tendency toward proletarization in Brazilian agriculture, but (b) there may have been such a tendency in the 1970s, in which case it would appear to be a reversal of an earlier trend in the opposite direction, and to have corresponded to declines in the importance of share-cropping and of unpaid family help, but not of the 'self-employed.' One obvious interpretation of a shift toward paid employment in the 1970s would be that it was a result of rising demand for wage labour, as reflected in the sharply rising wages (see table 7.3).

Some authors have suggested that, during the 1960s at least, labour was increasingly pushed into the smallest farms as the demand was stagnant on larger farms. Data from the agricultural censuses, although not comparable to and less reliable than those of the population censuses, do suggest such a trend over 1950–75, but with a still-to-be-explained reversal during 1975–80. The labour/land ratio was probably stable (as suggested by the figures in table 7.4) or falling for most farm-size classes over these thirty years,[19] being much higher on the smaller than on the larger farms, partly, of course, because of differences in access to market, land quality, etc.

Given constant or falling labour/land ratios, it seems highly probable that labour productivity was rising on the smaller farms as well as on the larger ones during this decade. Although data inconsistencies prevent any firm conclusions, it appears that, for agriculture as a whole, labour productivity was rising very rapidly in the 1970s, probably in the range of 3.6 per cent per year. Even if labour productivity on farms of below ten hectares fell from 43.5 to 37.3 per cent of the sectoral average between 1970 and 1980, as our figures suggest, if the sectoral average rose by say 50 per cent over the decade (a little over 4.0 per cent per year), these data would suggest an increase of a little under 30 per cent on the smallest category of up to ten hectares.[20]

Part of the improvement in the situation of the poorer people in agriculture suggested by the income figures reviewed earlier has been the result of a sharp change in the intersectoral terms of trade in favour of agriculture.[21] But increased labour productivity has, it would appear, also contributed significantly, and it is important to consider the factors that may have played a role in generating that result.

The wide gap in land productivity in favour of the smaller farms seems not to have changed much in the 1970s; the ratio of value added to the declared value of land remained, for example, about three times as high on farms of up to 10 ha as on farms of 100–1000 ha (Berry, undated). Over 1960–70 the increase in the share of land in farms with mechanical power was striking; for that decade the trends are not available by farm size. But during the 1970s, the rapid extension of the use of machinery to fairly small

TABLE 7.3
Brazil: distribution of the agricultural labour force by job position: 1960, 1970, and 1980

Job position	1960 No.	1960 Per cent	1970 No.	1970 Per cent	1980 No.	1980 Per cent
Total labour force	11,826	100.00	13,090	100.00	12,661	100.00
Employer	226.6	1.92	209.0	1.60	303.9	2.40
Self-employed	4,611.0	38.99	5,294.0	40.44	5,041.0	39.82
Paid worker	2,986.9	25.26	3,330.0	25.44	4,572.8	36.12
Share cropper	820.0	6.93	1,676.1	12.80	6,485.0	5.12
Unpaid	3,180.6	26.90	2,581.0	19.72	2,030.8	16.04
No information	0.8	0.90	–	–	63.9	0.51

SOURCE: The population censuses of the years in question

TABLE 7.4
Labour intensity (labourers/hectare) in Brazilian agriculture, by farm size, 1950–80

Farm size	1950	1960	1970	1975	1980
<10	0.608	0.642	0.644	0.713	0.702
<1	3.876	2.675	3.299	3.285	3.375
1–2	1.649	1.676	1.617	1.640	1.650
2–5	0.751	0.769	0.714	0.769	0.762
5–10	0.395	0.389	0.359	0.393	0.389
10–100	0.116	0.119	0.103	0.112	0.111
100–1000	0.0322	0.0296	0.0200	0.0238	0.0246
1000–10,000	0.0083	0.0075	0.0053	0.0064	0.0067
>10,000	0.00171	0.00141	0.00107	0.00145	0.00195
Total	0.0392	0.0506	0.0499	0.0514	0.0478

NOTE: Males and females, 14 and up, except 1950, where 15 and up
SOURCE: The agricultural censuses of the years in question, except for 1975, whose data came from the survey of that year

farms was striking; for example, the share of farms of less than 10 ha using such power rose from 2.4 per cent in 1970 to 15.7 per cent in 1980; for those of 5–10 ha, it rose from 4.35 to 24.55 per cent. For the smallest farms (under 10 ha), animal use seemed to be rising along with mechanical power, whereas for the larger categories, there was a decline in the use of animal power, machines presumably substituting for draft animals. Use of modern inputs (fertilizers, pesticides, animal feed, etc.) also rose notably over the period 1959–80, by perhaps fourfold on a per hectare basis. Use per hectare is more intensive on small farms than on larger ones, but the gap has narrowed markedly over the two decades; the ratio of modern input to output is greater on the larger farms. Still, one of the reasons for rising productivity on small farms is, no doubt, this form of modernization; depending on the price of deflators used, the per hectare use of these inputs has risen by two- and to threefold over the period.

Credit availability was, as one would expect, better for the larger farms; in 1980 the ratio of credit to value of production was 3–4 times greater on the farms of above 100 ha than on those of below 10 ha. Between 1960 and 1980, the per cent of farms receiving credit in the previous year rose from 8.3 to 21.0; the increase was most notable for farms of 10–1000 ha; it was not large for those of under 5 ha, where still less than 10 per cent had received credit, though the increase was considerable for those in the 5–10 ha range.

The evidence of change on small as well as on large farms might have owed something to improving education, but its level in rural Brazil remains strikingly low, and its advance was slow over 1960–80. In 1980 the share of persons 15 and up who had not completed grade 1 was around 50 per cent, down from 60 per cent twenty years earlier. For the cohorts of persons 15–19 years of age, who would by that age have received any lower-level schooling they were destined to get, the share failing to complete grade 1 fell from 53 per cent in 1960 to 36 per cent in 1980, a more marked improvement. But to have about one-third of the rural population not reaching school (a few would enter but not complete grade 1) is for a country with Brazil's per capita income very surprising. Many countries with per capita income far lower than Brazil's do better than this.

Over 1970–80 there was a considerable increase in non-agricultural employment in rural areas (about 54 per cent or 4.4 per cent per year), with doubling or near doubling occurring in manufacturing and in services. Including 'vegetable extraction' (rubber tapping, wood products, etc.) this category rose from 15.2 to 23.4 per cent of rural employment over the decade. Rural non-agricultural employment was more prevalent in the more developed regions of the country.

The message that seems implicit in the Brazilian story is that, even under a system of great built-in inequality, rapid growth can eventually produce a considerable trickle-down, to the point where the incomes of the bottom rural deciles could rise by 30–40 per cent or so over a decade. Together with the evidence from the 1960s, when growth was also fast but when it appears that less of its fruits accrued to the poor, this picture suggests that some sort of turning point was reached in the early 1970s – perhaps a marked tightening of the labour market. It remains to be seen how things have changed under the economic crisis of the 1980s.

c *India*

India's GDP growth averaged a very modest 3.5 per cent per year over 1960–80, but particularly striking was the unsatisfactory growth of agricultural output – 1.9 per cent per year (World Bank, 1982). The labour force in agriculture fell only from 74 per cent of the total in 1960 to 69 per cent in 1980 (ibid.) and thus rose in absolute terms at over 1 per cent a year, implying an increase in agricultural labour productivity of only perhaps 0.7 per cent or so per year. Though output in industry and services rose at an acceptable 5 per cent per year, the agricultural sector was clearly India's albatross over these decades.

Given this record, it is hardly surprising that little or no progress was made in the alleviation of poverty during these years, at least on a national level. A major issue of debate since the mid 1960s has been whether the advent of HYVs (high-yielding varieties) in India has been a boon to the poor or, as some have argued, perhaps even an additional scourge.[22]

The income-distribution impact of biological improvements (HYVs) is a matter of obviously great importance in LDCs; even a finding that the distributional impact is strongly negative would not imply that such improvements should not be sought because there seems little hope of winning the war against food shortages without them, but it would imply that different types of improvements should be sought or that the setting in which they are disseminated would perforce have to be changed.

The early evidence and analysis on this issue seem moderately reassuring, though for several reasons they must still be regarded as tentative. The most relevant research has focused on who adopts (especially by farm size and tenure category), what the implications of the new technology on labour inputs have been, and how wages have moved. Few, if any, studies have tried to link this type of technological change in any detailed way to trends in rural or overall income distribution, though doing so is clearly the final necessary step in throwing light on the issue.[23] Apart from the failure to take this final step, however, the results of the new technologies have thus far been analysed essentially in a short-run static framework, and there can be no assurance that the medium- and long-run impacts will be similar. Especially will it be important to focus on the impact on land distribution – any such effects are likely to show up gradually and probably be difficult to isolate – and on the second-round effects of technology change through mechanization or other processes set in motion by higher incomes.

These caveats aside, the evidence from India, the most studied and most important case, is, as noted above, fairly reassuring (Prahladachar, 1983). Although small farmers tend not to adopt HYVs as rapidly as larger farmers, the evidence suggests that in a fairly short time they tend to catch up or to substantially narrow the gap. Where the gap has not been pretty well erased after a few years, it seems often to reflect the inability of small farmers to buy pumps, finance fertilizers, and the like (Prahladachar, 1983).[24] Reviews by Vyas (1975) on wheat and Herdt (1980) suggest a tendency, though with lots of exceptions, for yield or net income per hectare of HYVs to be higher on large than on small farms. But the interpretation to be placed on such results is again not clear because variables such as irrigation and access to fertilizer were not generally taken into account and because many of the studies were no later than the early 1970s.

On the question of tenancy and adoption, the evidence seems much more limited, since some studies have failed to distinguish owner cum tenants from pure tenants. Parthasarathy and Prasad (1971), who did make the distinction in their study of a village in Andhra Pradesh, reported that owners had an advantage over tenants. Most other studies are ambiguous, so that issue remains one in need of further research. There seems no reason to believe that tenants *need* have any particular problem in adopting when the conditions are satisfactory.

It seems clear that the direct impact of HYVs on labour utilization (in wheat and rice, at least) has been positive.[25] A number of studies seem to suggest an increase in labour use in the range of 20–30 per cent (Prahladachar, 1983). Several studies indicate also a shift often interpreted as resulting from the need to carry out certain agricultural operations within a short, specific period of time. The labour-demand effect seems to be borne out by wage data. In his study of real wages in Indian agriculture, Lal concludes that whereas during the period 1956-7 to 1964-5, real wages were constant or fell in eight of the fifteen states of India, in the following 'green revolution' period, 1964-5 to 1970-1, they rose sufficiently to offset the earlier decline (Lal, 1976). A particularly interesting recent study by Nicholson (1984) attempts to isolate the effects of green-revolution technology by comparing Punjab with Gujarat state, which though dynamic economically has not had access to the benefits of the green revolution because it lacked the ample ground water and the good irrigation system that the Punjab had. He reports that over 1961-71 agricultural wages in the Punjab rose by 23 per cent to become the highest in India,[26] while those of Gujarat rose by 6 per cent. (Gujarat's agricultural output rose by 58 per cent during the 1960s, Punjab's by 78 per cent [Nicholson, 1984].) Nicholson argues that, in combination, the new technology and rural institutions slowed down long-term trends toward greater inequality that the dual processes of population growth and commercialization of the rural sector had set in motion. The favourable impact of the green revolution on the demand for labour was, according to the Day-Singh model and other analyses, counteracted from the outset by the trend toward mechanization and increasing capital intensification (Day and Singh, 1977, p. 142). But without the new HYVs, events would have unfolded less satisfactorily.

Though the literature clearly suggests that the benefits of the green revolution have usually been widely distributed, it seems to suggest also a worsening of distribution because of a substantial fall in the labour share. In one district, to illustrate, wages of hired labour were 33 per cent higher per acre of HYV than per acre of traditional varieties, while cultivator income rose by 76 per cent (Chinnappa and Silva, 1977). This is probably not a necessary and perhaps not even a general result, but it has thus far shown up with regularity. In areas where land distribution is relatively equal and social cohesion high, equality might not suffer; perhaps it could even be improved.[27] But where land is unequally distributed and labour in surplus, such a favourable outcome would be surprising.

An important question in the context of the Punjabi success story and its broader implications is the role played by rural institutions, in particular the co-operative. Nicholson argues that the new technology was so appropriate to conditions in Punjab that it is difficult to argue that rural institutions made any but a marginal contribution to its initial spread. He also disagrees with critics in judging that the rural co-operatives were highly equitable in delivering production credit to the smaller farms. Their role was marginal because other markets were able to do the job. Where conditions are less obviously 'right,' it is very likely that positive institutional developments would be important if not essential for fast advance.

It remains to be seen in India and elsewhere whether the green revolution has contributed or will contribute to income inequality and poverty through land concentration. In most countries the data needed to assess trends are woefully inadequate.[28] The problems of unclear, inconsistent, and incomplete data coupled with changing definitions are well laid out by Cain (1983). One can only hope that the effort to sort out these data will match the importance of the issue.

Tracing changes in land distribution over time is part of a more general need to monitor the longer-run and less easily discernible effects of the biological revolution in agriculture. It is intriguing to take note, from a different setting, of the Muda River Project in Malaysia, studied by Goldman and Squire (1982). In a very short period (1970–5) the availability of water permitted farmers both to switch from single to double cropping of paddies and to adopt improved varieties. The result was more than a doubling of output between 1969 and 1974. Goldman and Squire found no significant changes in the distribution of owned or operated paddy land. Rice was an import substitute so expanded output did not affect prices. Between the pre-project and immediate post-project situations, labour use per acre rose by 92 per cent. The authors report that all family-farm categories benefited greatly from big income gains. but, despite this dramatic beginning, all did not continue rosy in the project:

First, since 1977, there has been a substantial increase in mechanized harvesting and threshing, a development which will have eliminated many jobs for landless workers. Second, general inflation in the Malaysian economy has reduced the real income gains generated by the project. This has been exacerbated by two crop seasons since 1977 when drought left the project reservoirs with insufficient water for off-season water. Unrest among farmers has grown to the extent that in early 1980 violent demonstrations occurred in the area, involving farmers demanding an increase in rice prices, which are already supported above the world price level. (Goldman and Squire, 1982, p. 775)

What appears destined to remain unclear for a while longer is (1) whether the green revolution concentrates land distribution in a socially damaging way and (2) whether inequality of land distribution, together with other contextual factors, promotes employment-reducing mechanization with serious consequences.

3 Key Rural and Agricultural Policies Bearing on Poverty Alleviation

It is obvious that many of the things that Taiwan seems to have 'done right' will not come to pass in most LDCs; recent events in Brazil suggest that doing things differently from Taiwan need not preclude significant gains for the rural poor, though it will certainly make them more difficult. Trends in India and similar countries highlight the crucial need to get agriculture moving if there is to be any chance of eradicating poverty in a reasonable period of time. The poor in such countries are much more likely to pay a long-run price for their government's incapacity or lack of concern than are those in middle-income countries like Brazil.

Priority areas for policy focus will, naturally, vary by type of country. But some generalizations are hesitantly attempted in the remainder of this section.[29] Relative priorities naturally vary according to whether one focuses on the potential contribution of a particular policy in a technical sense or on its potential after allowing for social, political, and administrative obstacles to its successful implementation. As discussed in the introductory section, it is tautological to say that high priority must, in nearly all countries, be given to policies that raise productive capacity (among which policies to promote technological improvements are central) and to population policies. Land reform and other policies, which have the effect of redistributing productive potential, also appear to have great technical potential but are probably somewhat less essential than the other two, except where they are important contributors to successful pursuit of the other two, a definite possibility in many contexts. Other interesting policy categories involve consumption programs (food subsidies, health, education, etc.) and incentive policies (price policies). Each of these categories also can play a quite significant role, but, with the same caveat just stated, they seem likely to be of lower priority than the first two. Some consumption problems, of course, also raise the danger of a trade-off between poverty alleviation now and later.

A *Population*

In the numerous countries where the great bulk of the population remains in rural areas, yet the problem of population growth threatens to create a critical obstacle to economic progress, there is no assurance that the country can afford to wait for the processes of urbanization, industrialization, and education to slow population growth. The lucky developing countries already well along the development path, with the rate of population growth in most cases now decelerating, can reasonably expect that growth to fall to the point where it no longer threatens to derail the economic train. But for the poorer LDCs, many already seriously overpopulated and most lacking a really strong national resource base, to count on this easy way out could be to court disaster. In many such countries, success in development and poverty alleviation may require that population growth be stopped in the rural areas. This may be more important than anything else that happens there. Though genetic and other output-raising innovations have proved their capacity to raise agricultural output, it would be tempting fate to assume that such progress can go on for a matter of decades without running out of stream or putting the environment at risk. In some countries population growth must either slow down in the short run under the influence of public policy or in the longer run under the influence of poverty, the Malthusian outcome. A successful population policy has the advantage of virtually guaranteeing successful development sooner or later; no obviously attainable success in other policy areas can guarantee triumph in the face of population growth at 3–4 per cent per year.

What methods may be used to slow population growth and the potential success of the more gentle forms of control associated with provision of information, subsidized control devices, and so on remain to be seen. If they are not successful, the more aggressive approach pursued by the People's

Republic of China may become a major determinant of successful overall development.

Improved educational levels in the rural areas, along with greater instruction in the problems of large family size, would probably have some desirable effects on rural family size. If it remains impossible to get rural family sizes down to urban levels, encouragement of rural-to-urban migration could become one component of population policy. If it turns out (though the Taiwanese case argues the contrary) that population control is much harder even in a prosperous semi-industrialized rural setting than in urban areas, much or all of the advantage of achieving such a setting may be offset. Doubtless the debate will continue when population programs can have major impacts, but recent experience in a few countries, including Indonesia and Mexico, seems to imply that vigorous well-managed programs can have a significant input, even when they are much less Draconian than China's (Clinton and Backer, 1980). There seem grounds for optimism that, when countries' birth rates begin to decline, the rate of decline can be much faster than in the historical experience of now-developed countries (Kirk, 1971). Population programs probably have a greater impact when coupled with a socio-economic setting favourable to a desire for reduced family size, so creation of that desire becomes a central goal. Though analysis of the determinants of population growth remains a difficult and hazy area, both the importance of the issue and the evidence that policy may be able to make a difference suggests placing high priority on this matter.

B *Research and Technological Improvement*

Research on improved varieties, techniques of cultivation, machines, etc., will in most countries be the main single key to the advance of agriculture. There appears to be considerable scope for a country to choose the focus of its research and technological borrowing, and the orientation adopted probably has a considerable, perhaps even definitive, effect on the extent to which output growth contributes to poverty alleviation. A major distinction must be made between biological and mechanical improvements. In most countries, most new machine technology is imported and involves relatively capital-intensive technology – especially so for large tractors and associated machines. In the case of biological improvements, even if based on developments abroad, there must at least be adaptation within the country, so there is considerable freedom with respect to the directions to be taken.

As a broad category, technological change is at the same time essential and dangerous. Both mechanical and biological improvements are likely to be biased towards a society's power groups.[30] In the case of labour-saving machine technology, usually imported, one of the technician's objectives is to make sure that its price is not a subsidized one and that any price intervention goes in the other direction. Some inappropriate machine technology is financed by foreign aid; close and careful surveillance may help to impede it.

Biological improvements are most likely to be poverty alleviating when they involve staple food crops and are produced by small farmers and in labour-intensive ways. The well-known yield increases in rice and wheat were perhaps unrealistically expected to meet these conditions. Evidence from countries like India suggests that even if the benefits accrue disproportionately to the rich, as they are more than likely to do unless land distribution is equitable, the poor are likely to be co-beneficiaries. It remains to be seen what the long-run distributional impact of the green-revolution technology will be, both for reasons discussed earlier and because it is as yet unclear whether future research oriented towards finding varieties more suited to the small producer will be as successful as past efforts not so directed.

It is much to be hoped that the biological research process will be perceived as a mutual interest of the rural poor and of other groups: it is at the heart of the growth process; and also, as distinct from land redistribution, allocation of credit, etc., would seem not a likely candidate for conflict of interest between these groups. The frequently inadequate investment in this area seems to owe as much to the short time horizon of government policymakers as to any bias against such expenditures. To the extent that a lack of awareness of the pay-offs to such expenditures is a contributory factor, education on the issue deserves particular attention.

The question of appropriate mechanical improvements is only partially separate from that of biological progress and its impact. There seems to be no serious grounds for doubting the common view that the process of 'large tractorization' (with complementary machines) is a dangerous one – that such mechanization tends mainly to displace labour without raising output much. Clearly there are few third-world situations where such mechanization would occur in the context of an efficient agricultural sector and perfect factor markets. In those settings, small operated units would achieve high land productivity by heavy use of labour.[31] But in second-best situations, where large units are currently operating at low levels of efficiency, one must countenance the possibility that such mechanization will raise output and perhaps even increase the demand for labour at the same time.

Failure to predict an increase in labour-saving mechanization has an outcome of biological improvements seems to have underlain an overly optimistic view of the latter's impact on income distribution and poverty. As adoption of such varieties occurs, not only large farmers (who may in any case already be relatively mechanized) but fairly small ones as well may take this route. In the case of smaller farmers, investment in machines may partly respond to the increase in income generated by the high-productivity varieties, together with a lack of profitable outlets for savings.

The ultimate and only satisfactory gauge of how all these factors have worked out is the income-distribution evidence in their wake. Evidence on changes in the distribution of land and in the composition of the rural labour force as between the landed and the landless is also indicative, though by no means conclusive because a shift toward landlessness can occur in the context of growth of income opportunities (leaving a marginal plot for more lucrative paid employment, as, perhaps, in Brazil of the 1970s) as well as push factors (losing land one would like still to have). Unfortunately the record remains quite incomplete on both counts. When the agricultural censuses taken in or around 1980 in many developing countries have been carefully studied in conjunction with earlier ones, the degree and character of structural change will, one hopes, become clearer.

C *Agrarian Reform*

Land reform as the first step towards equitable growth has no substitute: it seems the key step in helping a country move toward a wide distribution of political power, a resulting equity in the access to education, and so on. The inertia built into socio-economic systems is tremendous. Even when the dominant group is virtually fully replaced – by a country's acquiring independence, for example – patterns of inequality can remain more or less intact, as in the case of Kenya.[32]

Major agrarian reforms are usually the result not of technical judgment or voluntary social interaction but of political upheaval of one sort or another. Some are associated with communist revolutions, others with non-communist revolutions as in Mexico and Bolivia, and others with extensive foreign involvement as in Japan and Korea. In only a few twentieth-century cases (e.g., Iran) have major changes occurred in non-revolutionary frameworks. For the most part, the non-communist reforms give evidence of the economic potential of the shift to smaller-scale family units, but the basic limitation of such reforms is suggested by the fact that the only fully successful ones – contributing to fast, equitable growth both in agriculture and economy-wide – are those where considerable outside control helped to steer the course. When the reform occurs in a revolutionary context, the outcome so far is either a communist take-over or a partial reform. Mexico and Bolivia are striking examples of the latter. Large amounts of land changed hands, and the reform sectors have remained more or less intact since the reforms, but the governments, instead of supporting the new peasant sectors, have focused their assistance on newly developing large-scale sectors. This danger of benign (or not-so-benign) neglect of small-scale agriculture by unsympathetic government[33] is a basic concern when one asks whether partial reforms – the only type likely to occur in non-revolutionary contexts – are worth much at all. This serious possibility raises the premium on full-scale reforms that are associated with, and can help to produce, major realignment of power groups in a society. While situations with the potential for such change are infrequent, one possibly valuable role for the international community and the aid agencies would be to provide timely financial resources and advice. Usually the context is one of strife and chaos (à la Mexico or Bolivia), of decision making under inadequate information, and of resource scarcity. Agricultural assets are often destroyed or lost during the uncertain period of transition. One hopes that better understanding of which agrarian structures and policies hold out the promise of successful growth would help decision-makers; possibly some financial resources from the outside could tilt the process more in favour of the poor.

On the information front, although it is probably not surprising that most LDC decision-makers involved with the agricultural sector have little confidence in the potential of small farms – and this is indeed the case – these views are perhaps more surprising when held by their counterparts in countries where reform has occurred (as in Mexico or Bolivia) or where governments have engaged or tried to engage in major restructuring of the agrarian sector (as recently in Tanzania and Ethiopia). Two major misconceptions seem to afflict the uninitiated in these matters, including most decision-makers. The first is that there are significant economies of scale in agriculture, putting small productive units at an automatic disadvantage. This belief flies in the face of the by now 'stylized' fact that land productivity is virtually everywhere higher on small farms than on large ones. It seems to originate partly in the observation that farms in developed countries are large, partly in the (irrelevant) fact that a family cannot earn a high income from a very small plot, partly from the higher marketed surplus from large farms, and partly from the fact that the most modern and capital-intensive farming does tend to be seen on (some) large farms. In classist societies it gets a big boost from the fact that decision-makers share their class with large farmers, not with ragged peasants. In any case this belief can incline the equity-oriented decision-maker away from the small productive unit and in favour of large private units, co-operatives, or whatever. The second misconception is that much can be expected of production co-operatives as a source of important economies of scale, above-average quality of management, or whatever contributes to economic efficiency.

Competent professional advice might matter in some of these cases, and observers have suggested the need for an international agency for agrarian reform, one of whose functions could be the provision of such advice – perhaps a counterpart to the role played by Wolf Ladejinsky for the U.S. government in the Asian post-war reforms. Such an agency could also help out financially; the capacity to buy off pockets of resistance could be important, as could the opportunity to buy time while the new reform units were achieving their potential – funds to assure adequate supplies of agricultural inputs, or even to import food to keep urban prices from skyrocketing, would be important.

The occasions when major reforms occur or are in the air are few,[34] so the major relevance of land reform is in non-revolutionary settings, where some land is transferred, some changes in tenancy arrangements decreed, or some other partial changes made. In these cases, the many ways in which good intentions may be sidetracked or sabotaged tend to reveal themselves. Particularly risky, it would appear, are reforms whose focus is the transfer of land from tenancy arrangements to ownership. Whether out of unconcern or incompetence, the supporters of such legislation usually fail to predict that it will create a powerful incentive for owners to discourage tenancy. Similarly, in reform-legislation guidelines laid down to determine which farms should be expropriated, 'adequate exploitation' providing exemption from expropriation is usually defined to include cultivation in capital-intensive ways but not share-cropping, even though from a social point of view, the latter is likely to be preferable.

Even without full-scale expropriations to redistribute land, it is likely that there is considerable economic potential in a well-designed land policy. A major aspect of how land policy in land-scarce countries will evolve in future involves the political power of landless and new landless, and the extent to which they influence the political process. The distribution of newly settled lands is in some countries quite important; changes in land values resulting from works of infrastructure are important in others. A law prohibiting the sale of land in large blocks would have a positive effect over time, while not seriously penalizing large holders. Rent ceilings with tenure guarantees seem to work sometimes. It is hard to imagine a successful transition to a relatively egalitarian rural income distribution without a reasonably equal distribution of rights in land.

D *Price Policy and the Development Squeeze on Agriculture*

Because it is the initial locus of economic activity, the early growth of the secondary and tertiary sectors of an economy is usually financed by a surplus from agriculture (Lewis, 1975). It may pass through financial markets, private portfolios overlapping both sectors, or the government; the transfer may also occur via the price mechanism, if agricultural prices are low. How resources are transferred between agricultural and non-agricultural, and intersectoral terms of trade patterns, constitute an important determinant of the distribution of incomes and of rural poverty, especially when labour is not highly mobile intersectorally. Mechanisms to encourage savings by lower-income rural people are obviously a more equitable way to effect the transfer than are regressive taxes. When migration out of agriculture is responsive to intersectoral earnings differences, the effect of tax or price policy on rural poverty or on poverty in general becomes unclear. If the poorest are the first to migrate in response to a fall in agricultural prices, for example, the effect on poverty could be very limited – in the opposite case it would be large. Some rural dwellers could benefit from controlled food prices also, if their earnings were less sensitive to those prices than their cost of living.

There are no doubt a variety of situations in which price interventions would, were they administered in the manner the technician desired, be good for the poor. But the dangers attendant on such interventions cannot be taken lightly. Neither economic theory nor the experience in success stories like Japan and Taiwan suggests that intervention cannot improve on market-determined prices; it is when the country lacks a coherent and firmly administered rural development strategy that such intervention is likely to be damaging. Bates (1981) makes the case persuasively, for the African context, that price interventions are systematically used for non-developmental political purposes. Low food prices are usually part of the 'urban bias,' a response to the greater political threat from disenchanted urban consumers than from disenchanted rural producers. Subsidized agricultural credit and input prices can be used to offset such farmer disenchantment but, better for the politican, serve also to strengthen political support when used in a discriminatory fashion to help the richer more-important farms, or one's political allies. The unfavoured mass of farmers are left out in the cold. In such settings even originally well-intentioned interventions are likely to become perverted. Where credit is subsidized, it will mainly find its way to large farmers; where subsidized inputs are available, they will be similarly directed; and so on.

In the context of price policy it is useful to raise the more-general question of the burden agriculture and in particular the rural poor are made to bear in the overall development process. There seems little doubt that in most LDCs agriculture has borne a large part of the burden associated with the transition to a modern industrial economy, through heavy taxes, unattractive intersectoral terms of trade, and relative neglect in government expenditure allocations. An important issue in this context is the strength of the economic or political factors that seem to make this the typical sequence of events.

In some low-income countries there appear to be valid economic reasons for focusing the development squeeze mainly on agriculture. Some versions of land tax have, in some countries, probably been easier and more efficient ways to collect taxes than available alternatives. The same goes for export taxes on agricultural products (often taking the form of a differential between the price paid to producers by a public-sector marketing board and the export price), especially when the country has some degree of world monopoly power in the product and hence some incentive to curtail its output. But these conditions appear to be met less and less. Few countries now use land taxes to any significant degree, and monopoly power in export-product pricing is probably less common than before. The maintenance of low terms of trade for agricultural products usually backfires; it discourages the output of those products and in the case of exports encourages inefficiency in the public-sector marketing agency. Avoidance of rising urban food prices is as likely to be regressive from a distributional point of view as progressive. The possible growth argument in support of such a policy is that low food prices are necessary to keep industrial (or non-agricultural) profits high – by keeping real wages expressed in non-agricultural products low – and to provide the needed incentive for expansion of that sector. This view could have some validity in countries whose food supply was price inelastic while industrial investment was sensitive to the profit rate. But the profit rate can be buoyed by other policies, including the level of protection from imports. It seems unlikely that there are many situations in which the tendency to squeeze agriculture as a whole could be defended on efficiency grounds. The same goes for the tendency to squeeze the rural poor, often the main victims. If their supply is price- or profit-inelastic, whereas that of the rich is elastic, such an argument could exist, for example, where small farms are already relatively efficient and large farms could be induced to raise their productivity by sufficient incentives. This may be a good way to characterize the practical alternatives for some labour-surplus countries, where land redistribution is not a feasible option. It raises the premium on countries learning how to facilitate the generation and channelling of the surplus in ways that are less regressive.

It has sometimes been argued that poor third-world farmers who are essentially unintegrated into markets are virtually unaffected by price policy. But the third-world farmers, even relatively small ones, are more integrated than is often believed, and much more than they were a few decades ago. And in spite of their famous and understandable 'risk aversion,' they are still victims of downward price movements, given their always precarious economic base. Further, the only proven route out of poverty does involve the production of a marketable surplus, so even a peasantry that is isolated now cannot afford to remain so.

Though judging just how important a good price policy is in alleviating rural poverty is difficult and probably quite country specific, some generalizations are possible. First, a low agricultural price policy, whether with the objective of benefiting urban consumers or not, is very dangerous; sooner or later (probably sooner), it will discourage output, innovation, and growth in agriculture, leading to food shortages. And it will keep rural incomes down. Only where rural land is held in a very concentrated fashion or where the country's comparative advantage in non-agriculture permits extensive food imports would there be potential logic to such an approach. Second, input subsidies (to credit, fertilizer, or whatever) may make sense in theory but are likely to be very risky in practice: subsidies are honey to which the better off are strongly attracted. Third, maintaining agricultural prices above world levels can be a sensible policy, within reason, as it may raise the incomes of the rural poor. But here, too, the benefits need to be carefully and well identified.

4 Direct Anti-poverty (Consumption) Policies

While it is evident that rural poverty (or any poverty) can only be dealt the coup de grâce by an increase in productivity, it is not immediately clear to what extent provision of government services is important as a complement to (or, in a partial sense, a substitute for) such progress. Provision of public education, health, water, and other services is certainly relevant; the question is the priority such expenditures should receive. In many countries if these services are not provided by the public sector they will not be provided much at all because of the importance of economies of scale.

Certain rural health expenditures seem to have a quite high pay-off; probably few if any investments can yield better returns than selected improvements in preventive health care in rural areas. The fact that countries like Sri Lanka and China, with per capita incomes of less than 300 U.S. dollars in 1980, could have a higher life expectancy (66 and 64 years respectively) than Brazil (per capital income of $2050 and life expectancy of 63) bears witness to this investment, although other factors – and most generally the distribution of income – also enter directly.[35] Education at least to the point of good literacy and numeracy is also no doubt a wise direction to go for the majority of LDCs, for whom the job of rural development will be inherently less easy than in land-abundant Latin countries like Brazil. Investment in this type of education would be especially beneficial where such expenditures are not at the expense of productivity-raising ones, as where broad budgetary allocations are made by ministry in the first instance and subsequent allocation occurs within the ministry, so that rural education is likely to be at the expense of some type of urban education. Most rural services are inexpensive, though this circumstance is, of course, in part a reflection of their poor quality. Their role in rural poverty alleviation may be significant partly because it can be rather independent of the evolution of the productive side of the economy and of agrarian structure. It is easier to provide broad access to rural health services than to land.

A related question is whether it is reasonable to expect the government to provide some sort of 'welfare net' in rural areas; social-security systems, food rations, and the like are usually urban oriented because they reflect rising income levels, because the urban poor and middle groups have more political clout than their rural counterparts, and because of economies of scale in the provision of the services. And it is indeed here where particular caution does seem to be warranted. Although there may be a moral imperative to save people who are starving in the wake of a drought, the long-run effects of such acts may be of little significance if underlying productive improvements are not put in motion. Food-subsidy programs also need careful assessment of their benefits and costs; their attractiveness stems, of course, from the fact that the benefits are immediate and obvious. The costs have to do partly with negative side-effects on the incentive for small farmers to produce and on their incomes, partly with the imperfect targeting of such programs[36] (they usually benefit urban residents more than rural ones), and partly with their high-profile character, which tends to remove them from political control and contribute to turning them into machines out of control that can eventually have very serious budgetary implications.

One powerful reason for giving very serious priority to rural nutrition and health programs is the possibility that both they and family-planning programs will be more successful if linked to each other. As Johnston and Clark (1982) note, 'the shortcomings of conventional family planning programs appear to be especially great in many of the low-income countries in tropical Africa, where the environment is so unfavourable that the cost-effectiveness of conventional programs is very low. In these countries, efforts to improve the survival prospects for infants and small children may be very effective in improving the context in which attitudes and motivations with respect to family planning are shaped' (p. 119). At the same time, nearly all successful health schemes 'have included the promotion of family planning because of the favourable effects of child spacing on the health of mothers and infants' (p. 131).

Food-subsidy programs have to jump a number of hurdles, some of them noted above, to be major successes. Nutritional interventions, designed to raise the level of nutrition without the large price ticket associated with major subsidy programs, seem also of limited promise, though certainly they have their place where specific deficiencies can be identified and dealt with. In general, though, there is little evidence of significant progress in reducing malnutrition in the rural areas of the lower-income developing countries through these techniques. This lack of progress may be related to the current view that protein-energy malnutrition is basically a result of in-adequate intake of food rather than a 'protein gap' associated with the com-position of food intake (Johnston and Clark, 1982). At the same time, small children and pregnant and lactating women do have special nutritional problems, which are not duly recognized in many societies. Attention to these problems could raise standards of health with little expenditure of resources, apart from those involved in the learning process.

5 The Crucial 'How To' Questions

In most LDCs, it would appear that success in rural development may de-pend as much on how well policies can be implemented as on the choice of superior policies.[37] Indeed, this is a misleading way to phrase an alleged dichotomy because, in any practical and detailed sense, rural policy cannot be made at all independently of its implementation, a point strongly em-phasized by Johnston and Clark (1982). Intellectual cogitation cannot pro-duce a blueprint for policy; inputs from the rural population and from the facilitators (extension agents, rural health workers, etc.) are likely to be just as important, especially in dealing with the rural population's most strongly felt needs and with feasible ways to organize the provision of services or in-puts and the co-operation (or at least non-conflict) of the rural population. There do appear to be some situations in which a sufficient condition for rural progress is the availability of a few great new crop varieties, which will spread on their own. But this simple blueprint is unlikely to provide a general solution, especially when one recognizes that a slowing of popula-tion growth is in most countries as important as an acceleration of output growth.

Because the answers to 'how to' questions are likely to vary a lot across settings, it is not possible to generalize much on administrative and institu-tional questions. But some distinctions can be validly made. There must be some way to meld the inputs of the planners at the centre (who deal with decisions on price policy, credit, research allocations) with those of the facilitators and the rural population. The system requires continuous communication and interaction among these groups, one requirement for which is a good dose of humility among the planners at the centre of the system. Broad-based rural development is a more complicated process than narrow-based growth; success in dealing with the 'how to' of the former is important to rural poverty alleviation.

6 The Package Approach and Integrated Rural Development

With the passage of time the recognition has grown that successful rural development involves many components – those noted above plus lots of others. And there has been widespread awareness of the inefficiencies associated with overlapping and non-cooperating bureaucracies, each of which focuses on its component of the package. Especially in the context of the new fertilizer and water-responsive high-yielding varieties has emphasis justifiably been placed on the need for a package approach to the provision of needed inputs. How much output may have been lost because of lack of integration among these services is not readily apparent. Broader ideas of 'integrated rural development' (IRD) – a term that seems to mean rather different things to different people – have also been prevalent in the last decade or so, in the context of the goal of broadly based economic advance in rural areas. The idea is doubtless a relevant one, but the thought thus far expended in this area has not yet produced a useful blueprint to assist in the process of equitable rural development. There seem to be two main reasons for this deficiency. One is that the pilot or limited-area application of IRD projects facilitates the resolution of many organizational problems (by providing centralized authority and atypically good access to resources) that arise when their generalization to the national level is attempted. The second is that understanding is still extremely partial as to what elements of a policy package are particularly complementary; indeed, the needed components and the relationships among them probably vary widely across settings.

A number of approaches to rural development have been based on the idea that the rural poor must band together to get anywhere (not per se implausible) and that such co-operation will be easily achieved. Experience has been generally unkind to these expectations; though there have been successes, it is now clear that success should not be expected unless rather stringent conditions are met. That efforts to organize the rural poor in self-help efforts have not been very successful results in part from the fact that the rural poor are usually a very diverse group, including landless workers as well as small, marginal farmers (Korten, 1980). Co-operative types of schemes have fared little better. Hunter (1971) noted that perhaps two-thirds of all co-operatives attempted in East Africa and India 'have proved unviable or semi-viable; and a large proportion of those which have succeeded have ... resulted in rewards for the ... "big men" of rural society as distinct from the humble farmers.' Johnston and Clark (1982, p. 10) note that 'Programs of community development, adopted with much to-do in their 1950 decade of prominence, delivered so little that most were terminated or drastically reduced as early as 1965. Nonetheless, under new names to hide the past, many of the same mistakes are being repeated in today's New Directions programming.'

It seems unfortunate that attempts should be repeated so systematically to pursue rural development in ways which have failed too frequently, when a very promising blueprint – the subject of section 1 – does exist.

Notes

1 Few of the earlier development economists ever claimed that it was; rather, they tended simply not to address the poverty issue in any formal or direct way; see, for example, Arndt (1983).
2 The only other setting in which such quick improvements seem to have been forthcoming for the rural population appears to be that of the communist countries, e.g., China and Cuba.
3 As of 1970, these three countries had the highest producer paddy prices of nine Asian countries studied by Timmer and Falcon (1975). Earlier, Taiwan's farmer price was lower, and Kuo (1983) attributes the diversification of Taiwan's agricultural sector in considerable degree to a low price of rice relative to other, less traditional crops.
4 See Kuo (1983), table 6.1. Possibly these figures exaggerate the decline (though the available estimate for 1953 is 0.56) because prior to 1964 the sources are not comparable. But there seems no doubt that a sharp decline in inequality did occur.
5 A recent reduction program had been implemented in 1949. The sale of public land to tenant farmers occurred in 1953, followed by the redistribution of private tenanted land to tenant cultivator (Kuo, 1983, p. 27).
6 The year 1968 was dubbed by Fei, Ranis, and Kuo (1979) as the time when labour surplus ended.
7 See Kuo (1983), table 6.1. The figures, taken literally, imply a growth of family income at 14.5 per cent per year over this period for the bottom 20 per cent. If the lowest quintile's share of total income had been 5 per cent in 1953 instead of the 3 per cent reported in the table, the annual income growth would still be an amazing 9.3 per cent per year.
8 A farm family is one whose head is registered as a farmer (Kuo, 1983, p. 134).

9 There is some ambiguity in the figures of Kuo's table 3.2 (p. 28) where farmers are classified only by tenure status, not simultaneously by size.

10 The enrolment of students in primary schools increased from 17,579 in 1901 to 670,000 in 1940. The post-war period also witnessed a rapid expansion in primary education, as attendance in primary school climbed from 850,097 in 1945 to 1,766,445 in 1960.

11 Ho has estimated the effects of the program on the income of an average tenant with one chia of medium-quality paddy land in Taoyuan Hsiom, concluding that in the absence of the reform his income would have risen by 16 per cent over 1948–59, whereas in fact it rose by 107 per cent (Ho, 1978, pp. 167–8).

12 Ho (1979), p. 77. Further, not only has industrialization been spatially more concentrated, but growth of commerce and services in rural areas has also been limited (p. 91), and the Gini ratio for Korea's farm households rose from 0.29 in 1967 to 0.32 in 1974 (p. 92).

13 Chinn (1979) used the 1967 farm-income survey data for the Taichung rice region to calculate the hypothetical loss in income if non-farm employment opportunities were lost to farm households. His calculations show that the percentage decline in income from the loss of non-farm employment was more than five times greater for farm households cultivating less than 0.5 chia (1 chia = 0.97 ha) of land than for those cultivating 3 or more chia.

14 Possibly this result is to some extent a result of the definitions of rural and urban used in Taiwan.

15 In 1970, the mean income of rural income earners was 37 per cent that of urban earners (Denslow and Tyler, 1984).

16 The most reliable source of agricultural incomes (partly because of better coverage of non-monetary incomes) is the 1974/5 national household expenditure and nutrition survey (EMDEF). It indicates that in all major regions of Brazil except the northeast, small farmers (farmers not hiring labour) receive on average about twice as much family income as wage labourers (Pfefferman and Webb, 1979, p. 69). (In the northeast the differential is minor.) The bottom quartile of families in the two groups seem to have similar levels of income however.

17 For paid workers, these figures indicate no clear change over the 1960s, with the possible exception of some increase in the bottom quartile. The decline estimated for the self-employed over this decade is probably not real, since income underreporting in agriculture appears to have increased markedly between the two censuses. The income increases for 1970–6 are probably overestimates, especially for the self-employed (where improvement in reporting of income was probably concentrated), but nevertheless suggest that substantial increases did occur for the self-employed as well as for paid workers.

18 Available indicators of the quality of housing and assets owned are generally consistent with the patterns just described. For example, the share of families owning a radio rose from 12 per cent in 1960 to 40 per cent in 1970 and to 72 in 1980.

19 The figures of table 2.4 are based on the agricultural censuses, which show a much more rapidly rising agricultural labour force than the more reliable population census data; the latter, however, are not available by farm size.

20 For details see Berry (1985). This result, or any other conclusion about trends in productivity by farm size, must be viewed as tentative until discrepancies in output figures between the agricultural census and the national accounts are explained.

21 Relative prices of agricultural produce were rising during much of the period since the Second World War. Pfefferman and Webb's (1979) three indexes of intersectoral terms of trade show marked increases between the late 1940s and 1960 and another significant jump from the late 1960s to 1977 (the last year for which they present data).

22 Nicholson (1984) summarizes the fears as follows:
   '1. The new technology increased the profitability of agriculture and, in consequence, led landowners to reassert control over their land, forcing tenants off. Land values rose, and this tended to squeeze small and marginal farmers off the land.
   '2. The beneficial effects of the new technology depended on the availability of cash to purchase needed inputs and the capital to invest in improvements such as tubewells. The small farmer therefore either was excluded from the new seed or operated at a disadvantage because of lower profits even if he did have access to credit.
   '3. Because of labor constraints, the need to maximize family survival possibilities, and the low profit margins of small-scale grain farming, the smaller farmers may have found the monoculture revolution centered on hybrid wheat or rice unattractive and unprofitable.'
   Each of these fears is backed by enough micro level evidence to lend it credibility.

23 Most attempts to study the effect of new technology on income distribution have used the farm as the unit of observation rather than the family, a serious limitation. For this and other reasons, including the variation of results from different studies, the overall distributional impact of the HYVs remains in need of further analysis.

24 In a village in the Punjab, Leaf (1983) describes the dramatic improvements that occurred between 1965 and 1978, and credits the new co-operatives, which took over much of the marketing function, with making it 'far more reasonable for small farmers to adopt new crops and methods at the same time large farmers do. Formerly it was much the wiser course for smaller farmers to lag a few seasons behind those better able to absorb a loss.'

25 See Bartsch (1977) for an extensive review of the literature as of that time.

26 Corroborating the favourable trends in the Punjab, Mundle (1984) reports that the per cent of population under the poverty line fell from 40.5 over 1963-4 to 1965-6 to 30.2 over 1971-2 to 1973-4. The improvements seem to follow, with a lag, gains in agricultural production, according to Mundle's recent analysis.

27 In his review of change in a Punjabi village over 1965-78, Leaf (1983) suggests that the gains in income 'have been accompanied by increased equity and political stability ... The gains have gone at least as much to the poorer villagers as to the wealthy' (p. 268). The data presented do not seem to demonstrate this, but they leave no doubt that all groups benefited substantially. A major question, though, is whether this quite positive outcome was a reflection of features of Sikh society not replicated in much of India. Leaf

refers to the farmers' identification of 'Sikh values of equality and independence with economic policies to support the activities of small scale independent peasant farmers' (p. 267).

28 To exemplify, Nicholson (1984) reports a dramatic difference in the evolution
of the distribution of operational units as between Gujarat and Punjab over
1961–71, with the Gini coefficient in Gujarat rising only from 0.52 to 0.55,
while in Punjab it rose from 0.38 to 0.63, as the number of small farms of
under two hectares increased dramatically. Meanwhile, according to Mundle
(1984), the Gini coefficient of the distribution of land ownership among
households in the Punjab increased a little over 1961–2 to 1971–2, although
the share with no land at all fell from 12.3 to 9.1 per cent. The Gini was also
about constant for the distribution of land by operator, though the share of
households operating no land rose from 39 to 54 per cent.

29 Its debt to such detailed studies as those by Johnston and Clark (1982) and by
Chambers (1984) will be evident.

30 Similar issues arise with respect to public investment in roads, storage, dams,
migration works, and the like. Most governments undertake such activities in
the interest of the larger, richer farmers, even though pay-offs would be
greater if the focus were different. Many of the points made in this section
hold also for these expenditures.

31 For a recent evaluation see John H. Sanders and Wayne R. Thirsk (1984).
These authors, after a detailed review of the evidence and the literature, conclude that it is mainly large crop farms that buy farm machinery and that
'most of the impetus for adopting mechanical technologies stems from the
subsidized cost of capital rather than the rising real cost of labour' (p. 54).
They also conclude that governments in Latin America have viewed mechanization as a relatively cheap method of stimulating the growth of crop output, whereas the biochemical technological improvements which would have
been more suitable on smaller farms would have required larger investments
before they come to be transferred to or developed for these economies
(p. 55).

32 How the elite and protected position of the large European farmers was
translated into a comparable position for an African elite after independence
is laid out clearly in Weys (1974).

33 Thiesenhusen (1984) distinguishes three broad reasons for the failure of land
reform in Latin America to live up to expectations in terms of reducing
inequality of income: (1) cases in which the reform itself introduces inequalities among beneficiaries or potential beneficiaries; (2) cases in which post-
reform policies (price policies, credit distribution, etc.) were inequity producing, offsetting any potential the reform itself had; and (3) counterreform – the
case of Chile under Pinochet.

34 Probably not many new cases will arise where substantially foreign-imposed
reform will really work (Japan, Taiwan [to some degree], and Korea worked;
El Salvador has not so far); where revolutions with substantial popular bases
will lead to thorough-going reforms (those of Bolivia and Mexico were too
partial) without Marxist authoritarianism (as in Ethiopia now); or where the
opportunity provided by independence in a country with considerable foreign
landholding will be taken advantage of (in Kenya much potential was lost; in
Zimbabwe it remains to be seen how things will work out).

35 China's 'barefoot doctor' appears to have provided broad access to basic health services in rural areas, in a very economical fashion. Even there, the usual bias of the medical profession towards curative interventions had to be countered by the personal intervention of Chairman Mao. See Maru (1977).
36 Johnston and Clark (1982, p. 16) include under this sort of indictment 'school lunch programs, which have been a popular element in aid programs throughout the developing world. The health gains secured by such programs have been positive but marginal, and often they have been offset by changed consumption patterns in the home. Moreover, when measured in terms of the forgone opportunities for improving the nutritional status of the most needy mothers and preschool children not reached by the lunch programs, the cost has been enormous. In an important sense the school lunch programs have been too feasible: they have provided a convenient outlet for the urge to "get on with it" and thus have reduced the pressure to search for more efficient and more effective alternatives.'
37 The question of the relative importance of policy selection vs policy implementation has received considerable discussion in another important aspect of development strategy – trade policy. The success of the outward-oriented approaches of Korea and Taiwan is attributed by some observers nearly as much to the organized and competent application of an export approach as to its choice in the first place.

References

Arndt, H.W. 1983. 'The "Trickle-Down" Myth.' *Economic Development and Cultural Change* 32: 1–10
Bates, R. 1981. *Markets and States in Tropical Africa*. Berkeley: University of California Press
Bartsch, W.M. 1977. *Employment and Technology Choice in Asian Agriculture*. New York: Praeger
Berry, A. 1985. 'Trends in Brazilian Agriculture during 1960–1980.' Draft (mimeo)
Cain, M. 1983. 'Landlessness in India and Bangladesh: A Critical Review of National Data Sources.' *Economic Development and Cultural Change* 32: 149–67
Chambers, R. 1984. *Managing Rural Development: Ideas and Experience from East Asia*. Uppsala: Scandinavian Institute of African Studies
Chinn, D. 1979. 'Rural Poverty and the Structure of Farm Household Income in Developing Countries: Evidence from Taiwan.' *Economic Development and Cultural Change* 27: 283–302
Chinnappa, N., and W.P.T. Silva. 1977. In B.H. Farmer (ed.), *Green Revolution? Technology and Change in Rice Growing Areas of Tamil, Nadu and Sri Lanka*, pp. 204–24. Boulder, CO: Westview Press; and London: Macmillan
Clinton, J.J., and J. Backer (eds). 1980. 'East Asia Review 1978–79.' *Studies in Family Planning* 11: 311–50
Day, R.H., and I. Singh. 1977. *Economic Development as an Adoptive Process*. London: Cambridge University Press

Denslow, D. Jr., and W. Tyler. 1984. 'Perspectives in Poverty and Income Inequality in Brazil.' *World Development* 12: 1019-28

Fei, J.C.H, G. Ranis, and S.W.Y. Kuo. 1979. *Growth with Equity: The Taiwan Case*. Toronto: Oxford University Press

Galenson, W. 1979. 'The Labour Force, Wages, and Living Standards.' In Galenson (ed.), *Economic Growth and Structural Change in Taiwan*, pp. 384-447. Ithaca: Cornell University Press

Goldman, R.H., and L. Squire. 1982. 'Technical Change, Labor Use, and Income Distribution in the Muda Irrigation Project.' *Economic Development and Cultural Change* 30: 753-75

Herdt, R.W. 1980. 'Changing Asian Rice Technology: Impact, Distribution of Benefits and Constraints.' CPS/Agriculture and Rural Development Department and Personnel Management Department. World Bank Proceedings of the Agricultural Sector Symposia, pp. 81-127

Ho, S.P.S. 1978. *Economic Development of Taiwan, 1960-1970*. New Haven: Yale University Press

- 1979. 'Decentralized Industrialization in Rural Development: Evidence From Taiwan.' *Economic Development and Cultural Change* 28: 77-96

Ho, Y.M. 1966. *Agricultural Development of Taiwan, 1903-1960*. Nashville: Vanderbilt University Press

Hunter, G. 1971. 'Research on Co-operatives in East Africa: Review/Note.' Overseas Development Institute, London (mimeo)

Johnston, B., and W. Clark. 1982. *Redesigning Rural Development: A Strategic Perspective*. Baltimore and London: Johns Hopkins University Press

Johnston, B., and J. Cownie. 1969. 'The Seed-Fertilizer Revolution and Labor Force Absorption.' *American Economic Review* 59: 569-92

Kirk, D. 1971. 'A New Demographic Transition?' In National Academy of Sciences, *Rapid Population Growth: Consequences and Policy Implications*, pp. 123-47. Baltimore: Johns Hopkins University Press

Korten, D.C. 1980. 'Community Organization and Rural Development: A Learning Process Approach.' *Public Administration Review* 40: 480-511

Kuo, S.W.Y. 1983. *The Taiwan Economy in Transition*. Boulder, CO: Westview Press

Kuznets, S. 1963. 'Quantitative Aspects of the Economic Growth of Nations: Distribution of Income by Size.' *Economic Development and Cultural Change* 11: 1-79

- 1979. 'Growth and Structural Shifts.' In Galenson, 1979, pp. 15-31

Lal, D. 1976. 'Agricultural Growth, Real Wages, and the Rural Poor in India.' *Economic and Political Weekly*, Review of Agriculture, June, A47-A60

Leaf, M.J. 1983. 'The Green Revolution and Cultural Change in a Punjab Village, 1965-1978.' *Economic Development and Cultural Change* 31: 227-70

Lewis, S.R. 1975. 'Agricultural Taxation in a Developing Economy.' In Richard M. Bird and Oliver Oldman (eds), *Readings on Taxation in Developing Countries* (3rd edition), pp. 389-400. Baltimore and London: Johns Hopkins University Press

Lipton, M. 1977. *Why Poor People Stay Poor: Urban Bias on World Development*. London: Temple Smith

Maru, R.M. 1977. 'Health Manpower Strategies for Rural Health Services in India and China: 1949-75.' *Social Science and Medicine* 11: 535-47

Mundle, S. 1984. 'Land, Labour and the Level of Living in Rural Punjab.' In A.R. Khan and Eddy Lee (eds), *Poverty in Rural Asia*, ILO, Asian Employment Programme (ARTEP). Bangkok, Thailand

Nicholson, N.K. 1984. 'Landholding, Agricultural Modernization, and Local Institutions in India.' *Economic Development and Cultural Change* 32: 569-92

Parthasarathy, G., and D.S. Prasad. 1971. 'Season-wise Progress of High Yielding Varieties in Andhra-Pradesh: Role of Economic Variables.' *Economic and Political Weekly*, Review of Agriculture, September, A117-A122

Pfefferman, G., and R. Webb. 1979. 'The Distribution of Income in Brazil.' World Bank Staff Working Paper no. 356. Washington

Prahladachar, M. 1983. 'Income Distribution Effects of the Green Revolution in India: A Review of Empirical Evidence.' *World Development* 11: 927-44

Republic of China, Directorate General of Budget, Accounting, and Statistics. 1984. *Statistical Yearbook of the Republic of China*

Sanders, J.H., and W.R. Thirsk. 1984. 'The Growth and Impact of Farm Mechanization in Latin America.' Report submitted to World Bank (mimeo)

Thiesenhusen, W.C. 1984. 'The Illusory Goal of Equity in Latin American Agrarian Reform.' In John D. Montgomery (ed.), *International Dimensions of Land Reform*, pp. 31-620. Boulder, CO: Westview Press

Timmer, P.C., and W.P. Falcon. 1975. 'The Political Economy of Rice Production and Trade in Asia.' In Lloyd G. Reynolds (ed.), *Agriculture in Development Theory*, pp. 373-410. New Haven: Yale University Press

Vyas, V.S. 1975. *India's High Yielding Varieties Program in Wheat: 1966-67 to 1971-72*. Mexico City: CIMMYT

Wyes, C. 1974. *Underdevelopment in Kenya: The Political Economy of Neo-Colonialism*. Berkeley: University of California Press

World Bank. 1982. *World Development Report 1982*. New York: Oxford

Index

adjustment finance: and the poorest countries, 45

adjustment policy: analysis of, 28–9; in Tanzania 1980–5, 37–8, 40; traditional, relevance of, 8

adjustment programs: components of IMF type, 6–7, 28–36; and development strategy, 35–6; and income distribution, 8, 23–4, 27, 36–43; indiscriminate application of, 7; and political unrest, 8; and public expenditure, 7, 9

agrarian reform. *See* land reform

agriculture: in Brazil, 186–90; development strategies in, 15–16, 176–8; growth potential of, 174; and implicit producer taxes, 146–8; and income distribution, 54; in India, 191–4; and land reform, 15–16, 198–200; and population policy, 15; and prices, 16, 154–5, 200–3; in Taiwan, 181–4; in Tanzania, 153–6

Bangladesh: and food subsidy, 14

basic needs: definition, 3; and economic stringency, 4, 42

benefit/cost ratio: private, for consumption of social services, 90

black market. *See* parallel market

Brazil: factor productivity in agriculture, 186–90; growth and income distribution, 184–5; rural development, 190; and trickle-down theory, 185–90

budgetary cut-backs: proportional, and income distribution, 26–7; and social services, 7, 33

Cali: and user charges, 58

Columbia: and user charges, 57–8

community development: and integrated rural development, 206–7

computable general equilibrium models: in analysis of adjustment programs and income distribution, 43–4

contraction, macro-economic: sources of, and effects on income distribution, 31–2

co-operatives: and integrated rural development, 206–7; as a rural institution, 193

credit: agricultural, in Brazil, 190; ceilings, and income distribution, 34; international, and the poorest countries, 45

cut-backs, budgetary: proportional, and income distribution, 26–7; and social services, 7, 33

data: for analysis of indirect tax effects, 71–2

devaluation: effects on income distribution, 29–30